Pursuing Peace in Godzone: Christianity and the Peace Tradition in New Zealand

Edited by
Geoffrey Troughton and Philip Fountain

VICTORIA UNIVERSITY PRESS

TE WHARE WĀNANGA O TE ŪPOKO O TE IKA A MĀUI
VICTORIA
UNIVERSITY OF WELLINGTON

VICTORIA UNIVERSITY PRESS
Victoria University of Wellington
PO Box 600 Wellington
vup.victoria.ac.nz

First published 2018

ISBN: 9781776561827

A catalogue record for this book is available from the National Library of New Zealand.

Printed by Ligare, Auckland

For Harry, Jake, Aria and Millie.

And for Jeffrey and Samuel.

Contents

Contributors

Jamie Allen is an Anglican priest and former Dean of Taranaki Cathedral. He is married to Suzy, and dad of four daughters—Danielle, Carrie, Katy and Roxanne. Jamie is currently part of the team at Tearfund New Zealand, an international aid and development organisation, and co-ordinator for a residential suicide prevention initiative based in Taranaki.

George Armstrong, PhD (Princeton), OV (Order of Vanuatu) is a priest and theological teacher in the Anglican Church, a veteran of the New Zealand and indigenous-led Pacific peace and justice movements, and a promoter of movements for interreligious and intercultural dialogue. He has taught in several seminaries and universities. His life work from 1965 has been as senior lecturer in Systematic Theology at the College of St John the Evangelist, Auckland, where his research and teaching included religion and society involvement.

Joseph A. Bulbulia is an evolutionary scholar and the Maclaurin Goodfellow Chair in Theological and Religious Studies at the University of Auckland. He is a co-curator of the New Zealand Attitudes and Values Study, a 20-year national-scale longitudinal study. He is also co-editor of *Religion, Brain & Behavior.* Joseph uses evidence-based methods to understand the links between religious commitments and social behaviours.

Manu Caddie lives with Tarsh and their children at Penu Pā near Ruatoria, where he is managing director for a biotechnology company developing health products from native plants, fungi, cannabis and shellfish. Manu is co-founder of the South Pacific Christian Anarchists network. Though full of personal convictions, and despite three arrests, to date he has no criminal convictions.

Jono Campbell is based in Christchurch where he works with rangatahi and whānau from across the city as General Manager of Te Ora Hou Ōtautahi (TOHO). He started in Te Ora Hou as a volunteer in 1990, became National Coordinator in 2002, then shifted into leadership of TOHO in 2004. Born in Southland, raised in the Far North, Jono is married to Vicki: their two girls claim Ngāpuhi, Ngāti Porou, Samoan, Niuean and European whakapapa.

John Chote is a career teacher of 35 years and counting. He has taught in primary, intermediate and secondary schools in New Zealand, the United Kingdom and India. His specialist subjects are religious studies, philosophy and music. He is currently Head of Religious Studies at Sacred Heart College, Lower Hutt.

Dorcas Dennis completed a PhD in Religious Studies at Victoria University of Wellington in 2016. She is an online co-ordinator at Florida International University, and section editor for the *Australasian Dictionary of Pentecostal and Charismatic Movements*. Her research interests include global Pentecostalism, religion and migration, transnationalism and diaspora studies—focusing on the religious traffic between Africa and the African diaspora in North America and Australia.

Elizabeth Duke is a former lecturer in Classics at the University of Otago. She became involved with the Quakers in 1967, and has held a number of voluntary positions, locally, nationally and internationally. She was employed from 1997 to mid-2004 as Associate Secretary, then General Secretary, of Friends World Committee for Consultation, the Quaker international networking body.

Philip Fountain is a Senior Lecturer in Religious Studies, Victoria University of Wellington. He was formerly a Senior Research Fellow in the Religion and Globalization Research Cluster at the Asia Research Institute, National University of Singapore. He received his doctorate in Anthropology from the Australian National University. He has published extensively on religion and development, disaster relief, non-governmental organisations, and the transnational service and peacemaking work carried out by North American Mennonites.

Karen Kemp is the Dean of Tikanga Pākehā students at the College of St John the Evangelist in Auckland. She has previously worked in nursing, community development, conflict transformation and theological education in Australasia, Chile, Mongolia and the United Kingdom. Karen currently teaches ethics, conflict transformation, New Testament studies and ministry formation. Her doctoral research through George Fox University, Oregon, focuses on leadership and spiritual formation.

Judy Kumeroa is manager and youth worker at Te Ora Hou Whanganui, where she has worked with Whanganui's young people for 25 years. She and her husband have fostered countless young people, and also volunteer for the community action event Stone Soup, which is held every eight weeks and attracts about 400 families for hāngī, games and music.

Adi Leason is married to Shelley, whom he met at Wellington Teacher's College in 1984. They have seven children and live on a small organic Catholic Worker farm outside of Ōtaki. Adi's political education was served by living in a Wellington City Council public housing complex for seven years and then in an urban slum in Southeast Asia. He and his family remain intrigued by the possibilities of manual labour, voluntary poverty, an open home and non-violent direct action.

Chris Marshall holds the Diana Unwin Chair in Restorative Justice at Victoria University of Wellington. He is author of many books, journal articles and reference work entries, and has a deep commitment to peace theology and peacebuilding in general. Chris has an international reputation for his contribution to restorative justice theory and practice and is frequently invited as a conference speaker and guest lecturer.

Peter Matheson is a religious historian whose main publications have focused on the German Reformation. He has taught at the Universities of Edinburgh and Otago, and is Principal Emeritus of Uniting Church Theological College, Melbourne. A retired

Presbyterian minister, of Celtic heritage, married to a German, he is active in peace and environmental issues, and fascinated by the dynamics of change, yesterday and today. Lives in Dunedin and loves it.

Tom Noakes-Duncan is a Lecturer in Restorative Justice at Victoria University of Wellington. With a background in theological ethics, his first book *Communities of Restoration: Ecclesial Ethics and Restorative Justice* (2017) highlighted the role of the church in promoting and grounding the restorative justice vision. His current work continues his interdisciplinary interests, bringing the theory and practice of restorative justice to bear on a wide range of issues.

Mike Ross (Ngāti Hauā) is a Lecturer in Māori Studies at Victoria University of Wellington, where his research focuses particularly on issues relating to iwi history, development and governance. Before coming to Victoria, he worked at Te Wānanga o Raukawa. Prior to pursuing an academic career, he spent many years in youth and community work.

John H. Shaver is a Lecturer in Religion at the University of Otago. He works on understanding intracultural variation in ritual behaviour, the relationships between religion and fertility, and the evolution of syncretic religions. He has conducted research in the Czech Republic, Fiji, Mauritius, New Zealand and the United States, and his work has appeared in anthropology, biology, neuroscience, psychology and general science journals.

Andrew Shepherd is a Co-Director of the conservation organisation A Rocha Aotearoa New Zealand, and a Research Affiliate with the Centre for Theology and Public Issues, University of Otago. His other writings on peacemaking and environmental themes include *The Gift of the Other: Levinas, Derrida, and a Theology of Hospitality* (2014) and *Creation and Hope: Anticipation and Promise in Aotearoa* (2018).

Chris G. Sibley is a Professor in the School of Psychology at the University of Auckland. He has published more than 250 peer-reviewed articles and book chapters, is the editor of the

Cambridge Handbook of the Psychology of Prejudice, and the lead investigator for the New Zealand Attitudes and Values Study.

Geoffrey Troughton is a Senior Lecturer in Religious Studies at Victoria University of Wellington. His research focuses on religion in New Zealand, the history of Christianity, and contemporary religious change. Major publications include *New Zealand Jesus* (2011) and various edited books—most recently, *Sacred Histories in Secular New Zealand* (2016), with Stuart Lange, and *Saints and Stirrers: Christianity, Conflict and Peacemaking in New Zealand, 1814–1945* (2017).

Pamela Welch is an Honorary Fellow and occasional lecturer in the Department of Theology and Religion, University of Otago. She studied English at Cambridge University and Theology at King's College, London, before embarking on a PhD in History at King's College. Her research interests include settler Christianity within the British Empire and diaspora, with a primary emphasis on Southern/Central Africa and Australasia; world Christianity (Africa); and the history of mission.

Acknowledgements

Issues relating to peace and conflict are always salient. In late 2017, however, as the proofs for this book were prepared, our project came into stark focus. Shocking exchanges between the leaders of North Korea and the United States raised the spectre of nuclear conflict—a threat that many thought had waned since the Cold War era, and only weeks after the International Campaign to Abolish Nuclear Weapons (ICAN) had been awarded the Nobel Peace Prize for their work in seeking to rid the world of nuclear weapons.

The present work is part of a larger project on Christianity and peace in New Zealand. It complements an earlier book, *Saints and Stirrers: Christianity, Conflict and Peacemaking in New Zealand, 1814–1945* (2017), picking up temporally where that volume leaves off. The two books differ in terms of tone and style, but deal with common themes. Readers will find their understanding of Christianity, peace and New Zealand's history enhanced by reading both together.

Both books arose as part of Geoffrey's research on the history of peace and Christianity in New Zealand—work that has been generously supported by the Faculty of Humanities and Social Sciences at Victoria University of Wellington, and by a Marsden Fund grant (ID: VUW1412). Philip has also worked extensively on the complex entanglements between Christianity and peace in other contexts—notably in his anthropological research on the development, relief and peacebuilding work of the Mennonite Central Committee, a North American service organisation in the Anabaptist tradition. Our interest in these issues and the compelling character of the stories themselves convinced us that this material needed to be told to a broader public.

We gratefully acknowledge the generous support we have received from many quarters in doing so. Friends and whānau have offered tremendous encouragement, and we have benefited from numerous conversations with colleagues in New Zealand and abroad. We are especially thankful for our colleagues in Religious Studies at Victoria, who form a remarkably sharp, witty and congenial group. Conversation with Matthew Bartlett was a great help in thinking about the shape of the book. Victoria University Press has been a pleasure to work with: Fergus Barrowman immediately saw the value of the project; Kyleigh Hodgson provided outstanding support; Rowan Heap produced another stunning cover. Two anonymous peer reviewers also provided outstandingly helpful feedback on earlier drafts of the chapters.

One exciting feature of this book has been the production of supplementary materials, which enrich the stories and may also be useful in various study contexts. A number of authors agreed to be interviewed on film about their chapters. We are grateful to them, and to Warren Butcher, Nathan Stewart and Matt Dennes from Image Services at Victoria, who were wonderful to work with in filming and editing these remarkable accounts. Thanks also to Te Herenga Waka Marae, St Michael's Anglican Church, Kelburn, and the Leasons and Troughtons for permission to film in their spaces. Sharon Ross Ensor and Anne van Gend were quick to recognise the value and appeal of the project for students, and have enthusiastically co-ordinated production of teaching resources that are available for use in high schools. Gregor Fountain, Mark Edgecombe, Ashleigh Milmine-Twist, Gillian Townsley and John Chote, among others, have all provided valuable insights into the ways the book may be used in classrooms.

These materials are all available online at a website spearheaded by Sharon and built by Lu Tang: pursuingpeace.nz.

A majority of the chapters that follow were initially delivered as papers at a lively and stimulating conference organised by Geoffrey Troughton and Chris Marshall, with support from Karen Kemp and Tom Noakes-Duncan, in November 2015. We hope that the energy and passion of those presentations is still discernable in the writing collated here. We acknowledge the support offered to that conference by the Religious History Association of Aotearoa New Zealand, the College of St John the Evangelist, the National Centre for Peace and Conflict Studies, University of Otago, and St John's in the City, Wellington. We especially express our appreciation to Chris Marshall, who has long been a remarkable source of inspiration and encouragement in New Zealand to think through the relationships of Christianity and peace.

In the 1980s, New Zealand established itself as a leading international opponent of nuclear weapons, most famously through legislation in 1987, which declared New Zealand to be a nuclear-free zone. This laudable Kiwi initiative took place in some significant respects because of the inspiring work of visionary Christian leaders who perceived nuclear weapons for what they are: inherently and unavoidably evil mechanisms of mass destruction. The recent events noted above remind us that recommitting to the practice of peace is a task that must be taken up by every new generation. It is for this reason that we dedicate this book to our children in the hope that they will embrace a proud tradition of pursuing peace.

Geoffrey Troughton and Philip Fountain
January 2018

1

Pursuing Peace in Godzone

Geoffrey Troughton & Philip Fountain

For many Kiwis, Anzac Day in 2017 began with attendance at dawn services to commemorate New Zealand troops who had died in action—a solemn form of remembrance that has grown in popularity in recent years. Later in the day, Anzac parades were held across the country with marching, bagpipes and other displays of military pageantry. The day was also marked, however, by small yet highly disruptive protests. These protests were part of a long tradition in this country of people opposing warfare and militarism under the banner of peace. Such opposition has always been controversial and the 2017 protests were no different.

In the capital city, protestors from Peace Action Wellington laid a wreath at the Wellington Cenotaph during the dawn ceremonies. They aimed to commemorate the deaths of civilians allegedly killed during New Zealand military operations in Afghanistan.[1] Initially provocative, the action won the protestors publicity in the form of an interview with Newshub, a nationally televised news programme. As two of the protestors were discussing their motivations, the interview was dramatically interrupted. A twelve-year-old, along with his father, sharply condemned the activists. Wagging his finger, the precocious 'tween' declared that it was 'wrong, wrong, wrong' to protest on Anzac Day and that they had been shamelessly disrespectful.[2] One of the protestors responded that Anzac Day should be a time to remember all those who died during war, including civilians. The exchange, which went back and forth for some minutes, was a broadcaster's dream and ignited a national debate that continued in the media for weeks.

The attention-grabbing Newshub clip dominated Anzac Day coverage, obscuring other dynamics, and also overshadowing protests carried out elsewhere on that day. In Whanganui, for example, a small group of Quakers, mostly elderly women, held a quiet peace vigil at the local Anzac parade. The Religious Society of Friends, as the Quakers are more formally known, is a small Christian denomination that has been present in New Zealand since the early nineteenth century. It is a historically pacifist movement which has long advocated for a forthright peace stance. Holding up signs declaring 'Honour the dead by ending war' and 'Build peace, cherish people, protect the planet', this unassuming group of protestors sought to articulate a vision for Anzac Day which mourned the destruction and loss of armed conflict. Their hope was that war might be relegated to history, remembered only as a past tragedy, and replaced by an expansive, comprehensive peace.

Tensions

These events on Anzac Day 2017 highlight some curious tensions in New Zealanders' attitudes. One tension relates to martial and pacific tendencies, and the pride that New Zealanders take in the nation's peacefulness as well as its legacy of military prowess. Another relates to the role of religion, and more specifically Christianity, in the contested spaces between conflict and peace.

Over the course of the twentieth century, and especially after the Second World War, New Zealand established a strong peace identity. This identity was forged at the state level through the nation's historic participation in the formation of the United Nations in 1947, and subsequently through alignment with internationalism, 'peacekeeping' mandates, and attempts to cultivate an 'independent foreign policy'.[3] The growth of grassroots activism was also crucial, particularly around anti-nuclear campaigning, which ultimately resulted in the landmark 'nuclear free' legislation in 1987.[4] Through these and other means, New Zealand came to regard itself as a 'good international citizen', valuing its reputation as a liberal, tolerant nation committed to peace.

A confrontation between university students and the Returned Services' Association (RSA) on Anzac Day in Wellington, 1971: the students wanted to lay a wreath at the Citizens War Memorial, which they did, but the RSA was opposed to the inscription accompanying it. Behind the wreath is Marian Logeman (later Marian Hobbs), Vice-President of the New Zealand University Students' Association; she later associated with the Quakers, and became a Member of Parliament, and New Zealand's first Minister for Disarmament and Arms Control from 2002 to 2004. Source: EP/1971/1799/18-F, Alexander Turnbull Library.

Pride in New Zealand's peacefulness was never only associated with opposition to war, however, or pursuit of what Johan Galtung and others have dubbed 'negative peace'—cease-fire, or the absence of direct violence and armed conflict.[5] New Zealanders have savoured for much longer the relative social harmony and prosperity that the nation has enjoyed. Colonial boosters touted New Zealand as an exceptionally beautiful and bounteous paradise, a land flowing with milk and honey. Comparatively open opportunity structures, relative freedom, support for egalitarian ideals, and legal and political stability lent credence to the image—popularised by Richard Seddon (New Zealand's Premier from 1893 to 1906)—of New Zealand as God's Own Country.[6] The peacefulness of New Zealand, its quaint serenity, has bestowed on it the distinction of being 'a great place to bring up kids'. In the contemporary era, indices measuring 'positive peace'—including factors such as co-operative values, equity and equality within society—suggest that the nation has indeed fared well in this regard. For example, New Zealand consistently ranks highly in the Global Peace Index (second in 2017), while in 2017 it also ranked eighth in the World Happiness Report.[7]

Yet this peaceable reputation and identity stands in tension with other starker trajectories. New Zealand has contributed extensively to military conflicts throughout its history, and taken considerable pride in doing so. Historian Keith Sinclair famously referred to New Zealanders as 'the Prussians of the Pacific' on account of New Zealand's militaristic national spirit.[8] Such militarism was expressed, he believed, in an over-eagerness for deployment in global military conflagrations. This tendency had been evident from the South African War through to the total war conflicts of the First and Second World Wars and beyond. It was also apparent in the valorisation of war and war heroes in the national imagination, and in the shocking and unusually harsh treatment dished out to pacifists and war objectors during both World Wars.[9] Tellingly, there is a far greater national historiography of war and war remembrance than of peace or peaceable protest.

Pride in New Zealand's peacefulness also tends to belie the extent to which the nation has been troubled by internal conflict. As scholars of nineteenth-century New Zealand have emphasised, modern New Zealand was forged in conflict and contestation. Colonisation was not peaceful. It was expressed in forms of structural and outright violence. Indeed, the New Zealand Land Wars of the nineteenth century must be regarded as wars of suppression that decisively shaped the nation's subsequent history.[10] Tensions have also erupted periodically along class, ethnic and sectarian lines. Pervasive expressions of violence remain embedded in societal structures and cultural patterns—as is apparent in New Zealand's troublingly high rates of domestic and sexual violence, and its abysmal statistics on youth suicide.[11]

In the tension between peaceable and martial narratives of New Zealand nationhood, Anzac Day occupies an ambiguous symbolic space. The landing of the troops at Anzac Cove on 25 April 1915, at the start of the Gallipoli campaign, has often been invoked as a key moment in the formation of New Zealand's national identity. Myths of origin are important: they ascribe meanings to past events in order to give form and shape to the future. This raises significant questions about the Anzac imaginary. Is Anzac Day an emblem of militarism and glorification of war? Is it a day for celebrating bravery and heroism, or one of remembrance—of mourning for suffering, sacrifice and loss? And whose bravery, which loss? Like most rituals, Anzac Day is susceptible to different interpretations—not all of which are compatible.

Little wonder then that Anzac Day is contested in New Zealand, and across the Tasman, where Tom Frame describes it as Australia's unofficial national day but also 'one of its most controversial cultural habits'.[12] The clashes of 2017 sit within a long, deep history of often heated debates about the meaning of Anzac Day, and concerning New Zealand's participation in military action more generally. These confrontations point to recurring tensions over New Zealand's national identity and the place of peace and violence within it.

Another tension from these stories concerns the role of religion in New Zealand culture and society. A striking feature of the Anzac Day dawn service is the extent to which it follows distinctively Christian patterns, including the singing of Christian hymns, despite New Zealand being thought of as a decidedly secular country.[13] The invisibility of the quiet Quaker protest mimics the dominant trend of marginalising religion within public discourse. Moral codes grounded in explicitly religious convictions are often regarded with suspicion, if not disdain, and are all too easily neglected. This displacement is regrettable because New Zealand's history is littered with colourful characters and remarkable events in which religious dynamics played a leading role.

Christianity and the Pursuit of Peace

This is a book about peace. It concerns ways that specifically Christian communities have engaged with peacemaking in New Zealand. The book explores the contours of Christian action on a range of fronts: ethical, institutional, theological. New Zealand Christianity is diverse, and Christian engagements with peace have reflected this diversity, in their varied conceptions of peacemaking and in the different methods they have employed. We emphasise questions of imagination and practice; the ways in which peace has been envisioned, embodied and enacted within particular communities, in connection with New Zealand society more broadly, and in relation to international currents.

Our focus is on the period from the Second World War to the present—the period in which New Zealand's peaceable image and reputation grew and flourished. Another recent volume, *Saints and Stirrers*, has examined Christian peacemaking and opposition to war in the period from 1814 to 1945.[14] Collectively, these two volumes establish the theme of peace as a vital dynamic in New Zealand history. Dreams of peace have animated communities' imaginations, leading them to passionately pursue their visions of a better world. New Zealand historiography has tended to locate war as a decisive shaper of our national identity, with our experiences of war informing our sense of nationhood and place in the world. But these volumes show that other imaginaries—other sets of values, symbols and structures for making sense of social existence—have been just as decisive. They also locate Christianity as a vital dynamic within this unfurling history.

Peace has motivated New Zealand Christians in compelling ways, resulting in some remarkable stories that are delightful, disturbing, provocative and challenging. These stories deserve to be told and debated. This volume includes some stories that have grabbed media attention and attained a degree of celebrity, or notoriety. Others have been virtually invisible to all but those most immediately affected. Some tales are told in first person by those who were directly involved. All of the chapters seek to capture a sense of the urgency and necessity of their protagonists. These are stories about commitment and humanity captured through evocative narrative. Taken together they reveal a multifaceted but deeply influential thread within New Zealand culture that illuminates distinctive outlooks and sensibilities.

Since the 9/11 attacks in the United States, 'religious terrorism' has become a regular subject reported on by the global media, such that it now seems like an everyday occurrence. These two words have become welded together, with religion being imagined as especially prone toward violence.[15] A dominant script asserts that religion breeds conflict and division. Yet religion is neither merely the 'angel in the house' nor an 'irrational maniac' that must be tamed, caged or eliminated.[16] It is clearly implicated in the full spectrum of our political and social relationships, and plays complex, varied and dynamic roles across diverse societies.[17] Rejecting trite stereotypes, this volume illustrates a more textured understanding of religion by focusing on the peaceable—if still highly political and frequently also disruptive—forces informing New Zealand Christianity.

The centennial of the First World War (1914–1918) has elicited a vast outpouring of literature and commemoration. Despite the diversity of this material, one effect has been to reinforce the centrality of warfare in shaping global geopolitics and national identities. Another effect has been to further normalise and entrench the institution of war. War and conflict are part of the backdrop behind many of the chapters in this volume, but the authors choose instead to foreground a different set of impulses; these reveal a more complex role for violence in society, in which it is alternatively embraced, subverted and negated. By attending to the impetus for making peace, this volume offers a valuable and necessary counterweight to the prevailing tendency to focus on war. Religious communities loom large as potential incubators of alternative imaginations and as agents of peaceable practices.

Framing Peace

As the preceding paragraph makes clear, peace is dynamically related to the question of war. The relationship can be oppositional, with peacemakers being deployed as anti-war agents. But peace also includes a broader spectrum of goals and practices. Peace can be thought of as being fundamentally about flourishing, wholeness and well-being. Conceptions of peace are rightly regarded as central to Christian Scripture, theology and ethics.[18] In the Christian tradition, peace includes: the absence of conflict and violence, and the overcoming of hostility of all kinds; the enactment of justice, including putting things right; and delight and joy in all our relationships—with God, others, creation, and oneself.[19] This expansive framing offers not a prescriptive set of tasks but rather a diverse repertoire of possible practices. Accordingly, a number of the following chapters are directly concerned with Christian peace commitments framed as opposition to militarism and war. Others address the question of peace in different forms, including in relation to bureaucratic infrastructure, ecological projects, community building and social justice initiatives.

There is something of a tension in Christian traditions over the primacy of peace understood as a matter of gift or of calling; that is, whether peace is primarily a divine action to be received and enjoyed, or a task that we must take up and actively pursue. While some would not preclude that peace may be a gift, the chapters in this volume are all weighted heavily toward investigations of Christian moral action. A striking feature is the common sense of Christian conviction that compels an activist stance toward the making of peace. Peace compels intentional, purposeful action.

Intentional enactment of peace can be achieved through a diverse set of methodologies. Indeed, peace in the Christian tradition is both end goal and method. In the final chapter, Chris Marshall presents a powerful argument for making the consistency of goal and method a decisive feature for a faithful Christianity. He contends that a forthright pacifism that disavows the use of violence is the only defensible Christian ethic. A number of the chapters present studies of activism inspired by such pacifist convictions. Yet New Zealand Christians concerned with peace have not solely couched their commitments in pacifist terms. This is striking, for example, in Dorcas Dennis's account of 'spiritual warfare' in a migrant Pentecostal church, as well as in Elizabeth Duke's account of New Zealand Quakers—a community that has deliberately styled itself as a 'peace church'.

Many of the chapters that follow record the evocative use of Christian symbolism in the pursuit of peace. Christianity has always been seeped in multilayered symbols, metaphors, images and analogies. This volume attests to the creative deployment of this repository in Christian peacemaking efforts. Adi Leason's dramatic narrative of a highly publicised protest, involving deflation of the radome covering an antenna at the Government Communications Security Bureau's surveillance base at Waihopai, near Blenheim, provides a conspicuous example. That protest had the hallmarks of a David and Goliath scenario: an unlikely standoff between ludicrously mismatched powers, with elements of improvisation and farce. Yet it was also deeply reflective and carefully planned. In this parable of confrontation, the weapons of war were disarmed by the tools of agriculture, thus enacting—albeit temporarily—the biblical vision of a day when nations would 'beat their swords into ploughshares and their spears into pruning hooks', and with this the cessation of war.[20] Many of the chapters show similar patterns of creative use of symbolic capital.

Actions like these must be viewed as products of moral formation. They do not occur unprompted, without deliberation. In each of the chapters below we find examples of communities that have regarded peace as a virtue, and sought to cultivate, inspire and inculcate it through peaceable habits, dispositions, theologies and actions. The forging and remaking of different kinds of communities is a central feature in a number of chapters. Andrew Shepherd, for example, addresses ecological restoration work as a form of collective action; at Karioi, such action required co-operation between often fractured communities and interest groups, but it also became a means for achieving co-operation. Mike Ross, Manu Caddie, Jono Campbell and Judy Kumeroa, in their chapter on Te Ora Hou Aotearoa, highlight the power of disenfranchised youth finding healthy communities that they want to belong to, and the importance of helping them to reconcile as best as possible with the communities in which they are already embedded. By contrast, chapters by Karen Kemp and Elizabeth Duke focus on the communities of particular national denominations—the Anglicans and Quakers respectively—and their significance in the work of peace.

The chapters illustrate a range of different peacemaking methodologies. Protest methodologies feature prominently, with their attendant sense of conflict and theatre. As with Leason's narrative, George Armstrong and Peter Matheson's accounts of Christian anti-nuclear campaigning during the 1970s and 1980s involve stories of public action, with peacemaking bodies placed visibly in confrontation with the powers that be. These are accounts of movements. Yet within movements, individuals play particular roles—often at considerable cost to themselves as well as their families. Tom Noakes-Duncan notes that Christian pacifists were the most vocal anti-war critics during the Second World War. For Ormond Burton, opposition to war led to a breach with his own church, and, along with Archibald Barrington, to imprisonment. Two of Pamela Welch's subjects—John Osmers and Michael Lapsley—suffered serious physical injuries, including lost limbs, as a result of letter bombs sent as punishment for their anti-apartheid campaigning in southern Africa.

Notions of reconciliation and restoration have a rich resonance within Christianity; such language is widely employed as a way of understanding the work of Christ, but also as an ethical imperative. Restoration and reconciliation methodologies are evident in Dennis's ethnographic vignette, which is partly a story about the overcoming of conflicts between ethnically diverse African Christian migrants in New Zealand. Significantly, though Welch primarily narrates their anti-apartheid activism, the later ministries of Osmers and Lapsley both gravitated towards healing, hospitality and reconciliation. In a moving account that weaves personal, institutional and community dynamics, Jamie Allen tells the story of attempts to reckon with Taranaki Cathedral's chequered history. The chapter describes reconciliatory practice operating on a range of fronts: within a church, between church and society, and notably between Māori and Pākehā. In this latter respect, the chapter highlights the central, distinctive roles of the Treaty of Waitangi and biculturalism in New Zealand's history of peacemaking.

Reconciliatory methodologies are often related with social justice, and many of the chapters point to this close relationship.

In their discussion of Te Ora Hou's work with Māori youth, Ross and his colleagues analyse the politics of marginalisation and address innovative attempts to respond to this displacement. John Chote's study of St Joseph's, in the Catholic Parish of Wellington South, is a compelling account of a church with a long history of commitment to peacemaking and social service. As in Duke's account of the Quakers, this interweaving between peace and social justice is so tight so as to leave hardly any space between them.

A final set of methodologies relate to the use of iconography and ritual in peaceable formation and practice. In Dennis's chapter, fighting the devil provides a startling example of Pentecostal ritualised action. There are also marked instances within other traditions, including the Anglican and Catholic churches. Allen's narrative hinges on the reordering of sacred space, and ritualisation of this adjustment through deliberate processes of community engagement. Chote's account of St Joseph's identifies a range of peace-orienting ritual practices that are ingrained in the rhythm of community life, as well as the crucial influence of the form and aesthetics of the church's facilities: its architecture, art and iconography.

All of these methods and actions raise important implicit questions about the success or otherwise of Christian moral formation in peacemaking. Expressed simply: how important is peace to New Zealand Christianity? How central has it really been? One of the concluding chapters in this volume, by John Shaver, Joseph Bulbulia and Chris Sibley, represents an attempt to address this question, offering an explanation for somewhat variegated and apparently conflicting patterns. Drawing upon rich quantitative data from the New Zealand Attitudes and Values Study, the chapter highlights a prevailing conservatism within New Zealand Christianity. The finding demonstrates the value of employing different analytical methodologies, and the insights they can yield. It also raises further questions, for we know that small traditions can also have effects out of proportion to their size, and that some dynamics are not captured by numbers alone.

How to Read This Book

Before moving to the chapters themselves, it is worth offering some clarifications about the book and guidance on how to read it. In terms of its contents, the book's chapters represent an impressively broad range of Christian engagements with peacemaking, but they do not aspire to offer a comprehensive account of such action. Many further examples could be identified and explored. Indeed, it is our hope that this book will help to open up this field and stimulate further research.

Stylistically, most of the chapters in this volume pursue a strongly narrative approach. This approach is intentional. On the one hand, stories are basic to the social sciences because they represent perhaps the most fundamental form of interpersonal communication. Readers should not be surprised to find stories told in a number of different ways, using a range of social-scientific methods, including ethnography, history and biography. Autobiography and first-hand accounts also feature, for many of the chapters are written by participants in the events described. This lends an immediacy and evocativeness to the writing. Readers should not expect each author to conform to the purported virtue of scholarly detachment, which is in any case largely mythical. Likewise, theologising has not been expunged from the text, though neither has it been required. This inclusiveness of the theological is out of a conviction that a mature conversation about religion will not blindside practitioners themselves. The hope is that this approach is provocative and stimulating for readers, regardless of their own locations. Those authors who own a theological position themselves represent a range of different traditions and perspectives.

In its attempt to furnish accessible, engaging accounts available to a broad readership, the volume can be read as a form of 'public history' or 'public anthropology'. A primary virtue of a narrative approach is the capacity of stories to engage a wide audience. Accessibility is further enhanced because of the brevity of each of the chapters. These are concise and focused interventions in particular themes, topics and events. References have been kept to a minimum, and are located in endnotes largely to signal places where those wanting further information might start.

In broad strokes, the organisation of the volume conforms to an historical arc, beginning during the Second World War and ending in contemporary responses to the Anzac Day commemorations. Despite this, the book is not necessarily the sort of volume that should be read in linear fashion from start to finish. Readers are encouraged to pick and choose and follow the strands they wish in the order they prefer. Each chapter stands alone, though we are confident that the value and significance of the volume adds up to more than the sum of its individual parts.

Our basic claim is that the will for peace, and peacemaking action, forms a more crucial element in New Zealand's history than analyses have typically allowed. We also contend that Christianity has been an important part of this dynamic. These are not claims for New Zealand's exceptionalism, or the uniqueness of Christianity. The collection of studies we provide here simply does not allow for adjudication over these issues. Nevertheless, our evidence does establish Christianity as a significant driver of peace action within New Zealand's recent history. This striking observation will, we hope, spark further conversations and debates in New Zealand and also further afield.

2

Barrington, Burton and the Challenge of Christian Pacifism in New Zealand

Tom Noakes-Duncan

> The time is coming even in these nominally Christian nations of ours when men will be tried, imprisoned and executed because their first loyalty is to Christ and not to any class or nation. . . . Have no fear—following Christ in the next twenty years is likely to be a stern, hard and bloody business.[1]

This omen, appearing in a 1921 booklet written by Ormond Burton for the Wellington branch of the YMCA, offers a glimpse of the Christian conviction that would, twenty years later, see Burton imprisoned for his uncompromising loyalty to Christ over nation. Burton was an outspoken defender of Christian pacifism at a time when his country was at war.

The story of Christian pacifism in New Zealand during the Second World War has been told before. Burton's biography has been written; the prison diary of his fellow pacifist inmate, A. C. Barrington, has recently appeared; the Christian Pacifist Society, which they formed together, has also had its story recorded.[2]

Yet this does not lessen the importance of engaging afresh with their theology of non-violence. By remembering not only those who fought in war but those who opposed it as well, we might become better prepared to pursue the peace that was their driving concern.

This chapter explores the challenges associated with living a commitment to Christian pacifism in New Zealand during this period by focusing on these two individuals, Archibald Barrington and Ormond Burton. In telling their story as a theologian, I will draw attention to the theological convictions that motivated them.

Barrington and Burton

Following the traumatic casualties of the First World War, the public mood in New Zealand was marked by uncertainty and insecurity. For many, this expressed itself in a collectivist mentality where the security of the whole depended on a tightening of the ranks. In such a conformist society, dissenting voices were suppressed and labelled as eccentric. For a minority, however, the post-war era led to searching questions of the political and legal establishment, and of militarism in particular. Burton, a decorated lieutenant praised as both a fearless soldier and a skilled war historian, was expecting a new age of world peace after the defeat of Prussian militarism. Instead, he was disillusioned by the post-war terms of the Treaty of Versailles, which struck him and many others as vengeful, and likely to sow the seeds for future conflict.

After a meeting with James Gibb, a leading Presbyterian minister who himself had undergone a radical conversion to pacifism,[3] Burton committed himself to pacifism as the only viable Christian response to war. He first made this declaration at a Student Christian Movement conference in Masterton, 1923, after which he published the booklet, *Shall We Fight?* He wrote,

> Let us face the gods of war with empty hands, but with the faith that moves mountains. Insisting on the solidarity of the human race, let us go up by every branch, suffering but causing no other to suffer, being slain but never slaying, proclaiming and practising the gospel of love.[4]

His conviction led him, along with Fred Page, to be the only New Zealand teachers to refuse to sign a new oath of allegiance to the Crown: Burton believed that signing the oath would conflict with his first duty to God.

Barred from teaching in the classroom, Burton became active in the Labour Party. In Burton's mind, faith and politics could not be compartmentalised and treated separately; they were woven together in a distinct blend of Christian Socialism in which every societal concern was an ethical one that could be addressed by following the social programme outlined by Jesus.[5] All that remained, he believed, was for men and women of courage to expound clearly the principles of faith, foremost of which was the universal 'brotherhood of man'. While Burton's social concerns were generally shared by Labour Party members, many of whom had opposed military conscription in the First World War, his uncompromising approach led him to leave the Party and stand for Parliament as an independent. Politics would not, however, be Burton's calling.

By 1935 Burton was serving as a Methodist probationer, taking up parish duties at Webb Street Methodist Church, in one of Wellington's poorest areas at the time. Burton's steward and lay preacher at Webb Street was A. C. ('Archie') Barrington. An accountant and professional secretary, Barrington was also responsible for the Methodist Young Men's Bible Class Movement, which had a national membership of 3,000–4,000, many of whom were self-professed young pacifists. Barrington had worked hard to get a resolution passed at the Methodist Conference committing the Church to an explicit and absolutist stance against war. When the Conference's resolution failed to meet Barrington's expectations, he and Burton decided to form the independent Christian Pacifist Society (CPS) in March of 1936.

Though predominantly made up of fellow Methodists, the CPS included a mixture of Presbyterians, Baptists, Anglicans and Congregationalists. Membership was only available to those who were communicant church members, as Burton believed that only committed church members could withstand the coming challenges of a pacifist witness. Burton was particularly wary of humanist inspired pacifism, as can be seen in his later comments to a university audience:

> Humanist-pacifism lacks the passion and the relation to reality which would enable it to grapple with the enormous difficulties of the human race. It tends to be an armchair philosophy and not of the nature of tears, blood and sweat. As with political liberation it is only able to provide amenities rather than a new structure.[6]

While perhaps not a fair representation, these comments point to the particularity of Burton's version of pacifism, which clearly had the church at its centre.

In the late 1930s there was already a feeling that war was in the air, and Barrington knew that New Zealand churches had a track record of giving their blessing to the Allied war efforts. Not long before, in the First World War, the Methodist Church had passed a resolution stating, 'We regard the British Empire, with all its defects, as being, in practical righteousness, the largest instalment of the Kingdom of God that has yet arisen among men.'[7] Churches across New Zealand had vigorously supported the war through providing chaplains to serve in the military, by using their pulpits as virtual recruiting stations, and by promoting the language of 'supreme sacrifice' as a way of making sense of combatant casualties. In general, New Zealand churches saw their role as blessing the established values of consensus and security, which in times of war meant loyalty to the Empire and willingness to sacrifice all for its cause.

Members of the CPS began to organise. Their first protest meeting was at a military display at Rongotai Airport on the King's Birthday, 3 June 1938, which was followed three days later with a march alongside the soldiers through the city, carrying sandwich boards with pacifist slogans. They also distributed a pamphlet called 'Come Down to Earth!' that renounced all war and its military methods, and which invited the Government to lay down arms and resume friendship and goodwill with all countries.[8] From the outset of their protests, the CPS encountered resistance from the police and the occasional passer-by, but people generally tolerated their presence.

The Wellington public was already familiar with the message of Christian pacifism. From the very first Sunday of taking up his position at Webb Street, Burton—and later his wife Helen (Nell), or Barrington—would spend every Sunday afternoon on his soapbox at the popular public grounds, the Basin Reserve, arguing the faith with passing agnostics, sceptics, rationalists and others. Burton's skill as an orator was such that he often drew a significant crowd. These debates about matters of faith became increasingly centred on pacifism.[9] For these Christians, pacifism was not a privately held belief but a question of public truth that needed to be proclaimed and defended, in the same way as their faith.

Wartime Dissent

On 4 September 1939, the day after Prime Minister Joseph Savage declared war on Germany, Burton, Barrington and other CPS members gathered near the grounds of parliament to express their opposition. Their speeches drew a crowd of about 200 before Burton and others were taken away, charged with obstructing police officers. It was arranged that Barrington would go home and write a report on what happened, which led to the start of their newsletter, the *Bulletin*. While held in the police station, Burton and his colleagues were charged with obstructing the police and opposing military recruiting. News of their arrest travelled quickly, and very soon none other than Peter Fraser, then Deputy Prime Minister and Commissioner of Police, visited them at the station pleading for them to stop their criticism of the war. No assurances were given, but nonetheless they were released until their trial.

At his trial for obstructing the police, Burton handed a statement to the Magistrate outlining his journey to Christian pacifism and why he and his fellow pacifists were in breach of wartime regulations. He concluded, 'We regret that this should be necessary but, belonging as we do to the Christian Church, there is for us a higher authority than that of the State.'[10] From this time, State pressure on the Christian pacifists to stop their 'subversive speech' increased, including police searches and seizures, and eventually prison time. When Burton was held in jail or prison, Barrington would have to fill his preaching slot at church. On some occasions a policeman would sit in the back row of the service with a typewriter, writing out everything that was spoken.[11] Barrington's house was searched more than once, but nothing was found. This is because he kept his files hidden under his daughter's cot, pamphlets under a pile of sand in his basement, and his stencils for making the bulletin behind a portrait of his father.[12]

Like many activist groups, the CPS were not always of one mind when it came to matters of strategy. In fact, at one point they were deeply divided, with tensions in the group reducing some members to tears. Shortly after New Zealand's entry into

Merle Hyland and Archibald Charles Barrington beside the 'Peace Caravan', which toured the country covered in anti-war slogans. Source: 1/2-037729-F, Alexander Turnbull Library.

the war, the Society organised a conference to discuss how they could show their opposition. Some, like Alun Richards, argued that the group needed to be more underground, and that its witness would be most effective through behind-the-scenes education.[13] Burton and Barrington disagreed, maintaining that a direct and open confrontation with the government was needed. The debate became personal, with Burton being accused of 'spiritual pride' and 'glorying in persecution'. Nevertheless, the CPS decided to continue with public protests, leaving it as the only New Zealand group maintaining a public opposition to war.[14]

The agitation caused by the CPS was evident when the Mayor of Wellington, Thomas Hislop, called these Christians 'peacemongers' and 'shirkers', and declared that he would do everything he could to prevent their meetings, telling the press that 'if they want a fight they can have it'.[15] This did not deter

Barrington, who made a tour of the North Island in a 'peace caravan'. He wrote of this tour:

> It was a lively journey. Some hundreds listened in the Square at Palmerston North without interference. Hardly anybody came to an advertised indoor meeting at Marton. But I was arrested in Wanganui, Auckland, and Gisborne. Returned soldiers, evidently primed for the purpose, marched me out of Stratford, Te Kuiti, and Tauranga. Tomatoes were thrown at Stratford, eggs at New Plymouth. In both cases the aim was poor. In fact, in New Plymouth I held the baby of an innocent spectator while he tried to wipe egg off his clothes. An angry policeman kicked my soap-box to bits in Hawera and, when I transferred to a Reserve, the Mayor appealed to citizens not to listen and to go home. I had a new 'soapbox' specially made that even a Bobbie couldn't put his boot through. Someone at the Wanganui meeting suggested I should be thrown in the river and by the time I reached Gisborne 'Truth' billboards screamed, 'We'll drown you in the river. Pacifists and angry crowds.'[16]

While Barrington toured the North Island, Burton went south in November of 1939 to deliver one of his most prophetic denunciations of the war. At the invitation of the Moderator of the Presbyterian Assembly in Christchurch, Burton spelt out why war would never be able to deliver a condition of lasting peace. In a time of war, then, Christians must follow:

> no other way than the way of the Cross—of Holy Love, suffering, and yet remaining utterly and purely Love, not penetrated by hatred. . . . As we practise this revolutionary way of Christ we shall lay heavenly foundations for a new civilisation that will be indestructible, enduring in mystical fashion through time into timelessness.[17]

Despite Burton's rousing message, the Presbyterian Church was undeterred in its support of the war.

The Methodist Church eventually withdrew its support of its pacifist members, especially Burton. The Church's Manifesto on Peace and War, first presented to the Methodist Conference in Dunedin in 1940, had as one of its principal intentions the banning of subversive utterances from the churches' pulpits—notably, including pacifist sentiments. While it was framed as a unifying document, bringing together people of differing viewpoints in common worship, Burton's refusal to accept the terms of the Manifesto eventually led to his dismissal in 1942 from both the Methodist Conference and his ministerial vocation. Writing of these events, Burton's biographer has argued that while Methodism 'gained in respectability and official approbation . . . it lost something of its own soul.'[18]

Burton's insistence on preaching the gospel as he interpreted it led him into direct confrontation with the religious and political leaders of his day. In this, he saw himself as continuing the tradition of the Protestant Reformation, while others likened it to following in the footsteps of Jesus. Barrington wrote of him:

> I think there is a curious parallel here with Christ's setting his face to go to Jerusalem. He could have avoided this confrontation and he might have been able to continue teaching, healing and creating his church. But there was a compelling force within him that could see beyond the ordinary, beyond the comfort of 'getting by' while avoiding complications.[19]

Only two weeks after his release from his first prison sentence, Burton informed the police of his intentions to speak again at the Manners Street Reserve. Meeting him there, a senior sergeant told him that he would not be allowed to address the crowd. Undeterred, Burton stood up and said, 'The words of the Lord Jesus Christ call us to peace', after which he was pulled down and arrested, this time being sentenced to three months of hard labour.

As the war stretched out and gathered in intensity, the CPS decided to hold more open air meetings, despite warnings by the police. This led to a number of arrests, most of which occurred after CPS members took to the memorial on Manners Street only to recite a few verses from the Bible. Burton began his meeting on 18 April 1941 before 400–500 onlookers with words from Romans 1:16: 'I am not ashamed of the gospel of Christ: for it is the power of God unto salvation.' He was immediately taken down and arrested. The Detective Sergeant asked him why he continued to speak despite warnings from the police. Burton replied, 'As a Christian man, I could do no other but preach

PEACE
MEETING
Every Friday
LOVE
YOUR
ENEMIES

Ormond Burton broadcasting the words of Jesus, 'love your enemies', at the front of a New Zealand Christian Pacifist Society parade for peace in Wellington, c.1940. Source: 1/2-152943-F, Alexander Turnbull Library.

the Christian gospel as I understand it. If that brings me into conflict with the law of the land, I deeply regret the fact, but my first obedience is to God.'[20] The policy of social control adopted by the police was meant to weaken the pacifist voice, but in reality it only strengthened their resolve.

Burton's third term of imprisonment at Mount Crawford Prison was quite unlike the first two, since this time there was a greater fellowship of pacifists and dissenters serving time together. On their first yard day they broke out in full service with singing and preaching—which was quickly broken up by the corrections officers. Barrington had also been sentenced to a year's hard labour for sedition, leaving behind his wife of six years and his three small children. The rhythm of work, fellowship and silence led both Burton and Barrington to write to their families likening their time in prison to that of being in a monastery, much to the dislike of the censors.[21]

With the introduction of conscription in 1940, approximately 3,000 people applied for exemption from military service. Of these, 800 were prosecuted for further refusing non-combatant service. Many of the men were sent to makeshift detention camps across the North Island, run by the military as a form of disciplinary action against 'defaulters'—those who were never granted Conscientious Objector status. One woman, Connie Jones, was jailed at Point Halswell in Wellington in 1941 for her outspoken pacifist beliefs. It is widely agreed that the way dissenters were treated in New Zealand was significantly harsher and more punitive than in Great Britain, Canada and Australia.[22] Whereas other countries saw freedom of conscience as what separated them from totalitarian fascism, the New Zealand authorities took the view that dissenters posed a direct threat to the public mood and therefore needed to be suppressed, even if that meant locking them up.

Barrington kept a diary while incarcerated in Mount Crawford. Because diary writing wasn't allowed, he wrote his journal entries in the margins of the many books that he kept in his cell—books like *Jesus of Galilee* by Frank Warburton.[23] They were then smuggled out of the prison by the family butcher in Kilbirnie, who also supplied the prison with meat. This journal was discovered many years later and was only published in 2016. It describes the harshness of prison conditions: they had to wear clothes that were filthy, full of holes, never fitted, and made them freeze in winter. They had a slosh bucket in the cell's corner to do their business, and there was lots of hard labour. They did, however, have concerts, plays, and even lectures in the prison.

Both Burton and Barrington faced one last trial each on the charge of distributing seditious material. While Barrington was released on a technicality, Burton was sentenced in October 1942 to two and a half years in jail despite the jury's plea for a merciful sentence. Barrington decried the sentence as a 'mockery of mercy'.[24] At his trial, Burton directed the court to rule against his Christian faith, since this is what he believed was on trial. In his concluding statement he wrote:

> In a small way, but at a great moment in history, it is my privilege to bear witness to the great tradition of the Christian Church that she must be free to preach the whole of her Gospel and live the fullness of her life. No doubt, Sir, you will be supported in your sentencing of me by the majority elements of the Church that are moving fast, as in Germany, to be decent ornaments of a Fascist State. Yet the living elements of the Church can live, and indeed find new life, in the gaols and, even when your fear grows to a certain intensity, in front of your firing squads. Therefore, Sir, I am prepared to receive your sentence without bitterness and, indeed, with cheerfulness, because I know that the good future lies with those who dare to practise a good freedom in a world grown insane with fear.[25]

Burton's belief that the life of the church might be discovered in the jails and before the firing squad is reminiscent of the great martyr tradition on which the church is built. The sad reality, however, is that his church was ultimately unsupportive of its members who held fast to their conviction that Jesus would not have them fight in war. The historian Allan Davidson put the matter clearly: 'The irony is that in cathedrals and churches, whose congregations follow the prince of peace, those who have fought in war are remembered, but those who took the other costly road and stood up for peace are usually ignored.'[26]

The Challenge of Christian Pacifism

As a theologian it is my task to consider both the work of God in the world today and the question of how we should live in a way that points toward, and participates in, God's activities. In conclusion, therefore, I want to provide some brief meditations on this remarkable story of costly Christian pacifism.

The first thing to say is that *Christian* pacifism is ultimately a matter of faith. When Barrington was tried for sedition after he left prison he was asked, 'What would you do if a savage, ravishing horde came to this country, molesting the women and children?' He replied,

> I wouldn't resist any invading force otherwise than by the way revealed by Jesus Christ. I believed this was adequate to all human situations. There couldn't, though, be any guarantee that in following this way there wouldn't be suffering or great hardship, or even death for some or for many. The way of war couldn't guarantee this either, or any good outcome.[27]

There are many reasons why people declare themselves to be pacifists, but Barrington makes clear that for him it had everything to do with 'the way revealed by Jesus'. In other words, if one interprets the life of Jesus as committed to non-violence, right up to and including his death, then it follows that the non-violence of Christians is predicated on how they understand God's purposes being fulfilled in Jesus.

The way revealed by Jesus is the way of the cross—the refusal to collude with violence, even when the cause appears just and good. On more than one occasion, Burton described his pacifism as 'a doctrine of the atonement', since it was for him a position closely bound up in his interpretation of the cross of Christ. Neither Burton nor Barrington were naïve; they knew that their pacifist stance would lead to suffering and possibly even death. Like war, it cannot guarantee a good outcome.

I would argue, however, that the Christian life is not ultimately lived with a view to making sure history comes out right. It is lived, rather, in trust that the social, political and ethical reality embodied in Jesus is now a present reality that can be laid hold of as people respond to the 'other'—stranger, friend, or enemy—with the compassionate, enfolding love that is God's.[28] If the cross on which Jesus died is interpreted as the end of his life, then Christians would have no ground on which to hope for something beyond death, in which case survival triumphs over all other goals. But if the cross is interpreted in the light of Jesus' resurrection, as Burton maintained, then it is Jesus' willingness to die for the sake of his convictions that becomes the ultimate goal to follow.[29]

This perspective reveals something else about Christian pacifism—it is not passivism. The commitment to pacifism is often confused with being passive in the face of violence or war, as if Christians should withdraw from engagement. But if pacifism is predicated on following after Jesus, then this requires Christians to actively take up the pursuit of peace. As Burton and Barrington exemplify: Christians are called to be relentless peacemakers, trusting that the outcome of their efforts has been assured in God's vindication of Jesus in resurrecting him from the dead, and believing that they have been freed for a purpose—to proclaim and embody Jesus' resurrection as the overcoming of all forms of death by violence.

This Christian witness to peace takes the form of a sacrificial commitment for others. Violence is the shutting down of dialogue; it is the refusal to let the enemy in, the inability to disagree without eliminating the other. In his trial, the prosecutor (himself a Jew) asked Barrington, 'You wouldn't expect us to love Hitler, would you?' Barrington replied, 'It's a very difficult job to love Hitler, but it's a Christian obligation to try—and there are lots of unpleasant people nearer whom we can practise on.'[30] Christian pacifists don't generally have a foreign policy for what to do with the likes of Hitler, Bin Laden, or Donald Trump for that matter. Rather, they have a commitment and an obligation to be as Christ to the world: to be committed to dialogue, to love their enemies and, even if that fails, to never resort to war as a way of settling their disagreements. For examples of what this can look like, I am grateful for the lives of those Christian pacifists who have gone before us.

3

A Historic Peace Church in Aotearoa New Zealand: Quakers and their Heritage

Elizabeth Duke

In Aotearoa New Zealand the Religious Society of Friends, or Quakers as they are more commonly known, are a small religious body in the radical Christian tradition. They are rooted in a movement founded in mid-seventeenth-century England that believed it was restoring the primitive, original Church and following Jesus in the power of the Spirit. Quakers believe that a radical faith alternative to 'the world' calls for an authentic peace.[1] They are known worldwide as one of the historic peace churches due to their longstanding emphasis on disavowing violence and pursuing proactive peacemaking.[2] This chapter examines how Quakers in Aotearoa New Zealand have sought to live out this call of peace, focusing primarily on the period after the Second World War.

Early British Quakers extended their reach initially to continental Europe and the North American colonies. Nineteenth- and twentieth-century service and mission work led to a worldwide movement, composed of self-governing bodies known as 'Yearly Meetings' or 'Friends Churches'. The Quaker body in Aotearoa New Zealand developed as individuals and families settled there from 1836. There was no external mission or formal attempt at church planting. Because nearly all these Quaker settlers came from Britain, the body here was part of the British Quaker structure until 1964, though national gatherings in Aotearoa New Zealand were held from 1909 onwards.[3] The present self-governing body is the Yearly Meeting of Aotearoa

New Zealand, Te Hāhi Tūhauwiri. There are approximately 1,200 people in contact with the Quakers in Aotearoa New Zealand today. Of these, about 500 are in formal adult membership. This is a very small body to manage the tasks of nurturing spiritual life and caring for its people while engaging in witness and service.

The Quaker Peace Testimony

Quaker theology is generally implicit rather than explicit. It is exemplified by lived practice, rather than embodied in doctrinal pronouncements. When Quakers speak of 'testimony' they mean bearing witness—as often through committed action as through words—to what they stand for. The earliest Quaker expressions of a peace testimony came from individuals, based on inner conviction and Scriptural teaching. William Dewsbury, one of the first Quakers, joined the Parliamentary army in the English Civil War (1642–51) because he believed that they 'fought for the gospel'. He was struck, however, by the profound spiritual ignorance of his fellow soldiers and soon left, recognising instead 'the kingdom of Christ to be within, and that its enemies being within and spiritual, my weapons against them should also be spiritual—the power of God.'[4] George Fox, a founding Quaker leader, was asked to be a captain for the Parliamentarians during the Civil War. He refused, saying that he lived 'in the virtue of that life and power that took away the occasion of all wars' and declaring that all wars arose from 'lust'.[5]

Under persecution, these individual commitments to peace gained collective expression. Following public declarations by early Quaker Margaret Fell, a group of leading Quakers could state in 1660: 'the spirit of Christ, which leads us into all Truth, will never move us to fight and war against any man with outward weapons, neither for the kingdom of Christ, nor for the kingdoms of this world.'[6] While this refusal to bear arms has become a central commitment for many Quakers over the ensuing centuries, the ways in which Quakers have understood their peace testimony have changed and broadened in diverse social and cultural contexts.

Wreath of white poppies made by Nelson Quakers and displayed in Nelson Cathedral for the Gallipoli centenary commemorations, 2015. The white poppy has been used as a symbol of peace—of grief and remembrance for the victims of war, and opposition to violence and war—since the 1930s. Photograph courtesy of Barbara Curtis.

Dilemmas of Peace

The Quaker experience of seeking to live out their peace testimony has never been free of complications and challenges. Peace churches today share the same dilemmas as the earliest Christians. How far do they support the social order, promoting what is good in it? Or to what extent are they counter-cultural, refusing to collude with the militarism and violence embedded in almost every nation state? Should Christians withdraw to their own separated community? How can they obey Jesus' instruction to 'render unto Caesar the things that are Caesar's, and unto God the things that are God's'?[7]

Quakers in Aotearoa New Zealand have struggled with and found differing answers to these dilemmas, as the following two examples illustrate. In 1985 the New Zealand Government established a Defence Committee of Enquiry that included

Kevin Clements, a Quaker. Though in this role Kevin was generally supported by Friends, he also received hostile messages from fellow Quakers accusing him of undermining their peace testimony. In a written response, entitled 'What is a Quaker like you doing on a Committee like this?', Kevin stated:

> Personally, I ascribe to an absolute pacifist position and will not take up arms against anyone. I believe very strongly, furthermore, that it is absolutely essential that groups such as Friends, and other Peace Churches, maintain a vocational witness to non-violent alternatives to war. Having expressed my position, however, I am conscious of the fact that my views are not shared by all the community, and for the foreseeable future, therefore, we can not expect to dismantle the armed forces. In this situation, I am in favour of working to ensure that the New Zealand armed services see themselves in defensive, non-aggressive terms alone, and work in ways which cause no offence to anyone.[8]

Following the dissension surrounding Kevin's involvement in the Defence Enquiry, the Yearly Meeting in January 1987 addressed a statement on peace to the nation. It was unequivocal:

> We totally oppose all wars, all preparation for war, all use of weapons and coercion by force, and all military alliances; no end could ever justify such means. We equally and actively oppose all that leads to violence among people and nations, and violence to other species and to our planet.

Just as firmly, the Yearly Meeting proclaimed the foundational Quaker understanding of 'that of God in everyone', stating: 'We may disagree with the views and actions of the politician or the soldier who opts for a military solution, but we still respect and cherish the person.'[9] Personal attacks are themselves unpeaceable.

Marian Hobbs, a Quaker who served in the Labour Cabinet (1999–2005) and was New Zealand's first Minister for Disarmament, recognised the hard challenges of working in public office.[10] She experienced an 'awkward and constant compromise of clashing values'. As a member of a political party and as a cabinet minister, she was part of a team that made decisions that she had to stand behind, even decisions that she had doubts about. Her Quaker commitment to peace was sometimes pivotal to her experience of clashing values: 'although I have never really had to face the challenge of personally taking another's life, I have felt the weight of Government decisions which may well have led to loss of life, such as sending soldiers to Afghanistan and to the Solomon Islands.' Such clashing loyalties exemplify how difficult it is to discern what is rightfully Caesar's and what is God's.

Pursuing peace involves working through such complex dilemmas. Yet Quakers in Aotearoa New Zealand have remained committed to living out their peace testimony in a variety of ways. Peace in the biblical tradition is *shalom*—right relations with God, humanity, our planet and its life. It includes resistance to war and militarism, prevention of war, healing the wounds of war, building social justice and honouring all life on this planet. Quaker testimonies emerge from a direct relationship of all with God, 'that of God in every one', as George Fox asserted.[11] In the remainder of this chapter I illustrate how Quakers in Aotearoa New Zealand have understood and practised these five facets of peace.

Peace is Refusal to Fight and Kill

Seeking peace fundamentally requires non-violence, the refusal to take up arms. This decision becomes more challenging in the face of heightened wartime patriotism. Already in 1909, New Zealand had introduced compulsory military training, against which Quakers made representations from the start. During the First World War, the implementation of forced mass conscription in 1916 imposed sharp challenges on individuals. Quakers, as members of a peace church, could be granted alternative service. Three young Quaker men from Dunedin were among those who served in wartime Europe in the Friends Ambulance Unit established by British Quakers. On their return in 1919 the Dunedin Meeting recorded:

> The conscientious objectors of our Society, and others likeminded have fared badly; but some of our members considered it right to help our Empire in its hour of need, and chose ambulance work. Three members of our meeting, Henry and Cecil Wardell and J. H.

> White left New Zealand to assist in ambulance work, and we are pleased to record that their work was appreciated by the state.[12]

The last phrase, and the words 'to help our Empire', reflect the powerful influence of the contemporary social climate even on decisions of conscience.

During the First World War, conscientious objectors without a church backing were harshly punished.[13] Those Quakers who refused alternative service as collusion with militarism also experienced detention or prison, but they were strengthened by mutual support. Edward Dowsett writes of John Brailsford, a fellow Quaker prisoner:

> It was John Brailsford who refused to let any of us give way to self pity; it was John who helped us think first of our fellow prisoners and to refuse all concessions that were not also granted to the outlaws from society serving sentences for crimes of a different kind from ours.[14]

Quakers in the Second World War who refused any form of alternative service also experienced detention.

Quakers have not seen the refusal to fight as relating solely to decisions made by individual consciences, as important as these decisions are. Instead, they have sought to ask questions about the societal acceptance of the necessity of violence and also provided support for those choosing to do otherwise. New Zealand Quakers have promoted the universal right of conscientious—and not only religious—objection, and done so by various means, including: representations against compulsory military training; opposing the presence of cadet units in schools; and providing counselling to conscientious objectors in both World Wars. They have also given employment to some who lost their jobs on account of their refusal to fight in wars, and provided support for detained conscientious objectors and their families. Jos Brusse, who had suffered German occupation in the Netherlands, is one example of a Quaker who offered counsel to young men facing the draft after the Second World War. He informed them 'on the rights and responsibilities of conscientious objectors and that it was not a soft option.'[15]

Peace is the Prevention of War

Since the Second World War, Quakers have individually served on various peace bodies in New Zealand that have advocated for and worked toward the prevention of war. These include the Women's International League for Peace and Freedom Aotearoa, Peace Movement Aotearoa, the Foundation for Peace Studies Aotearoa/New Zealand, the Campaign for Nuclear Disarmament (NZ), the Christian Pacifist Society, War Resisters International, the Fellowship of Reconciliation, and the National Centre for Peace and Conflict Studies at the University of Otago. Through individual participation and corporate financial support for such groups, Quakers have sought to enlarge their own work for peace.

Individual Quakers have found their own way to oppose war and build peace. Betty Duffield served as a military nurse in the Second World War. In 1990, fearing the imminent Gulf War which commenced in August of that year, she concluded that if 'all the Quakers in the world' got in between the opposing forces, the war would be prevented. Failing to persuade other Quakers, Betty heard of a peace camp planned for the Iraqi/Saudi Arabian border and, aged 80, set off to join it. The international volunteers were hospitably received in Baghdad, but the conditions affected Betty's health, and she was unable to stay for very long.[16] On her return home, Betty spoke to a number of groups about her deep concern for Iraqi women and children. Another example of a Quaker 'getting in-between' is Christina Gibb, who, already a grandmother, spent four three-month periods from 2003 to 2006 with Christian Peacemaker Teams in Hebron, Palestine. Through their presence the teams sought to prevent or reduce harassment of Palestinian children and families, and to listen to Palestinians and Israelis talk about the conflict.

Another way of seeking to prevent war is to resist the glorification of fighting in media, music, monuments and public life, and the militarisation of society. Quakers have sought to engage effectively and charitably with the centenary commemorations of the First World War. In 2014, the Yearly Meeting stated:

> On the eve of commemorations of World War I, Quakers in Aotearoa New Zealand are concerned that history is not reinvented to glorify war. We remember the loss of life, the destruction of the environment, the courage of soldiers, dissenters and conscientious objectors; we remember all those who still suffer the ongoing trauma of war. We also note the increasing use of scarce resources for war. In Aotearoa New Zealand over ten million dollars a day is being spent to maintain our armed forces in a state of 'combat readiness.' We actively support alternative processes for resolving conflict and violence both within and between nations.

Peace is Healing the Wounds of War

In 1947 the Friends Service Council and the American Friends Service Committee, both prominent Quaker organisations, were awarded the Nobel Peace Prize for their efforts in attempting to heal the wounds of war through relief and construction work in Europe. The Friends Ambulance Unit, mentioned already above, combined a testimony against war with tangible relief for its victims. Although initially active only in Europe, during the Second World War it expanded its geographical horizon to meet the desperate needs in China. A number of New Zealanders, mostly Quakers, joined the Unit in China from 1945 to 1951.[17] Of those who served in the 'China Convoy' delivering medical supplies and other services, Margaret Jackson and Neil Johnson, together with Mary Campbell, who undertook the group's logistics,[18] went on to work for the relief of suffering with the Council of Organisations for Relief Service Overseas (CORSO). This was launched in 1944 by Quakers, the New Zealand Red Cross, and the National Council of Churches.[19]

One way of healing the wounds of war is to recognise the humanity in one's 'enemy' and extend care to them. During the First World War, John Howell was the director of the Christchurch Technical College. He resisted official pressures, and stirred up a storm, by continuing to offer prayers for the enemy at the College's daily assembly.[20] In 1940, while Howell was director of the Wellington Technical College, he requested permission to visit 'enemy aliens' interned on Somes Island. With fellow Wellington Quakers, including Margaret Wadman and Richard Harris, Howell saw to the needs of the internees and their families. Harris went on to support and care for Japanese prisoners of war.[21]

Peace Requires 'True Justice'

In his book *True Justice*, British Quaker Adam Curle argues that the absence or ending of conflict is not enough. 'Without justice there is no peace', Curle concludes. Peacemaking works for a just society by 'altering what was exploitative or oppressive into something nurturing human growth and the fulfilment of potential'. It involves treating all 'with love, respect and intelligent concern'.[22] Aotearoa New Zealand Quakers seek to work in accordance with these principles, building social justice in diverse ways.

Building upon their involvement in wartime emergency relief, Quakers became involved in a variety of development initiatives. In addition to helping found prominent New Zealand development organisations, including CORSO, the Yearly Meeting works through its own Quaker Peace and Service Committee (QPSANZ), which seeks to engage with peace, justice and development issues around the world. The QPSANZ Committee recognises that development and justice accompany peace. In 2015 it supported a diverse range of initiatives and organisations, including peace and development centres in Mexico City and Capetown, earthquake relief in Nepal, a water project in Zimbabwe, a girls' school in India with students from poor tribal communities, a development body in Guatemala, a documentary on inequality in Aotearoa New Zealand, a Quaker peace centre in Indonesia, and a study on pacifist women in this country. The Committee regularly supports Peace Movement Aotearoa, Christian World Service, international peace and disarmament work, and Quaker work at the United Nations, which includes peace and conflict resolution, human rights and refugees, trade and economic equity, and climate change concerns. It also advocates to the New Zealand Government on peace and justice issues.

In 1998 a group from QPSANZ perceived a calling, during a time of heightened tension and violence in Indonesia, to train Indonesian police in human rights and non-violent conflict resolution. A decade later, when the project concluded, they

Mary Campbell (right) with Tayeko Yamanouchi, a Japanese Quaker, in May 1950, possibly at the Quaker Centre in Shanghai. Campbell was one of a number of New Zealanders who served in the 'China Convoy', providing medical supplies and relief services after the Second World War. Source: PAColl-6162-03-01, Alexander Turnbull Library.

had helped to develop and evaluate police involvement in the Master of Peace and Conflict Resolution programme at Gadjah Mada University and, with funding from the New Zealand Aid Programme, arranged workshops for senior police on non-violent conflict resolution and community policing.[23]

Another area that Quakers have had longstanding involvement in is penal reform. This concern originated with their own early experiences of imprisonment, reinforced by more recent detention of conscientious objectors. Quakers also observe that the current penal system too often breeds violence, fails to rehabilitate, and does not recognise the humanity of all involved. Quakers hold penal reform seminars and support penal reform organisations, including the Howard League and the Robson Hanan Trust. As a small gesture of friendship and remembering Quaker conscientious objectors imprisoned there, every Christmas the Mt Eden Quaker Meeting gives flowers to each sentenced inmate at Mt Eden Prison.

In 1991, New Zealand Quakers fostered the Alternatives to Violence (AVP) project as an attempt to encourage inmates and community members to value themselves and others, and to develop co-operative and non-violent responses to conflict. AVP was launched some years earlier in New York by prisoners, with Quaker help. In New Zealand, the initiative is now independent, although Quakers remain involved, and while it is not currently accepted in penal institutions it continues to operate in the wider community.

Quakers believe that a commitment to peace and human rights in this country must necessarily involve a commitment to Te Tiriti o Waitangi / the Treaty of Waitangi, since Quakers were also settlers and therefore under the Crown, the tauiwi (non-Māori) partner to the Treaty. An 'Advice' from British Quakers in 1840 urges: 'Earnestly, therefore, do we desire that all those under our name, who may emigrate to such settlements, may be careful neither directly nor indirectly to inflict injury upon the natives'.[24] Quakers are part of a society which has failed in this, but the Quaker Treaty Relationships group continues internal education, and representations to Government on Treaty-related issues. Quakers in Whanganui offered support to Māori occupying Pākaitore (Moutoa Gardens) in 1995 to protest historical grievances. They also helped form a citizen circle between the occupiers and police. When two young occupiers were sought on other charges, a Quaker, Lizzie, accompanied them to the police station, in order to prevent a provocative police intrusion.

In terms of economic justice, Quakers in New Zealand have recognised that personal simplicity sows awareness of the need for social and economic equity. Quakers support the contemporary Living Wage campaign and engage in advocacy to the Government on social issues. A crucial challenge today is the interrelation between the nation state, militarism and global capital; in the face of this powerful alliance it is hard to find effective interventions. The Yearly Meeting and its groups endeavour to invest ethically by carefully selecting where their investments go.

Finally, Quakers have also brought attention to issues of eco-justice. According to the *Quaker Handbook*: 'A full testimony to peace includes a harmonious relationship with the many life-forms and diverse riches of our planet, and a commitment to live as part of earth's systems, not as their proprietors.'[25] Quakers in this country urge strong measures to mitigate climate change, but also struggle on a personal level to transform their own behaviour. In order to reflect this concern, they have agreed that food at Quaker events should be mainly vegetarian. They wrestle with whether to attend international and national gatherings, given the emissions impact of air travel. They have urged the Government to raise climate change at the United Nations Security Council, and to welcome people displaced by climate change, especially from Pacific countries.

Concluding Reflections

How can a small body faithfully live the gospel of peace and seek to heal the world? This is no easy task and requires continuing careful and prayerful discernment of right action. I see the basis of such discernment as a Good Samaritan theology.[26] The Samaritan on the Jericho road came across a man who had been attacked by robbers. He did not set off to catch or disperse the robbers. Nor did he explore the Bethlehem road to find someone in greater need. Instead, he decided to do justice and love mercy, in the opportunity before him, with the abilities and resources he had. To discern peace witness is to recognise the need which is to hand, one's own capability, and how to serve. To be a historic peace church in Aotearoa New Zealand is to seek, through struggles and failures, to live the gospel and to embody the realm of God where we are and as we can. While Quakers continue to have their own distinct vocation, all Christian bodies are called to be peace churches, and to recognise the voice of God in the world around us and in its people.

4

The Peace Squadron Revisited

George Armstrong

Action . . . Cameras

On 19 January 1979, the nuclear powered and armed submarine USS *Haddo* barrelled its way through a thick tangle of 200 small boats, dinghies, sailboats, rafts, bodies and surfboards in Auckland's inner harbour. Police boats amongst them added to the confusion. The submarine was hell-bent on reaching its berth in the very heart of Auckland city. Equally hell-bent was the flotilla of protestors, who deliberately placed themselves in the submarine's path. Among the protestors was journalist Terry Bell, whose small kayak was swept down the side of the surging submarine, in imminent danger of being chewed to pieces in its huge propeller thrashing astern. Seeing Terry's danger, experienced daredevil Pat McQuarrie steered his motor boat alongside *Haddo*; Stephen Sherie, a mild-mannered steel worker crewing for Pat, leaned out to grasp the hand of the imperilled Terry, hoisting him to the safety of Pat's boat. In the process, however, and on pure impulse, the bespectacled Stephen leaped onto the prow of the submarine. Stephen turned and eyed the *Haddo*'s astonished captain, Commander Minns. 'Turn this bloody thing around,' shouted Stephen. From high above in the conning tower, Minns exclaimed: 'What the . . . is he doing there?!'

Pat McQuarrie's team had made several earlier runs at the *Haddo*, liberally daubing its menacing snout with eggshells full of bright yellow radioactive-warning paint. After the testy remarks exchanged between Stephen and the commander of the submarine, a craft which Stephen had now more or less commandeered, Stephen was left to ride the submarine right to its berth—for all the world like a surfboard rider finding himself suddenly in charge of a sea monster. The whole thing was eagerly captured by a thousand cameras, including those wielded by police.

For Terry Bell, the game was by no means over. Saved from the submarine to Pat McQuarrie's motorboat, he was out of a frying pan and immediately into a fire. A large police launch had been hot on the tail of Pat's boat, and in the uncontrollable melee alongside the *Haddo* it rode right over the stern of Pat's vessel. Its bow hung there for a few seconds before mercifully slithering backwards. Terry, fearful of the situation and his imminent arrest, jumped overboard. He dived deep and long, only to surface near an unceremonious police boat hook. He was bundled off to the cells for questioning, clad only in his red underpants—all that was necessary for comfort and decency in his kayak. When the police later released him, he made his way thus garbed down Queen Street—with more to think about than the cut of his cloth.

This scene and the improvised actions of Stephen, Terry and Pat, along with hundreds of other like-minded protestors, were typical of the Peace Squadrons which were active in various ports around New Zealand in the late 1970s.[1] In their demand for a 'Nuclear Free' country, they engaged in daring, adventurous actions. These protests were pure sociodrama. While the actors, scene and kaupapa (agenda or purpose) were established, the plot unfolded according to the dynamics of the day. They were unscripted and only lightly choreographed. The best lines wrote themselves, emerging in the midst of full-blooded active life. Undeniably chaotic, this kind of public liturgy also had a potent and compelling moral force, drawing diverse audiences into a collective longing for peace and a pristine environment.

I had become a spokesperson for the Auckland Peace Squadron and so it was one of my jobs to try to articulate to the public what it was that we thought we were doing. The task was made easier by a New Zealand media that clearly relished our antics and were thoroughly caught up in the spirit of it all. There was ceaseless media coverage and I was constantly being asked for interviews or soundbites. Print journalists and editors could not resist headlining the spectacles that regularly attended US navy visits through the late 1970s and 80s. For example, after Stephen Sherie's occupation of the submarine, the *Auckland Star* obligingly composed the perfect postscript. The 'words of the prophets' written that afternoon on ocean waves were blazoned unforgettably across that night's front page: 'Boarded! Hot Welcome For Yellow Submarine.'

Hoodlums or Heroes?

The only curious thing outside the hospitable Methodist parson's house in a dark and quiet suburban street one night in 1976 was the extraordinary number of cars parked there. Inside the house was a different matter. The lounge, designed to seat perhaps seven people, was packed wall-to-wall with seventy. All were vigorous, purposeful people, almost all entirely new to one another, certainly new to me as convenor. It was the first meeting of the Auckland Peace Squadron skippers. Lawyer Barry Littlewood, with clipboard, was taking names. 'We don't want any spies in here,' he explained. The media were also excluded, confined to the entrance hall, which was crammed full of photographers and television cameramen trampling impatiently. The meeting's business was to discuss how we were to 'so fill' the harbour that there would be 'no room' for the nuclear cruiser *Long Beach* when it tried to enter in two days' time. Two intense hours of discussion later, not without fear and trembling, I summed up as best I could the direction of the meeting. After a short silence, somebody said 'Yup, that's it', and there was a chorus of agreement—a kind of non-church 'Amen'. Then they all got up to leave and I went out to meet the eager media in the hallway.

From the beginning, the Auckland squadron's core of boat skippers was very conscious of our responsibility for what might happen on the harbour. In Auckland, where most of the main squadron actions took place, the skippers looked to me for some initial leads, since I had initially convened them. But they insisted that we should together articulate a written policy. I became its reluctant draftsperson. It was like doing theology in a committee—and doing theology on your own is demanding enough! In the process we came to agree with great clarity on what we were doing and why we were doing it. The basic aim, as we stated it, was: 'So to fill the harbour with life that there would be no room for death.' Labour MP Matiu Rata nicely illustrated this central policy when, as he joined the flotilla on Ranginui Walker's launch, he hung a fishing rod over the stern, thoroughly enjoying the picnic.

Fundamental responsibility resided neatly where universal rules of seamanship laid it: with individual skippers. The more experienced skippers were magnificent and capable figures. An incipient Peace Squadron had already begun assembling over the past decade among the skippers who had sailed their boats east of New Zealand to Tahiti, to protest French nuclear testing.[2] On the western edge of the Pacific, Japan had been the first country to witness the use of nuclear weapons in times of war when the US dropped atomic bombs on Hiroshima and Nagasaki in 1945, attacks which killed over 200,000 people.[3] Immediately after the end of the Second World War, the US carried out the first of 23 nuclear tests at Bikini Atoll in the Marshall Islands. The New Zealand public had been outraged at the use of our Pacific backyard as a nuclear testing site. The fight against nuclear weapons was to become a defining political issue for a whole generation of New Zealanders. One-time head of Moruroa Testing Facility, Jean Montpellier, noted this broad-based sentiment when he visited New Zealand in 1983: 'Most New Zealand people had a kind of quasi-religious hatred of nuclear things.'[4]

The reason the Americans were so insistent on sending their nuclear warships to New Zealand harbours is embedded in a long history of close military co-operation between the two countries. New Zealand had fought alongside the United States in both World Wars, and during the Cold War it was part of the ANZUS (Australia, New Zealand, United States) alliance. New Zealand dutifully sent troops to Korea and Vietnam to fight

Overleaf: Stephen Sherie atop USS *Haddo* during the Peace Squadron's anti-nuclear protest against this submarine in Auckland, January 1979. Source: EP-Navy-Warships-USS Haddo-02, Alexander Turnbull Library.

alongside the Americans.[5] A more immediate cause of American interest in New Zealand ports was the forced withdrawal of US forces from Vietnam following the American defeat in 1975. US Pacific strategies were forced to change. The mighty US navy now slipped away from Asian shores into deep Pacific waters: an 'American Lake.'[6] The US sought to maintain and extend its dominance in the region by deploying its forces from one end to the other. For the US admirals, any refusal by New Zealand to harbour their nuclear ships could inspire other allies to do likewise, and their brand-new version of their nuclear-based Cold War policy would fall apart before it could be put into place. It was imperative that the New Zealand government was seen as a willing host. It was this willingness, more than anything, that we sought to disrupt.

All Sorts and Conditions

The basic idea of a boat blockade came from a handful of Baltimore activists. Influenced by Quaker pacifism and Martin Luther King's non-violent direct action, they had paddled canoes into the path of the freighter *Padma* in 1971. The *Padma* was loading a cargo of munitions at Port Covington, which the US government was secretly supplying to the Pakistani military for use in their dirty and bloody war against East Pakistan (soon to become Bangladesh). The protestors decried this injustice and aimed to draw public attention to the issue. They succeeded in doing so, and their protests eventually led to successful legal action to stop the lethal shipments.[7] I watched the entire drama unfold on the television while I was finishing up my doctoral studies at Princeton Theological Seminary in New Jersey. I was also captured by this simple yet profound display of Christian hope for peace. When I returned to Auckland in 1972 to renew my work as a lecturer at the College of St John the Evangelist, the national New Zealand Anglican seminary, I began to look for others who might be interested in doing something like the Quakers' action in New Zealand. I found immediate support among students and staff at St John's, as well as at Trinity Methodist Theological College. Together we launched the idea.[8] Although the Peace Squadron in Auckland began as a Church initiative, its development depended upon attracting all sorts of people of goodwill and good faith. We expected and sought the broadest possible membership. And we achieved it.

When the USS *Long Beach* visited New Zealand in 1976, Phil Amos, a Cabinet Minister from the previous New Zealand government, was one of several sailors blocking its entrance to Auckland Harbour in their small boats. He was arrested by the police, and escorted to the wharf where various dignitaries, including the US Ambassador, were waiting with their red carpet to greet the senior officers of the cruiser. The welcoming party had to cool its heels while the *Long Beach* disentangled itself from the un-welcoming party out in the harbour. The US Ambassador had known Phil personally in Phil's recent high office as Minister of Education. Seeing Phil come ashore, he clasped him warmly, assuming that, like himself, Phil was there to welcome the US navy. The handshake was broken by the arresting police officer, who clasped Phil with a rather different kind of warmth: 'Excuse me Mr Ambassador,' explained the policeman, 'but this man is under arrest.' Phil was later defended in court by David Lange, soon to be Prime Minister of the subsequent New Zealand government.

Phil Amos may have been the most eminent of the assorted sailors, but perhaps the most prominent was two-year-old Lief, who eyeballed Commander MacDonald of the *Pintado* from his mother's arms in 1978. Lief's parents were from Waiheke Island, a short ferry-ride out into the Hauraki Gulf which forms the approaches to Auckland's magnificent inner harbour. Lief's dad rowed their dinghy right onto the prow of the submarine while his mother held the child out in appeal to its commander.

The Peace Squadron received strong support from Māori, who increasingly became involved in nuclear-free activities. From nearby Takaparawhā (Bastion Point), Māori protestors, who were well into their 506-day occupation, looked out approvingly as the peace flotilla blocked the path of visiting navy vessels.[9] A number of Māori leaders spoke powerfully about the

Overleaf: The Peace Squadron surrounds USS *Haddo* in Auckland Harbour, January 1979. Source: EP-Navy-Warships-USS Haddo-01, Alexander Turnbull Library.

NEW ZEALAND
5
POLICE

NO
99
UCLEARFREE

obscenity of nuclear weaponry. They argued that the way the American ships forced their way into Auckland harbour was a re-run of the original colonial invasion that had systematically dispossessed and marginalised Māori. Māori and other indigenous Pacific peoples were at the forefront of the emergence of the Nuclear-Free Pacific Movement in the 1970s. Many came to see the independence of every Pacific territory—including New Zealand—as inseparably connected with their capacity to become or remain nuclear free. Along with colleagues from the Pacific Conference of Churches, I was heavily involved in the Pacific regional movement from its earliest days, and experienced remarkable new partnerships from it. In the process, I became much better educated on regional and indigenous concerns. Through these experiences I also became a more competent priest and theologian.

Trade unionists were another sturdy component in the opposition to nuclear ships. When the cruiser *Truxtun* visited Wellington in 1976, one of the first nuclear visitors to New Zealand, it was not permitted to dock at a wharf. It was instead forced to anchor in majestic isolation in the centre of Wellington Harbour because the trade unions withheld their wharf labour during its visit. The same thing happened in Auckland with the *Long Beach*. Public sentiment at that point was already shifting towards refusal of ship visits. The image of isolation, unpopularity and danger helped firm up the public's developing understanding that these ships were unwelcome visitors, kept waiting on the doorstep. Other actions were equally remarkable. On one occasion while I was walking down a Wellington street, a stranger, a man of few words, handed me a fat envelope of money for the Peace Squadrons. A visiting seaman, he had taken up a collection around his mates in solidarity with our protests.

Doing Christianity

We theologians and seminarians never claimed any sort of Christian 'ownership' of the Peace Squadron. The movement was open and embraced all comers. But for me the specifically Christian connections ran very deep. It was not that we ticked all the right creedal boxes—believing in all the right things. Nor that we had a high-minded moral tone. It was more intuitive than that. Our role in encouraging, supporting and resourcing the movement was important, and valued. We had announced the first boats of the Auckland Peace Squadron with a telegram to Prime Minister Bill Rowling, bearing signatures from Trinity and St John's Colleges. The launch of the first boats clearly exhibited these Christian links. That morning we celebrated a public Eucharistic Communion Service at Takaparawhā in the grounds of the Michael Joseph Savage Memorial. The children then led a procession down from there to the water below. There was a blessing of the harbour by a Māori priest. And then the boats were launched. This was a modest beginning, involving just a few boats, including one rowed by a couple of theological students and my own Boston Whaler, powered—if it could be persuaded to start—by an ageing outboard motor. St John's College in Meadowbank was often used as the venue for planning and debriefing sessions, and many a party and barbecue were held there. But when some folk expressed their discomfort with the ecclesiastical setting we shifted our meetings to other locations.

Those of us who held strong Christian convictions didn't feel the need to preach this from the pulpit or the street corner. Instead, we found ways to express our faith in imaginative, parable-like direct actions. After much over-speaking by churches and religious people, we recognised that it was now time for some straightforward doing: to *do* the truth rather than just speak it. It was time to apply our spirituality rather than just enjoy the experience and talk about it in religious meetings.[10] It was time to practise what we preached and let any preaching flow from that.

The media called the Peace Squadron a 'mouse that roared', an image that reworked the Bible's narrative of David, a young shepherd who confronted the giant Goliath.[11] Both images express a truth central to Christianity about the power of humble human goodwill, even, or perhaps especially, in all its weakness. Such vulnerability can bring down the mightiest from their seats. The phenomenon of unarmed human weakness nakedly confronting armoured human power is as central to the Christian gospel as the experience of personal redemption and restoration. By setting out unarmed in our little dinghies and kayaks to face down the mighty nuclear ships of the world's greatest navy, we declared again, in an embodied parable for a new age, that real strength does not come from brute force.

David McTaggart, a Canadian who eventually became the head of Greenpeace, experienced a wordless doing of Christianity first hand when he visited New Zealand as part of the mission to stop French nuclear testing at Moruroa. As he worked to prepare his yacht for the long protest voyage, he received extensive help from locals:

> In the midst of the steady hum of activity, I paused often during those days, astonished by how much love I felt around me. I was used to groups that were competitive, raucous, defiant, proud. But here was something different. Here was something that I didn't want to even try to put into words. There was an almost religious atmosphere—not a revival, no sermons. It was quiet, whatever it was.[12]

For me what McTaggart describes was the Peace Movement at its best: Christianity, humanity, at its best. I often felt that the Auckland Peace Squadron was the best church I was ever pastor of.

The Peace Squadron's actual reception within the institutional Church was always mixed. I found strong support among some colleagues and students at St John's and Trinity Colleges, and many other Christians found ways to express their support. But others thought the movement was mistaken, if not offensive. Edward Norman was the Bishop of Wellington throughout the period of the Peace Squadron's protests. A much decorated and respected former military officer, Edward vigorously opposed the Peace Squadron, as well as my role as an activist theologian at St John's College.[13] When he was finally persuaded to have a cup of coffee with me, he frankly shared how much my actions had offended him. I appreciated his forthrightness. To me Edward appeared as a kind of high priest, championing and sacralising the secular powers around him. To Edward I appeared dangerously unlawful, a stain needing to be cleansed from his version of the pristine Anglican temple.

Reflecting on the radical protests of that era I am convinced that in many ways the 1960s and 70s were trying to shock us and our churches into wider perceptions of the significance of Jesus and of Christianity. Certainly, many of us at Trinity and St John's felt that God was speaking to us through the secular dynamics of our world. The Bible and the newspaper illuminated each other, and sometimes the newspaper shone clearer than our conventional understandings of the Bible.

Diving Deep and Surfacing

The visits of the nuclear submarines *Pintado* and *Haddo*, in 1978 and 1979 respectively, brought more than themselves to the surface at the entrance to the Waitematā Harbour. The giant cruisers, such as *Long Beach*, had an undeniable and massive dignity about them. Not so the sinister black submarines. They appeared every inch true death ships, with nothing redemptive about them. Barely visible amongst the peace flotilla brouhaha, they sneaked into the harbour, at once furtive and forceful. But it was the protests around the submarines that tilted the balance in favour of the Peace Squadron.

Prime Minister Robert Muldoon was determined that the American navy vessels would reach port, and he summoned the resources of the armed and police forces to make this happen. On the *Pintado*'s visit, the submarine was led in by the New Zealand naval frigate *Waikato* while air force helicopters flew overhead. These hovered mast-high, clearly intending to disrupt and capsize the protestors' boats with their battering downdraughts. The blown-about yachts, at least one of them capsized right in the path of the *Waikato*, littered the boiling sea, making the situation even more dangerous for those on the water. This added to the spectacle spread before the curious or rapt Aucklanders gathered in considerable numbers around the natural amphitheatre that was Auckland's inner harbour. The country's armed forces were being used against the country's own citizens and—to add insult to injury—in a foolhardy and counterproductive manner. The veteran *New Zealand Listener* journalist Geoff Chapple captured all this in a careful article at the time, titled 'The Balance Tips'. Geoff believed that the helicopter behaviour had tipped the balance of public opinion in favour of the Peace Squadron's actions. Between 1978 and 1983, polls showed citizen support of the Peace Squadron's aims relentlessly rising above 50 per cent. By the end of election year, 1984, scores of New Zealand towns and boroughs had declared themselves nuclear free.[14] Submarines surfacing in New Zealand discovered 'something in the water down there', as *Time* magazine loftily opined. And it proved to be much more insoluble than the 'residual opposition' that the US navy anticipated in one of their Fiscal Year Reports.

In 1984 the Labour Party, led by David Lange, bundled Muldoon out of office. Riding on the back of a wave of nuclear-free conviction, steeled by many years' struggle, Lange had promised to challenge American nuclear visits. When the US tried to bully Lange into a deal, the Labour Government responded in 1987 with legislation outlawing nuclear weapons full stop. This appeared effectively to bar state-of-the-art American fighting vessels from visiting New Zealand, as they adhered to a 'neither confirm nor deny' policy about the presence of nuclear weapons on board their vessels. The ANZUS treaty was put on ice and, publicly at least, highest-level nuclear-related military co-operation came to an end. In passing the legislation, Lange pointed to the clear public will of his electorate. But Lange further displayed his genius and spirit in his speech at the Oxford Union Debate in March 1985 on the proposition that 'nuclear weapons are morally indefensible'. Lange's brilliant performance against prominent American religious fundamentalist Jerry Falwell won an unprecedented standing ovation from a British audience not easily swayed by rhetoric.

To assuage the growing fears that New Zealand was the tip of an anti-nuclear iceberg, Lange assured the nuclear powers that the New Zealand policy was 'not for export'. But the Prime Minister was fully in concert with longstanding Labour policy on a nuclear-free Pacific zone. Under Norman Kirk's memorable leadership (1972–74) the New Zealand Government had twice sent New Zealand warships to Moruroa to express its opposition to nuclear testing. France eventually retaliated by a terrorist bombing of the Greenpeace ship, *Rainbow Warrior*, on 10 July 1985, while it was moored at a wharf in Auckland. The ship was sunk by explosives attached by French secret service divers, and a crew member was killed. The extraordinary behaviour of France and the deafening silence of New Zealand's supposed friendly nations and allies in the face of such behaviour woke New Zealanders up to the deadly seriousness of what we were doing. Our allies had their fingers on the nuclear trigger and were already far gone in nuclear madness. It was a mark of our peculiarly New Zealand form of sanity to refuse, in our shrewd innocence and our right mind, to co-operate with nuclear weapon systems deployment.

For New Zealand Christianity, the growth of this public anti-nuclear sentiment was accompanied by a dawning appreciation of peace and justice issues as central to its gospel. It possessed an apocalyptic urgency equivalent to a call to conversion of individual souls and persons. Indeed, it ultimately required radical conversion—both private and public. For behind the whole nuclear panoply sheltered grossly unjust social and economic disparities and injustices globally. These injustices implicate us all. A whole world systemic and structural, as well as personal, transformation and salvation was needed, and these would not necessarily come only by one-by-one conversions of individuals. At this point, there was a remarkable coming together of every stripe of Christianity, from the most evangelical to the most liberal, from Protestant to Catholic, from believers who believed a lot to believers who seemed wedded to outright disbelief in their conventional traditions.

So both secular and religious communities were feeling their way towards something quite contrary to all conventional wisdom about the necessity for violence and war. To conventional political and military leaders, often angrily assailed for their attachment to war-fighting and preparation, this passion for some sort of transformation seemed itself a form of unrealistic, idealistic madness. Yet both the New Zealand Government and the New Zealand churches reached the same ethical and perhaps the same spiritual conclusion about nuclear weapons: that at best they were unnecessary, and at worst they were a madness to be avoided at all costs. New Zealand continues to have a large vocation to fulfil in ensuring that we retain and build upon this strange sanity. Its churches and religions also have a special share and role in that vocation.

The New Zealand National Anthem, remarkably, includes the phrase: 'Peace, not war, shall be our boast.' The notion of 'boasting' fits perfectly the exhilarating spirit of a Peace Squadron enterprise. With the eventual banning of all nuclear weapons from New Zealand we—and the world with us—indeed had reason to boast of peace. It is my hope that we continue to have reason to boast on, modestly, into the future.

5

Revolution at the Kitchen Tables: Churches and the 1980s Peace Movement

Peter Matheson

The polarising Springbok Tour in 1981 was a watershed event that everyone who experienced it remembers. Families and communities were split down the middle, with police and enraged fans locked against protesters blocking the rugby field. These images of a conflicted New Zealand were flashed across the world, giving great encouragement to those fighting apartheid in South Africa. Yet the burning conviction during the Tour that change was needed and was going to happen, come hell or high water, did not come out of the blue. Successive waves of protest had been mounting for years: Māori had had enough; women had had enough; at Manapōuri and Aramoana, conservationists had had enough. And then along came the Peace Movement in the 1980s, and it changed the cultural and political landscape of New Zealand forever.

I was fortunate enough to experience the Peace Movement's dynamism, having just arrived in Dunedin from Scotland in 1981. What my German wife, Heinke, and I were drawn into was a grassroots movement of passionate, informed, utterly determined people, mainly young, mainly women, often drawing on marae or Pasifika roots. Folk with no money at all to spare made it to national gatherings up and down the land.

In Scotland, Heinke and I had been deeply involved in Parents for Survival, a group aiming to increase awareness of the danger posed to children from nuclear weapons and the arms race. I had travelled across the Iron Curtain to East Germany, Poland

and Hungary, linking up with the unofficial Church peace movements there. And now we met incredible people here: the anarchist, peace and church groups, and the Topp Twins. We took part in street theatre performances and sat around innumerable kitchen tables. I remember the dining-room table of that wonderful epidemiologist, Dr Ian Prior, groaning under the medical evidence he had accumulated about nuclear testing. We knew we were up against it. The establishment—political, military, legal, business—was powerful and dismissive of us. But with gracious experts like Ian Prior behind us we were ready for anything.

Why did the Peace Movement succeed? That's the fascinating question, so relevant to us today as we face a real risk of environmental meltdown. Any 'explanation' of this revolution in values, with its political, social and religious dimensions, has to be tentative. The reality of it, however, is not in doubt. Between 1975 and 1987, New Zealand abandoned the nuclear deterrent policy of its traditional Western allies, which consisted of stockpiling ever greater numbers of nuclear weapons, and embraced an independent nuclear-free stance. Those involved in the Peace Movement experienced this turnaround as miraculous, given New Zealand's long alignment with British and US policies, and the generally patriotic attitudes and unquestioned values of most New Zealanders. After all, practically every school, church and civic centre across the land boasted its war memorials. Instinctive values were framed by patriotic songs, stories, flags, cadet training at the schools, and Anzac Day rhetoric of sacrifice for the good of the nation. Yet in less than a decade, the counter-culture of small, marginalised peace groups had morphed into the consensus of middle New Zealand. New Zealanders now realised we were different, independent, and we set our own course.

In the early days of the Peace Movement it often felt, though, like an uphill struggle. It was a prolonged, bitterly contested process. The New Zealand Nuclear Free Zone, Disarmament, and Arms Control Act 1987 only came about after an unprecedented efflorescence of popular protest up and down the country. The élan and rapid growth of the Peace Movement, as it came to be called, took the political institutions and the gatekeepers of conventional mores by surprise. It developed new networks, long before the social media revolution, and leapt over social and racial barriers. The broad spectrum of people involved and the creative imagination evident in street theatre, song, visual culture, literature, workshops and new patterns of consensus decision-making are vividly described in Marie Leadbeater's recent *Peace, Power and Politics*, a history of New Zealand's nuclear-free movement.[1]

A glance through the back copies of *Peacelink*, the monthly or bi-monthly periodical produced by volunteers in Dunedin, illustrates the wide palette of interests. In amongst arguments for pacifism and a nuclear-free Pacific are articles on women's rights, inner peace and anti-racism. We sensed we were at the cutting edge as we all sat up until late at night putting *Peacelink* together. The nuclear threat gave us nightmares, and emphasised the urgency of our task.

In its grassroots appeal, its fairs, its wharfside protests, its flotillas of boats, its national gatherings, the New Zealand Peace Movement was as unpredictable as any movement of the spirit. It was a highly diverse movement, troubled at times by personality clashes. Yet it transcended all of this, and ran on the sacrificial energy and generosity of literally thousands of volunteers. While it boasted outstanding charismatic leaders, Māori and Pākehā, female and male, and itinerant apostles like Jim Chapple, chugging in his Mobile Peace Van from one centre to another, its success lay in the roots it struck in local communities—inner-city, suburban, small-town and rural. Kitchen and cosmos came together. It was astonishingly interdisciplinary. Professional groupings such as engineers, doctors, teachers and lawyers stood side by side with the Maori Women's Welfare League, Pasifika groups, traditional lefties and tiny pacifist organisations. What was the glue that held them together?

A common core set of concerns lay at the heart of the Peace Movement. The Movement was ardently educational, armed with the researches of Ian Prior, Owen Wilkes and others. Because we knew what we were talking about, we punctured the traditional ANZUS rhetoric in thousands of talks to Rotary groups, churches, rural women's groups and schools. The Campaign for Nuclear Disarmament epitomised the rational dimension. We were contemptuous of the lunacies of mutual assured destruction (MAD) nuclear gamesmanship. A powerful moral impulse shaped the Movement. We were outraged at the diversion into the arms race of resources desperately needed elsewhere for basic needs and humanitarian causes.

But the Movement was always a coalition of diverse groups who participated in it for their own reasons. For many women, the struggle was inseparable from other aspects of male violence and hegemony. The strength of support from women was apparent in May 1983 when 25,000 of them gathered to march down Queen Street in Auckland to celebrate the International Women's Day for Nuclear Disarmament.[2] Young parents were fired up by the vision of a different future for their children, and by desperation about the consequences of a nuclear holocaust. While some of those involved in the Movement were hardened activists with years of experience organising and participating in protests against the Vietnam War and for other causes, others were new to this form of political and social engagement.

Many Māori and Pasifika folks read the nuclear threat as a manifestation of neo-colonialism. In 1985, Anglican Archbishop Paul Reeves told a peace commission in Washington, DC, that the Pacific was becoming a 'nuclear sewer' for foreign powers. For Reeves: 'It is a Pacific experience that behind every racial oppression, every economic exploitation and every neo-colonial manipulation lies military force and national security logic.' Reeves told the commission that Māori saw the land as their mother, as their 'right to life, to power and to eternity.'[3] Others argued that this was true not just for the land but also for the ocean. Since the 1940s, American, French and British nuclear tests had devastated parts of the Pacific, and Pasifika peoples were alarmed at the poisoning of their lands and seas and the effects of radioactive contamination on infants.[4] In 1981 the Pacific Conference of Churches called for a nuclear-free Pacific, and resistance to nuclear testing was henceforth intimately linked to self-determination in the Nuclear Free and Independent Pacific Movement.

Peacelink magazine covers from April 1983 to February 1985, showing the wide range of issues that concerned the peace movement. Source: Owen Wilkes Papers, Alexander Turnbull Library.

The Peace Activism of the Churches

Religion has often, not least in recent times, been associated with conservative values and an instinctive nationalism.[5] But the churches in New Zealand in the 1980s were one part of the establishment that bucked the trend. They played a key role in a momentous, counter-intuitive transformation of values, not dissimilar to the role of the churches in overcoming apartheid in South Africa and in the civil rights movement in the United States. I had seen at first hand the skill of the East German Protestant Church in exploiting every little crack in the totalitarian regime there, contributing to the fall of the Berlin Wall in 1989. New Zealand's churches proved to be equally adept at inspiring a longing for peace.

This crucial role of the Christian churches in the New Zealand Peace Movement, however, remains largely unrecognised.[6] It could not have been predicted. The pacifist stream in New Zealand Christianity was weak, though the Parihaka tradition was never wholly forgotten. In the wake of the First World War, leading churchmen such as the Presbyterian James Gibb threw doubt on the just war theory and passionately supported the League of Nations as a mechanism for advancing the prospects of peace. The Quakers and small Christian pacifist societies ensured that non-violent alternatives were never entirely lost sight of.[7] Mainline churches, however, both Catholic and Protestant, had willingly marched under the national flag and had tended to see themselves, in Allan Davidson's terms, as 'chaplains to the nation'.[8]

From the mid-1950s on, though, the mainline churches began to forsake their unquestioning support of the state and moved towards a liberal internationalism. The 1956 Suez Crisis, the Korean War (1950–53) and the Vietnam War (1955–75) sharpened critical discernment for church leaders such as Allan Pyatt, the Anglican Bishop of Christchurch. As early as the 1950s, reflection on the nuclear bombing of Hiroshima and Nagasaki had led a growing minority in Student Christian Movement circles and elsewhere to reject nuclear weapons. Ministers such as James Matheson, of Knox Presbyterian Church in Dunedin, took part in public protest and told the Parliamentary Petitions Committee in 1957 that the churches were moving towards a more radical position than those advocated by the Campaign for Nuclear Disarmament itself.[9]

For two decades, a lively debate took place within the mainline churches, especially the Methodists and the Presbyterians. Roman Catholicism, too, edged away from its previous preoccupation with the Communist menace. Peter Sutton, the Anglican Bishop of Nelson, denounced the French nuclear tests in the Pacific in 1966 as 'a wanton disregard of international opinion'.[10] From 1975 onwards, the Presbyterian and Methodist churches advocated a nuclear-weapons-free zone in the Pacific, and by the early 1980s, majority opinion was moving towards 'nuclear pacifism'. The threat of the use of nuclear weapons was seen as a sin against God, humanity and the entire created order. In 1982, the *New Zealand Herald* remarked on the passionate commitment of the Christian community to nuclear disarmament.[11] They had become, again in Davidson's words, less chaplains to the nation, more 'prophets at the gate'.

The role of a few outstanding Christian leaders within the Peace Movement is relatively well known. George Armstrong, an Anglican clergyman and theologian, was a familiar face in representing the Auckland peace flotilla to the media.[12] Ray Galvin, a Presbyterian minister with a special ministry for peace, authored *A Nuclear-Free New Zealand*.[13] John Murray, later a Moderator of the Presbyterian Church, was prominent in campaigns against racism, Springbok Tour protests, and more generally within the wider Peace Movement. Less widely recognised is that at a grassroots level the churches were developing a distinctive profile on war and peace. Both Catholic and Protestant mainline churches began to educate and mobilise their members on peacemaking. Although some remained bastions of conservative support for the status quo, in fact many New Zealand churches in the 1980s emerged as crucial incubators for protesters and activists.[14]

The churches had great advantages. Their halls and kitchens were natural social centres, located up and down the land, and linked by established communication channels. Articles on peace and justice jostled with more predictable reports in the monthly church publications, which were read by hundreds of thousands of people in the 1980s. Catholic Justice and Peace groups boasted a formidable network, and Catholic schools mediated the new insights to the next generation.

Many parishes began to observe Peace Sunday around 6 August, Hiroshima Day, and declared themselves Nuclear-Free Zones. This was the step made in 1992 by St Matthew-in-the-City, an Anglican church in Auckland, which declared itself a Nuclear Weapons Free Zone and designated its chapel a Peace Chapel, though not without controversy.[15] A wide political spectrum was represented in congregations and national bodies, but members were generally prepared to listen to one another, and to their priests or ministers, because of their common faith.

National figures such as Archbishop Paul Reeves simply could not be ignored. He spanned the Māori and the Pākehā worlds, and with his humour and silver tongue got across to most people. In the 1980s the churches still represented a large constituency. On their national committees sat lay representatives from every corner of the land. They had access to Parliament. Synods, Conferences, and Assemblies sent off well documented, pragmatically argued submissions to government ministers and departments. It was not easy for politicians to dismiss such church advocacy as 'left-wing' or 'extremist'. Church leaders' submissions in 1982 to the Select Committee on Disarmament and Arms Control were of particular importance.

The churches' international connections—with Rome, Canterbury, Geneva, the United States and the World Council of Churches—were invaluable for inspiring alternative political imaginations. The Church did not stop at the Iron Curtain, and because of their links with churches in Communist countries, Cold War presuppositions came under scrutiny. The mantra of the defence of the 'Free World', fiercely criticised in the Peace Movement as a whole, made even less sense from the perspective of the Church universal, which embraced Russian, South American and Palestinian Christians as well as Western ones. The language of material circulating globally in the Church at the time could be startlingly strong: the state was 'the devil disguised as Almighty God', the *Kairos Document* argued.[16] One's ultimate allegiance was not to the Warsaw Pact or the ANZUS Alliance. The menace of the USSR was a fantasy.[17]

Clergy and lay people, both women and men, travelled across the world and reported back to local synods and parishes about the activities of other peace movements. Jan Cormack, for example, used her position in the Presidium of the Christian Conference of Asia to advocate for peace, and Jocelyn Armstrong, an Anglican laywoman, was a strong peace presence in her leadership roles in the ecumenical movement in New Zealand and in the World Council of Churches. On one particular expedition, twenty clergy and lay people visited Russia and other Eastern Bloc countries as part of a tour organised by the New Zealand National Council of Churches.[18] The traffic also went in the other direction. In 1986, Bishop Károly Tóth of Hungary, a powerful advocate of Christian peacemaking, toured New Zealand and spoke with numerous church groups. I had met him some years earlier in Budapest. The Nobel Prize winner Carl Friedrich von Weizsäcker, who advocated a conciliar process to unite the Christian churches at every level across the world, and was an advocate for peace, justice and the integrity of creation, was another highly influential visitor to New Zealand, in 1987. The churches' committees on international affairs were impressively informed about the arms race and nuclear strategies, and about the worldwide Christian reaction to them, and they made vigorous efforts to transmit this information right down to parish level. The strong ecumenical movement also ensured that the various churches supported one another through interdenominational organisations, including the National Council of Churches.

The churches, then, proved an effective sounding-board. They also raised consciousness about nuclear issues in the wider society through their rich tradition of religious symbolism. Vigils, fasts and Eucharistic celebrations spoke to people at a deeper level. This constituted, in George Armstrong's terms, a 'public liturgy'.[19] The distinctive dimension of the churches' input to the Peace Movement, however, went deeper. It stemmed from their biblical, ethical and theological basis. Their input had a language all of its own. It talked of an ultimate divine authority and of nations ceasing to be human when they transgressed certain limits. Its ethical engagement rested on foundational understandings of creation, salvation, and the work of the Spirit. As the churches co-operated together on the question of peace, the wider Peace Movement took notice. Half of the December 1982 issue of *Peacelink* was devoted to an unprecedented gathering of Roman Catholic, Quaker, Anglican, Methodist and Presbyterian leaders who set peacemaking at the centre of the churches' ethical engagement.

Theology began to matter as traditional cultural values were challenged. Age-old political maxims were now questioned. New hymns, prayers and sermons nudged church members towards alternative understandings of national security. Lay people were urged to wrestle with what St Paul called the 'Principalities and Powers', and not to restrict discipleship to personal piety. In countless church halls, 'middle New Zealand' sat around candlelit tables and talked theology and politics.

Theological centres such as the Anglican College of St John the Evangelist in Auckland and the Presbyterian Knox Theological College in Dunedin were at the forefront of the Peace Movement. Their ordinands were fired up with a peacemaking message. The Bible, the Presbyterian Public Questions Committee argued, had consistently challenged cultural idolatries and structural injustice. Serious theological reflection, already evident in resistance to the 'heresy' of apartheid and the 1981 Springbok Tour, provided church members with a powerful justification for peacemaking. Thorough debates in Synods, General Assemblies, and Presbyteries meant that when it came to convincing a wider public, the arguments of peace advocates had already been well honed.

The churches became the producers and disseminators of peace resources that gained wide distribution across the country. The booklet *A Call to a New Exodus*, produced by the Pacific Council of Churches, was also widely disseminated across New Zealand.[20] It argued from a Pacific perspective that the whole earth and the vast expanse of its oceans were sacred, a gift to be stewarded for future generations, and that the nuclear arms race was 'demonic' and idolatrous in its potential for indiscriminate destruction, grotesque wastefulness, and testing and dumping of waste. This Pacific input wove a theology of creation into liberation theology's prophetic call for justice. Traditional concerns for redemption and mission fired a peaceful crusade for social and political transformation.

Peacemaking: The Christian Imperative, prepared for local congregations in 1986 by the Methodist-Presbyterian Workgroup for Peace, defined peace as the experience of justice and freedom, as *shalom*.[21] A cessation of hostilities was a mere *Pax Romana*, a faux peace that didn't hack it. The booklet presented the global arms race as a frightening centralisation of power, contrary to the interests of ordinary people, especially indigenous people. It constituted theft from the poor. It begged the question: what happened to one's soul if one relied on nuclear weapons for security?

Two members of St John's College run onto Rugby Park, Hamilton, while two supporters of the Springbok Rugby Tour try to stop them, 1981. Photograph by Peter Black. Source: Te Papa Tongarewa Museum of New Zealand.

This linking of justice, peace and the integrity of creation was echoed in countless sermons, worship services, hymns, talks and newsletters up and down the land. In 1987 a set of worship resources on these themes was provided to churches and church schools. The resources were thoroughly international, with, for example, prayers from Papua New Guinea and hymns from France, Germany and the United States. These peacemaking packs drew extensively on the progressive thinking of the Second Vatican Council (1962–65), Latin American liberation theology and the World Council of Churches.

The theology of hope in particular proved a powerful antidote to the sense of powerlessness and resignation which the threat of an imminent holocaust could induce. The Resurrection gospel pointed the way from death to life; the old order had lost its power. These eschatological dimensions of the biblical message offered the Peace Movement as a whole a welcome dollop of buoyancy, complementing the dire warnings of a Larry Ross or a Helen Caldicott.[22] A particular strength of the churches' peace advocacy was that its re-reading of the political situation was yoked to new insights from Scripture. The peaceable Kingdom was at hand! Love and self-sacrifice, the renunciation of violence and war, were the appropriate way to anticipate God's New Creation.[23] *Peacemaking: A Christian Calling*, a widely circulated discussion paper by the International Relations Committee of the Methodist and Presbyterian Churches, called for decisive and committed action. Christian hope offered a way forward, a defiant response to the menace of the nuclear holocaust.

Courageous Engagements and Moral Authority

The churches played a key role in mobilising public support and tipping the balance in favour of the Peace Movement as a whole. Their leadership, both clerical and lay, was politically liberal, at times radical, and welcomed alliances with peacemakers with very different perspectives. The churches learned massively in the process. Alone they could have achieved little, but in company with campaigning doctors, scientists, engineers, lawyers and teachers they helped to win over the middling classes of New

Zealand society. Their religious perspectives were not shared by all, but they took the debate beyond the purely political sphere, and offered a coherent theological base for courageous engagement.

After the passing of the nuclear free legislation, interest moved, both in the secular community and within the churches, to the ecological issues which had always been part and parcel of the Peace Movement's concerns. An imaginative 'Earth Charter for the Churches of Aotearoa New Zealand' was prepared, for example, by a Taupō-Rotorua work group in 1993. Parallel, however, with this shift in commitment was a drift away from ecumenism and socio-political involvement, and a growing emphasis on internal issues of church growth and divisive debates about human sexuality. The theological mood changed. A significant minority of the churches' membership had never been enamoured of the Peace Movement, suspecting that political objectives were flying under the pirate flag of theology.[24] Perhaps activists like myself had pushed too hard, and neglected or alienated the conservative and evangelical heartland, though there is always, of course, an ebb and flow in church pieties and theologies.

I would argue in conclusion, however, that the spiritual and theological undergirding of the churches not only broadened the appeal of the Peace Movement, but also deepened its moral authority. The resultant broad swell of public opinion was what transformed the cultural landscape and 'inscape' of this country. New Zealanders woke up, rubbed their eyes, found they had a different take on war and alliances, and congratulated themselves on their good conscience about this new state of affairs.

6

The Treaty, the Church and the Reconciliation of Christ

Karen Kemp

Overlooking Hohi in the Bay of Islands stands a lone stone cross commemorating the beginnings of a settled Christian presence in New Zealand. The cross also marks the establishment of a relationship between two peoples. In 1814, Ngāpuhi chief Ruatara hosted the Reverend Samuel Marsden and the first missionaries of the Anglican Church Missionary Society (CMS) mission to New Zealand. On Christmas Day, Marsden preached from the second chapter of the Gospel of Luke: 'Behold, I bring you good tidings of great joy'. Those 'good tidings' concerned the gospel of peace and reconciliation for all.

Twenty-six years later, in 1840, in nearby Waitangi, Māori rangatira (chiefs) and representatives of the British Crown signed the Treaty of Waitangi (Te Tiriti o Waitangi). The Reverend Henry Williams, the leader of the CMS mission, and his son Edward were responsible for translating the English draft of the Treaty into te reo Māori. Williams senior then promoted it as, in one interpreter's words, 'a spiritual covenant and guarantee of political protection and "fostering care" by the British government'.[1] The Treaty had been a response to the growth of independent British settlement, and increasing complications in the relationships between those settlers and their Māori hosts, the tangata whenua, or 'people of the land'. Anglican missionaries like Williams were involved in every aspect of the Treaty's development and subsequent signing. Consequently, the Church and the gospel of peace and reconciliation were inextricably bound up with the Treaty from the outset. The 'covenant' of the Treaty has, however, been relentlessly challenged and tested over the ensuing 175 years.[2] This subsequent history has had enormous implications for Māori and for the nation, and also for the Anglican Church.

In this chapter, I seek to explore how the Anglican Church has responded to legacies of colonisation in Aotearoa New Zealand, and how it has struggled to implement the promises undertaken in the Treaty of Waitangi—particularly through the introduction of a three-tikanga structure. These are, I argue, issues that are fundamentally about peace. My focus is on church bureaucracy. This may not seem a likely location to encounter peacemaking in action, or an especially exciting one. Nevertheless, if peace is to have any meaning at all, it must be realised within our institutions, structures, resourcing and power relationships. Bureaucracy—as the configuration of institutional infrastructure—is fundamental to the organisation of social relationships; the possibilities of our co-existence are enabled, sustained and potentially destroyed by the ways in which we structure our communal life. In New Zealand, questions concerning the peace and justice of our institutions invariably lead back to the Treaty.

Learning to Honour the Treaty within the Church

Despite the aspirations of the Treaty, New Zealand's history after 1840 was marred by contestation and outright violence over land, including unlawful confiscation; te reo Māori was denigrated, and impoverishment of Māori occurred; there was also a steep decline in the Māori population during the nineteenth century. All of this had severe ongoing consequences. Māori were never merely passive in response to this history of colonisation and marginalisation, but after the Second World War an emerging generation of urban and university-educated Māori engaged in new and dramatic forms of public protest. Many Māori took issue with the government's ongoing failure to honour the Treaty. Some called it a fraud: public debate heated up. Perhaps New Zealand did not actually have the 'best race relations in the world' after all.

This debate intensified in the 1970s. Key events, such as the 1975 Land March on Parliament and the 506-day occupation at Takaparawhā (Bastion Point) in Auckland in 1977–78, focused public attention on Māori grievances. The New Zealand government established the Waitangi Tribunal in 1975. Though at first it was quite limited in scope, with a mandate solely focused on contemporary issues, in 1986 the Tribunal was granted retrospective powers to address grievances dating back to 1840. With this much wider mandate, awareness of the importance of the Treaty grew considerably, especially in the education and health sectors.

Renewed interest in the Treaty led to a growing restlessness as Māori in church and society searched for self-determination: they sought the mana (authority, prestige) that they believed was rightfully theirs as tangata whenua and signatories to the Treaty. As John Bluck details, in 1975 Māori clergy expressed their growing impatience at a national hui (gathering) at the College of St John the Evangelist, Auckland, recommending that Māori Anglicans leave the Anglican Church.[3] Although this did not eventuate, the recommendation was nevertheless a wake-up call for Pākehā: Māori concerns had to be addressed. One concrete outcome of this time was the consecration in 1981 of Bishop Te Whakahuihui Vercoe, the first Bishop of Aotearoa to be elected by Māori. Vercoe became a significant figure in the emerging discussions about institutional change; he repeatedly called on the Anglican Church to honour the Treaty by reversing Māori marginalisation.[4]

In 1984, the General Synod (the representative governing body for Anglicans) established the Bicultural Commission to examine the Church's relationship to the Treaty.[5] The Commission established that the Church had a duty to honour the Treaty of Waitangi in its structure and policies, and to be committed to bicultural development. It made a series of recommendations to the General Synod in 1986, calling for proactive steps to be taken. Even so, it was not until 1992 that General Synod approved the constitutional revision. The new constitution, known as Te Pouhere, provided for three self-governing tikanga or strands: Tikanga Māori, Tikanga Pākehā and Tikanga Pasefika. They were to be equal partners in decision-making and resourcing, yet free to exercise mission and ministry in culturally appropriate ways within each strand—hence the use of the term tikanga, which refers to correct protocols, plans and procedures. General Synod would be the place where all three came together, and decisions would rely on consensus between tikanga, as well as between houses of clergy, laity and bishops.

Interviews with three senior Anglican leaders in 1994 suggest that Māori Anglicans welcomed Te Pouhere with hopes for self-determination and exhilaration at the freedom to participate fully in the governance of the Church.[6] For Pākehā the mood was more sober: they would need to create space for Māori to develop in their own way, requiring significant adjustment and a fresh exploration of their own identity as Pākehā. The late inclusion of Polynesian Anglicans, amidst controversy around the implications for the allocation of resources and the challenges of a three-tikanga structure with a bicultural partnership at its core, made Tikanga Pasefika a tentative partner from the outset. These issues resurfaced as recently as the 2014 General Synod, and led to a formal yet moving apology from Tikanga Māori to Tikanga Pasefika at the May 2016 General Synod in Napier.

Te Pouhere and Peacemaking

Te Pouhere's peacemaking intent is clear in its Preamble, which recognises strained relationships and the complicity of the Anglican Church in New Zealand's troubled history. It speaks of the 'pain and anguish, aspirations and hopes of the Māori people in the Church'.[7]

The creation of the Three Tikanga Church was an explicit attempt to address structurally the power imbalance within the Church, and to restore relationships that had been broken through the dishonouring of what many regarded as a sacred covenant between two peoples. The new constitution's solution involved a deliberate move away from Pākehā-dominated decision-making processes and control of resources. Rather, equal partnership would be a new core principle: equal partnership in governance and access to resources would enable each tikanga to flourish. The new structure reshaped all aspects of the Anglican Church in New Zealand, including financial decision-making, theological education, liturgical resources, disciplinary practices and church governance.

Te Pouhere is culturally defined and organised. Yet, paradoxically, it affirms that the Church provides 'for all God's people the tūrangawaewae, the common ground',[8] and that the Church's unity is in Christ. In his address to General Synod in 1992, Archbishop Brian Davis articulated early hopes that the new constitution would help bridge divides and foster relationships of mutual respect and care between cultures. He referred to Te Pouhere as 'a new cultural partnership' that sought to honour 'cultural diversity'.[9] The model represented an innovative, and in many ways unique, approach to Christian peacemaking in Aotearoa New Zealand. Te Pouhere sought not only to redress the injustices of the past and restore fractured relationships, but also to provide a structure in which reconciled parties could be self-determining.

How the Three Tikanga Church 'Works'

Over the years the three-tikanga partnership has been variously interpreted, experienced and evaluated. Te Pouhere not only changed the make-up of General Synod, it also shifted the decision-making processes away from parliamentary-style adversarial debating to a kōrero approach, involving dialogue and consensus akin to that used in a hui on a marae (meeting place).

A close reading of the Proceedings of General Synod in the years since Te Pouhere was adopted suggests that the structure does indeed provide for robust conversations across all three tikanga. These conversations are often painful: consensus takes time. Nevertheless, genuine understanding and partnership continues to be built in the process. A biblical understanding of peace suggests that peace occurs when truth, justice and mercy come together in both addressing the wounds of the past and building a peaceable future.[10] This future is only possible where relationships are reconciled and renegotiated through ongoing kōrero. The three-tikanga structure was intended to create an architecture that would facilitate this end.

Three archbishops, representing the three co-equal tikanga (cultural strands) of the Anglican Church in New Zealand, at the opening of the diocesan synod, or church council, in St Paul's Cathedral, Dunedin, 2007. They are, from left: the Most Reverend William Brown, Te Pihopa o Aotearoa (Tikanga Māori); the Most Reverend David Moxon (Tikanga Pākehā); and the Most Reverend Jabez Bryce, Archbishop of Polynesia (Tikanga Pasefika). Source: *Otago Daily Times*.

So, how does the Three Tikanga Church 'work' in practice? A theological hui in 2005 was provocatively themed as 'Anglicans in Communion: Rhetoric or Reality?' Not surprisingly, one report on the hui contended that it had 'exposed and underlined the theological differences which exist in our church'.[11] Nevertheless, the report affirmed Te Pouhere's intent to 'restore right relationships across all aspects of the Church's life' and concluded that theological hui could be instrumental to 'resource and stimulate a *new spirit of koinonia* [fellowship] in this Church'. The process of talking through theological differences deepened understanding and strengthened inter-tikanga relationships, at least amongst individual participants.

Hui and other church events are locales where the Treaty itself continues to be discussed and fresh resolutions adopted to strengthen the Treaty's place in the life of the Church and the nation. The 1998 General Synod set up the Constitutional Arrangements Commission to explore models for a Treaty-based constitution for Aotearoa New Zealand as a nation, based on the three-tikanga partnership. This idea has not gained traction and the original Commission has subsequently morphed into a series of others dedicated to strengthening the bicultural partnership in both the Church and the nation. However, it did lead in 2001 to a Special General Synod on the place of the Treaty in the Church, which resolved to deepen inter-tikanga life and protect the place of the Treaty in New Zealand society and governance.[12] The peacebuilding aspects of this Commission were expressed by the Venerable Winston Halapua of Tikanga Pasefika, who commended the Anglican Church for actively seeking out ways to 'paddle our canoe in the same direction'.[13] Also using a maritime metaphor, Jenny Te Paa Daniel has eloquently called attention to the relational implications of Te Pouhere: 'To say my fate is not tied to your fate is like saying, "your end of the boat is sinking".'[14] Peace in this understanding is about recognising those on your waka (canoe) and seeking to work together for the sake of everyone on board.[15]

A Critique of the Three-Tikanga Model

The three-tikanga model has been extensively debated within the Anglican Church. Some commentators, like Christopher Tremewan, have been highly critical of the racial politics and basis of the new structure.[16] Others have focused on different effects, including various perceived benefits and weaknesses. In 2009, Rangi Nicholson evaluated the effectiveness of Te Pouhere in terms of bicultural development, with the Church being assessed as a place for Māori language and culture regenesis. Nicholson argued that the new constitution had not provided enough financial and human resourcing to empower Māori community and ministry development.[17] In contrast, writing around the same time, Bishop Muru Walters claimed that the three-tikanga model had contributed to a general flourishing of those in the Tikanga Māori church. For Walters, the 'model allows for Māori to be empowered and gives our people the ability to stand on their own two feet in catering for their own needs.'[18] Clearly empowerment and self-determination are needed to 'paddle in the same direction'. But how can this be measured? Ongoing debate about just what constitutes equitable distribution of resources across the three tikanga suggests that this is a key indicator of the effectiveness of Te Pouhere in addressing injustice, especially for Māori in regards to the Treaty relationship, and pursuing reconciliation.

The distribution of resources and its impact on the flourishing of Māori is not the only aspect of the Three Tikanga Church which draws critique. For all its contributions in facilitating self-determination and inter-tikanga dialogue at the General Synod level, there are questions about the three-tikanga model's theological foundation, and its appropriateness for New Zealand's increasingly multicultural context. Is the church 'silo-ed' in its resources and its theology? Some say it is and lament.[19] With the exception of General Synod, Common Life Conferences (intended to gather members of each tikanga around common concerns such as mission) and the national seminary, St John's College, the three tikanga are largely separate.

A robust theological foundation was largely missing from the outset in 1992, other than in the general terms outlined earlier. While this has drawn criticism,[20] inter-tikanga commissions and hui have enabled greater collaboration in the fields of contextual theology and education. Perhaps the most explicit theology written for the Three Tikanga Church was *A Trinitarian Theological Reflection* by the then Bishop of Waikato, David Moxon, in 2005. He argued that the primary question was not about the possibilities of Canon Law—the Church's own institutional rules—but rather 'What are the potentials of friendship?'[21] Moxon looked to the logo of the Anglican Church in Aotearoa New Zealand and Polynesia, the woven flax cross, as a symbol of the care needed in order to weave together the tikanga in harmony and unity.

A theology of 'the potential of friendship' reminds us there are now new voices in the Treaty partnership: Chinese immigrants to New Zealand are technically Tikanga Pākehā; African and Melanesian students study at St John's College. The voices of these and other newcomers to the Treaty partnership and the Three Tikanga Church keep alive questions around theology, identity and belonging, especially within Tikanga Pākehā. Lasting peace is always relational, and the hospitality needed to facilitate relationships can only be offered and received where there is an 'at home-ness' on the part of the host and acceptance of those being welcomed. Greenaway and McIntyre explore this dynamic in a paper on migrants and the Three Tikanga Church, and note the important place of the tangata whenua in such relationships. They argue that the possibility of welcome is dependent on the honouring of Māori 'as God's guardians of the Taonga [treasures] of the nation'.[22]

Writing as a faculty member at St John's Theological College in 1997, Philip Culbertson has also highlighted the challenge presented by new migrants, alongside two other considerations that he claims were ambiguous from the start:

> At least three problems were left unaddressed by the new three-tikanga structure: the role of tikanga Polynesia, the third partner in a church committed to equity between two Treaty partners; the place of ministry by and to the growing Asian and other immigrant populations of New Zealand who do not easily fit into any of the three tikanga; and the creation of 'horizontal' structures which facilitate, or even allow, communication between the three parallel ethnic streams.[23]

Not surprisingly, subsequent General Synod Proceedings reveal that the voices of non-European migrants remain largely unheard in the Three Tikanga Church. And as recently as September 2015, Jenny Chalmers echoed Culbertson's critique about the lack of grassroots interaction between the tikanga: 'many Anglicans live out their church life within their own Tikanga without necessarily coming across the others.'[24]

A related, persistent critique of Te Pouhere is that the energy and resources required to function as three tikanga has distracted the Church from its call to mission.[25] This is despite the three-tikanga Common Life Conferences, which are intended precisely to foster collaborative ministry and mission. However, supporters point to the Hikoi of Hope in 1998 as an example of an initiative which drew the three tikanga together as they joined others in walking for change in Aotearoa New Zealand.[26] Bishop John Paterson noted that the hikoi (walk):

> [Brought] people together . . . and in the walking and the talking the people found that they themselves were being changed. The Hikoi of Hope brought the three Tikanga together as never before. It exposed for many a lack of understanding of how different we are, and how differently we go about many things, and how blessed we are in those differences.[27]

Nevertheless, observors like Nyasha Gumbeze, a Zimbabwean-born priest in the Anglican Church in New Zealand, claim that the three-tikanga structure fundamentally inhibits mission—not simply because of the energy and resources needed to sustain the structure, but also because of its ethnic rigidity. By hampering preparedness to reach out to migrants, the structure limits an important opportunity for ministry, given that the non-European migrants Gumbeze interviewed perceive 'the church to be the only place where they can receive unconditional care'.[28] If Gumbeze is correct (recent census data reveal very few non-European migrants in the Anglican Church, which suggests that she is), then this is a sobering critique. It would be a sad unintended consequence if structures designed to empower and facilitate ministry and mission actually detracted from it.

Into the Future

These critiques will no doubt continue to be debated. They reveal that the transformation of relationships in the Three Tikanga Church is far from over. Te Pouhere was not an end point, nor was it intended to create rigidity. Rather, Te Pouhere is a staging post on a journey together that began at Hohi in 1814.

Structurally, Te Pouhere allows the Anglican Church in Aotearoa New Zealand and Polynesia to wrestle with different understandings of theology, identity, bicultural partnership and the mission of the Church, in order to heal the wounds of history and build more genuine partnership for the future. General Synod records since 1992 reveal that at times it has felt more like grasping nettles than smoking a peace pipe—and yet in each informal conversation and hui there is a deepening understanding and commitment to journey and work together in

Young people from the Diocese of Polynesia (Tikanga Pasefika) bring the 'gospel vaka' into Auckland's Holy Trinity Cathedral during the service for the consecration of the cathedral on 28 October 2017. Source: *Anglican Taonga*.

ways that enable the flourishing of each tikanga.[29] Institutionally, at least, it seems Te Pouhere can be celebrated as a peacemaking initiative.

It must also be acknowledged, however, that these conversations are more often than not dominated by people within the leadership structures of the Three Tikanga Church. The structure holds the conversations, but unless those who are in it stay vitally connected to the rest of the Church and to its overarching mission they risk being constrained by the very mechanism which was intended for flourishing. Gumbeze and Nicholson articulate critical voices which need to be heard. Gumbeze's conclusion in 2010, after interviewing migrants, lay people and clergy across the three tikanga, still stands as a challenge today: 'The three Tikanga as experienced as divisive has fostered mutual neglect rather than mutual interdependence.'[30] In 2017 there are hopeful signs that bishops and clergy alike are seeking to foster inter-tikanga mutuality at diocesan and parish levels. Yet in many places the longing for deeper understanding and partnership at the grassroots remains.

Finally, if this three-tikanga model is to build and sustain a genuinely inclusive and peaceable church, the conversation must include the voices of those who still migrate in their modern waka to Aotearoa New Zealand and seek a place to stand in a church that claims to welcome them with manaakitanga (hospitality). How the Church responds to these new waves of non-European migrants remains a pressing theological and practical concern.

The story of the Treaty, the Church and the reconciliation of Christ continues. The changes the Anglican Church initiated in 1992 were a response to a particular set of historical and contemporary circumstances. That context was shaped especially by the Church's historical role in the creation and signing of the Treaty of Waitangi, and a period of intense national wrestling with the need to honour the Treaty. The Church's new constitution emerged as a gospel-inspired peacemaking endeavour, and it remains as a unique exemplar of the place of structural change in the peacemaking vocation of the church. Te Pouhere articulates an explicit goal of building lasting peace. Nevertheless, it would be naïve to presume that the structure is itself evidence of this goal being reached. Twenty-five years on, it is clear that the Church faces fresh challenges: grassroots relationships across the tikanga require attention, and there are questions about the place and needs of new migrants within the existing structures. Some members also feel that a stronger theological foundation is needed, and hope to see a greater missional focus established within the Church. These dimensions are all relevant if the Church is to continue fostering peace and promoting the flourishing of all its members.

In 2014, at Hohi in Rangihoua Bay, Māori and Pākehā descendants of those present two hundred years ago gathered to celebrate the bicentenary of the first preaching of the gospel—'behold I bring you Good News'. My direct ancestor Thomas Hansen was there in 1814 as the captain of Marsden's ship, and I was there with my family in 2014. Anglicans from across Aotearoa New Zealand and Polynesia, along with many from other churches, celebrated the legacy of friendship first evoked in the hospitality Ruatara offered to Samuel Marsden. They pledged themselves again to live out the reconciliation of the gospel so that it will indeed be the 'glad tidings of great joy' for all who live in these islands. The lesson of Te Pouhere is that such commitments need to be embodied within the structures of institutions. They also need to be renewed, so that the spirit of reconciliation can be pursued in the changing circumstances of history.

7

Taranaki, Coventry and the Paths of Peace and Reconciliation

Jamie Allen

Ki tō tātou Kaihanga, me whakakorōria tōna ingoa i ngā wā katoa.[1]

You don't need to be a regular pew-dweller to guess that a congregation of over 1,000 for Sunday worship in an Anglican church in Taranaki is pretty rare. I've personally experienced it twice. The first occasion was at the consecration of New Zealand's oldest stone church (St Mary's, New Plymouth), when it changed from being a parish church to a cathedral in March 2010. The other was three years later. This was another moment marking the culmination of many years' preparation and prayer, but with a very different kaupapa—a purpose that gathered kaumatua (Māori elders), military, social activists, international visitors, the press, politicians, educators, bishops, peacemakers, community leaders, and Māori and Pākehā alike to church. They came in droves to enact and embody a drama of reconciliation along a path which was begun in the 1840s, when this small but robust place of worship was built and then consecrated on 29 September 1846 by the settlers of New Plymouth.

New Plymouth was a site of early Māori–Pākehā interaction. The site of the town had been occupied by Māori for hundreds of years before the establishment of a Pākehā trading station in 1828. In 1841 the arrival of the first Plymouth Company settlers signalled the beginning of planned settlement. It had long been an area of contestation. By 1860, tensions over a disputed land sale in the nearby Waitara area sparked the first shots of the Taranaki Wars on 17 March 1860. A series of wars then raged through the region on and off for 21 years. At stake was ownership and authority over the land. Contested ownership would shape the future for both Māori and Pākehā, particularly following government confiscations of land under the New Zealand Settlements Act of 1863. Well over 700 people were killed in Taranaki during the wars of this period, on both sides, and several thousand over Aotearoa New Zealand as a whole.[2] Many more were wounded and many more again had their livelihoods permanently disrupted. Meanwhile, St Mary's—a fledgling place of worship—was sited at the base of a beautiful pā site, sacred to Māori, which was levelled off and became the site for the barracks of British imperial regiments. It took on the role not only of a garrison church, but also a sanctuary for Pākehā in this conflict. A strong alliance therefore formed between St Mary's Church, settler society and the state. This allegiance extended to the storage of munitions within those sanctified walls, stones and timbers—stored ready to spill the

The Taranaki Cathedral Church of St Mary, built in 1846, the oldest stone church in New Zealand. Photograph by Paul Scott, http://paulscott.info.

blood of Māori. Margaret Alington's history of St Mary's, *Goodly Stones and Timbers*, includes a record of the wartime memories of a child who was '"hurriedly stowed in safety" within the barracks on the dismal winter's night of 27 June 1860, when 60 bluejackets and marines were landed from the warships lying at anchor, and marched with their brass 12-pounder up to St Mary's Church where they were billeted.'[3]

Painful Memorials

A significant subplot in this terrible drama began, for St Mary's, in 1878. A local clergyman, Archdeacon Philip Walsh (1843–1914), was commissioned to paint a hatchment—a large, diamond-shaped coat of arms—as a memorial to one of those same regiments. Once finished, Walsh's work of art was received with delight by the folks of St Mary's, and he was duly persuaded to press on with a further 16 hatchments, to acknowledge each of the regiments that fought locally on the side of the settlers. On 28 April 1904, a number of the hatchments were unveiled by the Governor General, Lord Ranfurly, alongside the Native Minister, James Carroll, and other dignitaries. Bishop Neligan of Auckland dedicated them. Captain Robert Falcon Scott of the Royal Navy, who later died in Antarctica, was also present. The intention at the time was purely to honour the imperial and colonial soldiers who died. Walsh, in a sermon referring to the hatchments, said, 'there is no evil greater than that of war. There is no department in life in which its evil effects are not felt.'[4]

Over a number of years, the hatchments were faithfully painted, dedicated, and hung from the walls of the church, alongside colours which were laid up from the various regiments. Their arrival took place during a period of imperialist pride. Their legacy, however, came to symbolise the position of the church as a supporter of settler interests during the conflict—a conflict which may have been over in military terms, but whose outcomes still divide us. As Andrew Moffat writes:

> Few seemed troubled that they were one-sided markers of the conflict. As with most memorials of the day, Māori were excluded, apart from those deemed 'friendly' to the colonists. The hatchments thus became a source of mamae (pain), strong

Hatchments on the walls of St Mary's, commemorating the regiments and 'friendly Maoris' that fought for the settlers during the Taranaki Wars. Photographs by Paul Scott, http://paulscott.info.

> reminders of bloodshed and loss. These sentiments were swamped for generations by the mainstream Pākehā view of the memorials, but strong undercurrents of feeling remained, bubbling occasionally to the surface.[5]

With such a wounded history, the journey towards finding common ground was never going to be simple. Indeed, it has included some incredibly courageous initiatives. Amongst these, the creation of a beautiful memorial, unveiled in St Mary's in 1972 'to the Glory of God and in memory of the Maori people of Taranaki who died during the conflicts of 1860–1870.'[6] This impressive and striking Māori artwork boldly affirms that there are two peoples to be commemorated, and expresses sadness that the differences resulted in bloodshed. Its carved figures tell the true story of two warring Taranaki tribes, reconciled through the love of two young people, Takarangi and Raumahora, whose descendants included Te Whiti o Rongomai and Tohu Kākahi.[7] Its subtext is that, by mutual acceptance of the God of Love, two peoples can live together in common respect and peace.

When St Mary's finally became a cathedral in 2010,[8] the church's change of status was full of sparkling potential—as new beginnings often are. During the consecration service, an apology was lovingly offered by the Bishop of Taranaki, Philip Richardson, on behalf of the Pāhekā Church for the sins of our history. Silence was held in deep and humble confession, and then Pie Jesu—a medieval Latin hymn asking Jesus to give rest to the departed—was sung by Danielle Allen, my daughter, to symbolise the hope that this family would be peacemakers. It is significant to note that the gift of forgiveness was offered that day by the giving of a precious gift by our kaumatua—*before* the apology was made.

I was the person licensed to be the first Dean of that new cathedral. I came to this position open and eager, committed to the task of reconciliation. Yet I was soon confronted with the extent of my limitations, partiality and ignorance—and how much I had to learn. One incident vividly illustrated this point. During my time as Dean of Taranaki, one of my tasks was helping to prepare a commemorative panel which would hang in perpetuity in the cathedral. The panel was to bear the words:

> As a community we pay tribute to the many Māori and Pākehā who are both commemorated and forgotten here. Of these; one who lies at rest in the Vicarage garden was Taiporutu, leading chief in the Māori King movement, along with his 20-year-old son, Hemi. His dying words were, 'Let, I say, the white man and the dark skin dwell together in peace.'

This last sentence was quoted from a history book, which was in turn quoting from a *Taranaki Herald* account of the dying speech of Wetini Taiporutu, purportedly delivered in 1861. I thought it spectacularly impactive. However, some outstanding research by John O'Leary reveals the entire text of this speech to be a flagrant and shameless fake.[9] It turns out to be a kind of dramatic monologue. The piece purports to be the poroaki (farewell address) of Taiporutu. However, it is nothing of the sort. It was concocted for readers of a Pākehā newspaper.

This repulsive and crude interpolation—a sentence of which I received in good faith, and naïvely believed—continues to serve as an object lesson for me: whilst I might think I'm providing objective copy, I am doubtless overlaying my own rendering to this account, even here and now. Interpolations may come, in part, from my own messy formation—which includes a connection with Coventry, where I was ordained. Indeed, this is the right time for Coventry to enter our narrative, because through the mysteries and grace of God, Taranaki and Coventry cathedrals were to form a permanent bond in the years that followed 2010.

Coventry Connections

Coventry Cathedral also has a painful history. In November 1940, during the German Luftwaffe's 'Operation Moonlight Sonata', the beautiful medieval building was bombed and destroyed. The provost of the cathedral famously wrote 'Father Forgive' on the smoke-blackened wall of the sanctuary (not 'Father forgive *them*', to people's surprise). From the ruins, a cross was formed using three huge nails which had fallen from the broken roof. After the cathedral was rebuilt in 1962, the original cross remained, becoming a symbol of reconciliation. Later, other crosses of nails were presented to Kiel, Dresden and Berlin, cities shattered by Allied bombing. Out of the ashes grew a trust and partnership between Coventry and the German cities. These relationships, bent on peace, catalysed a worldwide peace and reconciliation movement—and the establishment of the Community of the Cross of Nails (CCN) in the 1970s. The CCN network consists of over 170 partners in at least 35 countries (including many of the world's major conflict areas). Members can be churches, reconciliation centres, prisons, NGOs or schools. Indeed, any body of people may apply to be received into the CCN if they can demonstrate an active and ongoing commitment to this threefold vision: to heal the wounds of history; to learn to live with difference and celebrate diversity; and to build a culture of peace.

CCN members are presented with a large cross of nails as a physical sign and reminder of their vocation; the crosses are modelled on the original, and are constructed by prisoners serving life sentences in Germany—a powerful reminder that reconciliation is an ever-ongoing journey, not a destination. It was surely the pain of conflict so early in the life of St Mary's—and the signs of suffering so present in its DNA—which began our sense of a congruence with the story of Coventry, and the Community of the Cross of Nails. At first glance, it seems remarkable that Taranaki Cathedral should be presented with such a cross, given its past. Yet that did indeed happen, and the next few parts of the Taranaki story were pivotal to that end.

Reconciliation in Action and Symbol

Another significant step was our approach, in 2010, to the people of Parihaka and the many communities around Mount Taranaki to help us make an altar cloth dedicated to peace. We asked representatives of each community to contribute an image expressive of their community identity. The 37 eclectic images received were then transformed into a single work of art, symbolic of our unity in Christ. The contributions included the likeness of a wedge of cheese; depictions of hands, and of children climbing a tree; and images of a teapot, a waka, a splash of stars, water, and the sacred maunga, Taranaki. Central to the single combined image were the white feathers of the raukura of Parihaka—that sacred sign of peace. The presence of this beautiful symbol was gifted to the cathedral by Lindsay MacLeod, visionary, man of grace and great mana, kaumatua of Parihaka.

The cathedral's physical proximity to the Māori community of Parihaka is of note. In 1881, around the same time that the paint was drying on the first hatchment to adorn St Mary's, an invasion was mounted on Parihaka, which lay just a little more than 40 kilometres away. Government forces were met at the papa kāinga (village) by children, teens, women, men and the elderly, who were singing, dancing, and all expressing that they would offer no resistance to the invasion. In response, the soldiers raided and ransacked the village; they pulled down and burnt the houses, stole taonga (treasured things), and raped women.[10]

Visitors to the cathedral—of any age—were then invited to lay their hands on the cloth, pray for peace, and sew a stitch (or stitches), to build up the picture as a collective expression of prayer. As they stitched, they talked, prayed, and sewed peace. The finished cloth was stunning—some might say surprisingly so, given its means of creation. A flax cross was woven by Whero O Te Rangi Bailey and applied to the altar frontal, with the strands of dyed flax and the embroidered feathers giving it a depth of beauty that, quite literally, causes you to gasp. The completed tapestry commemorates Te Whiti o Rongomai, Tohu Kākahi and their followers. The last stitch was sewn on 11 September, and the altar frontal was then dedicated to the Glory of God on Te Whiti's day (5 November) in 2011. It now permanently adorns the nave altar at the cathedral—poignantly so, that being the place where the greatest sacrifice and reconciliation is recalled. People are invited to come and lay a hand upon it, and continue this ministry of prayer for peace.

None of us expected on 6 March, when the first stitch was sewn in the Peace Altar Frontal, that we would be celebrating the last stitch sewn on 11 September 2011, the tenth anniversary of the 9/11 terrorist attacks. With the atrocities of 9/11 and the nineteenth-century pillaging at Parihaka in mind, a group of prayers for peace—of sewers, embroiderers and artists—gathered to pray with thanksgiving for every stitch, for every prayer that the Peace Altar Frontal represents.

The Peace Altar Frontal at St Mary's, featuring the white feathers of Parihaka and a flax cross woven by Whero O Te Rangi Bailey. Photograph by Paul Scott, http://paulscott.info.

Yet, imagine as the backdrop to that constantly deepening kōrero (conversation) of peace and reconciliation—of a faith community weaving te reo Māori (the Māori language) regularly into their liturgy—those 17 hefty chunks of black wood still hanging there, each hatchment the size of a large road sign, crowding the inside walls of the place of worship. Superficially, the church was reminiscent of a teenager's bedroom, where a lack of restraint with posters had ended up with a takeover of all available real estate. More deeply, the spiritual 'weight' of these emblems of warfare—championing one side in a bloody conflict—suggested the building's own fatigue at bearing the burden of these tokens of a conflict not yet fully resolved.

The Shifting of the Hatchments

Jesus said, 'Blessed are the peacemakers, for they shall be called children of God.'[11] For justice to be done, the next move was obvious, but far from easy. So it was that, over 130 years after the first hatchment was painted, more than 1,000 people gathered in March 2013 to see them shifted. It was tempting to burn them or deposit them in a museum somewhere—particularly the hatchment to the 'Friendly Maoris', those tangata whenua who fought on the side of the settlers. But it was clear that to be shot of them was to risk repeating mistakes which cost far too many lives. Tuck them away and we would soon forget the suffering they recalled us to with their presence. Cathedrals must be places of abundant welcome to all; each person who ventures across the threshold must know that the place is somehow their own, including those of direct lineage to any who were killed, injured or marginalised in war. So, instead of a burn-up, we concluded that all 17 hatchments would be relocated from the positions that dominated and darkened the entire worship space, to form two simple displays with explanatory signs. One such display would be through a door out of the worship space, in the gathering area for the ministers and choir. The other display would be laid on the walls of the transept (or side-arm) of the building. Most (but not all) of the congregation were yearning for the day when these artifacts of war would no longer define the community's prayer space, but would be noted as unique taonga of historical significance, part of our common journey and heritage, and properly displayed and documented as such.

In the darkness of the evening before the crowded service, as part of our preparation, a group of us nervously began taking down the hatchments one-by-one from the walls, and gently dusted and cleaned them. So it was, on the morning of 3 March 2013, in the context of Holy Communion, that the hatchments were passed hand-to-hand to their new positions: a real-life drama of peace and reconciliation, in which those present discerned something far deeper taking place. For some, the events of the day came as long-awaited joy and liberation. Others were uncertain, or bearing grief more profound than words. There were many tears shed, and words of anger were exchanged. The Eucharist was the well-appointed setting for this—the presence around the table which represents the eternal love of God, made perfect only through sacrifice. This historic occasion was introduced with these words:

> The hatchments will now begin to be moved. This is a sacred moment; allow the Holy Spirit to touch you. There is no need to remain silent—although you may wish to do so.

People then began to pass forward the hatchments, which wove their way through from one pew to the next until they were received at the front, to be hung in their new positions. The children made a human chain from the very front pews to the destination of the hatchments.

As the movement of the hatchments began, a school kapa haka group responded with passion, and then there was a period of deep silence, followed by a Canticle of Praise, led from the front by children. We then again stood together and continued to pass the hatchments, concluding with the sharing of 'The Peace'. This ritual involves turning to one another and exchanging words and a gesture or sign of peace, such as a hongi, handshake or embrace—and its potency was not lost on us.

We had set up ladders and scaffolding because the hatchments were to be rehung during the service itself (a health and safety nightmare, but the entire act needed to be begun and ended together). I looked up at one point to see that matters had been taken in hand by a Pākehā museum curator (who had ascended the scaffolding), a Māori parish councillor (who was halfway up the ladder) and a school principal (also Māori), who was passing the hatchments aloft to him. The significance of the wider community's ownership of the entire healing act was thus most clearly demonstrated through the relationships involved.

Four experiences in particular affected me during this process. The first was the returning memory of a Tuesday, almost three years prior, when I had propped up a ladder next to one of the hatchments, intending to take it down for an hour or so. I was planning to talk about its history to a visiting school group. 'Ooh, careful! What are you doing, Dean? We don't touch those,'

A hatchment being passed from hand to hand through the church to its new position, 3 March 2013. Source: Fairfax Media NZ / *Taranaki Daily News*.

said an angry parishioner's voice as I wobbled on the ladder. Beautiful chunks of wood they may be, but these hatchments had gained a power and authority that was unintended by their maker, or by his Maker, for that matter. Yet now, here we were, permitted by the church's faculty system to take them all down, and to address an unhealthy power balance. I was speechless at the courage that the Holy Spirit had enabled in people.

The second event happened as we re-entered the building that evening, and gazed about after the last hatchment had been taken down. Of course, the building 'felt' lighter simply because several square metres of black painted hangings had been stripped from the walls. But something much more significant had happened—a spiritual lightness had arrived, and it was somehow as if the nave was breathing out and rejoicing in sheer liberation from what it had been required to shoulder for so long.

The third was the exchange of hongi with a beautiful, wise Māori priest. Somehow, mystically, a vision came vibrantly to me as my nose touched hers and our breath mingled, and the vision said this, with the voice of some ancient ones: 'from us all, thank you to your people for what you are doing.'

The fourth, strictly speaking, was after the event, when we kept discovering a buzz around our region that 'something had happened'. At hui, people would mention, 'the cathedral moved those banners' as an indication that a change was coming about in our midst. It has been exciting to see where new stems and buds now blossom.

Nails of Suffering and Hope

Here, in closing, I must name a further pivotal relationship in this journey. Six months prior to the move of the hatchments, my darling 12-year-old daughter Carrie lay dying of horrific, rampant, soft-tissue cancer. A life-loving, boundary-pushing, faithful-to-God young woman, her tough, barely used body was engaged in a gruelling head-on with rhabomyosarcoma, and she was bravely enduring the final stages of a massive relapse. Our family asked that, should things not go the way we hoped, the old St Mary's graveyard—which had been closed since 1861—might be re-opened. Carrie was enfolded in love and compassion, prayed for and upheld by thousands worldwide, as well as many Pākehā and Māori alike in Taranaki—including the community of Parihaka.

Tragically, there was no miraculous healing. When Carrie died, in grief beyond words, her coffin was gently lowered to rest upon two whāriki, or woven mats, within the church graveyard. The whāriki were prepared by those with immediate links to Parihaka—the community by which her kawe mate was graciously received,[12] as she had no marae of her own. Like the flax strands on the Peace Altar Frontal, the interweaving of tikanga Māori into her farewell (as the 'daughter of the Dean') was pure grace from all who brought their culture and common humanity to the graveside. Her headstone honours her in te reo Māori first, and in the English language second; a headstone set amongst so many which bear inscriptions speaking hatefully of the tangata whenua. Her photograph has a place at Te Niho Marae o Parihaka, close to that of Te Whiti o Rongomai. The ache and understanding of Māori of the loss of the apple of our eye perhaps opened a channel for healing which fine words and gestures could never do.

A year later, a community Garden of Remembrance was installed which includes, centrally, three tall sculptures echoing those three white feathers of the raukura of the community of Parihaka; sculptures carved by the giver of those whāriki on which Carrie lies (and of the Bishop of Taranaki's crosier, and of Carrie's headstone), Moewai Terry. The raukura are sacred signs of peace—and it is hard to believe that they now are so spectacularly present in the grounds of a place with such a divided past. Once again, they speak more than words ever could. The garden is symbolic of new life and hope. Its Māori design expresses unity and the next chapter of moving on together; our challenge is to continue, even in the laying to rest of our loved ones.

Taranaki Cathedral's mission statement reads: 'To be as Christ to the Community'. That means it must continue to look outwards to serve, and to be a place of grace and welcome for all. I believe that the Church should be positioned to set an example in cultural unity, justice and peace. After the establishment of the Garden of Remembrance we knew that our membership of the Community of the Cross of Nails would stir us to be still more active in such work—particularly as we considered this to be our core vocation, not just for our city but, in a small way, for our nation.

St Mary's therefore submitted an application to join the CCN as a partner; and in 2015 this was approved. Visiting to present St Mary's cross of nails around the anniversary of the moving of the hatchments, Dean John Witcombe of Coventry Cathedral spent three weeks in Aotearoa New Zealand. At the conclusion of his visit, he wrote:

> I see a significant contribution from NZ to the Coventry Cross of Nails Network, with its working out of reconciliation issues in a small, and relatively new country, which makes the stories perhaps easier to grasp. The Maori/Settler history has tragedies, but also triumphs—the story of Parihaka deserves to be known across the world.

We know that there are countless communities, churches and organisations in Aotearoa whose vocation is similar, and who may also consider the possibility of becoming part of the network. We hope that Taranaki Cathedral will establish a hub—a local base, as Coventry is so far away—open to others wanting to seek membership; and that its people will continue to express their vocation against the inspiring backdrop of a worldwide movement for peace and reconciliation.

Aroha mai, aroha atu
Love received demands love returned

8

Maungārongo ki te Whenua: Te Ora Hou Making its Peace

Mike Ross, Manu Caddie, Jono Campbell & Judy Kumeroa

The Māori ceremony of welcome, the pōwhiri, traditionally began with a challenge, performed by a selected, capable warrior. This was conducted on the community courtyard, the marae, in the domain of Tūmatauenga, the deity of conflict and war. During the challenge, both parties were given space to declare their intentions and rules for engagement, either for peace or conflict. It was only once a person or group had gone through the domain of Tūmatauenga that they were able to join the tribe in the Wharenui (tribal house), within the domain of Rongo, the deity of peace.

This chapter discusses the peacebuilding activities of Te Ora Hou, a youth organisation with Christian and Māori values working in mainly Māori communities. It outlines the youth-centred club programme, and reflects on its practice, results and challenges. It then presents a joint community and Te Ora Hou project called Stone Soup, and finally describes a relationship with a Nepalese youth network. Each story reflects the movement from uncertainty and conflict, the domain of Tūmatauenga, toward security and peace, the domain of Rongo, for individuals, whanau and communities, with the ultimate goal being maungārongo ki te whenua (peace on earth).

Te Ora Hou means 'The New Life' and refers to the Christian roots of the organisation and the intention to share a new way of approaching life with young people in socially and economically struggling communities. It began in the mid-1970s in Dunedin under the guidance of Youth for Christ, a Christian organisation working with young people, which has been active in New Zealand since 1950. Te Ora Hou quickly spread to many cities and towns throughout the country and by the mid-1980s hundreds of indigenous young people were involved.

The mid-1990s was a pivotal period in Te Ora Hou's development. Four factors had a particularly profound influence on the organisation's ethos and direction at that time. These were:

1. awareness of rangatahi (youth), and Māori in general, experiencing intergenerational social and cultural poverty;[1]
2. development of a mission theology that promoted an indigenous faith and church for and by indigenous people;[2]
3. recognition that youth work in a Māori context was relational and included seeing rangatahi as part of a whānau (family) and community;[3] and
4. the rise and importance of the Treaty of Waitangi obligations in the social and political life of the nation.[4]

Recognition of these four factors challenged the predominantly Pākehā leadership of Youth for Christ to consider culturally appropriate practice and an ethical response to Māori poverty and the Treaty. After intensive discussions, the leadership of Te Ora Hou concluded that it could not respond effectively if Māori voices, practices and thinking remained on the margins of Youth for Christ; it proposed a dynamic move forward as an independent organisation. The Youth for Christ leadership agreed, although there were hesitations on both sides, and Te Ora Hou established itself as an autonomous collection of centres unified by the intention of indigenous mission to indigenous communities.[5]

Rōpū Rangatahi

The common component of Te Ora Hou has always been its 'club' programmes that offer after-school activities for mostly Māori youth. While many things have changed over the years, in response to changes in youth culture, needs in the community,

A neighbourhood event in Whanganui co-hosted by the community and Te Ora Hou Whanganui. Source: Greg Tichbon.

A Youth Work event in Whangarei organised by local young people with support from Te Ora Hou. Source: Te Ora Hou Northland Inc.

the passion of volunteers, and government policy and funding, the core principles of the clubs remain the same. A Christian adult builds relationships with a small group of young people, once a week they pick them up in a van, go out and play some games, the youth worker tells them about Jesus, then drops them off home . . . occasionally battered and bruised from the physical rough-and-tumble activities, but generally intact and happy.

The pursuit of peace is not a turn of phrase that naturally roles off the tongues of Te Ora Hou kaimahi (workers). Rough and ready, loud, organic and chaotic are words that sit more easily with those who have journeyed with Te Ora Hou, as young people or kaimahi, during its 40-year history. Nevertheless, the pursuit of peace in the lives of rangatahi has been an essential component in Te Ora Hou's philosophy and practice.

Clubs are about fun. Young people love to laugh with and amongst themselves. The role of Jesus as a peacemaker included finding the humour that was present. Often that desire for humour can be utilised to defuse a situation and gently encourage people to learn to laugh at themselves. Evening events often involve physical combat disguised as games—activities such as Storm the Heights, bullrush, rugby league—high in energy, low in planning, and often ending in tears for someone. There is the usual posturing and language of teenagers fuelled by the volatile mixture of testosterone, hormones, overconfidence and self doubt. The movie *Boy* captures the mood and dialogue perfectly, with so many club nights having a 'you're a egg'. . .'you're a major egg' exchange.[6]

To the uninitiated it would seem that much of what takes place perpetuates the macho culture that many of these rangatahi come from. Consequences for swearing are push-ups—straight out of the boot-camp manual. There are initiation pile-ons (everyone 'piles' onto an individual), and the Jandal of Justice (a playful slap attack with jandals) may be liberally used to welcome unsuspecting newcomers into the group. Key phrases include 'go hard or go home', 'one in, all in', and the ubiquitous 'harden up ow!'[7] Scratch a little bit deeper, however, and the initial appearance of an out-of-control, disrespectful group proves to be deceiving.

Many of the young people involved in Te Ora Hou have a background of disenfranchisement and alienation in urban environments or state housing, and some have family gang connections. Young Māori people in deprived suburbs or depressed rural areas are more likely to use and abuse alcohol and drugs earlier, leading to harmful effects on their social life and educational and employment opportunities.[8] Family violence within Māori communities has also been said to be 'of epidemic proportions'.[9] In these disruptive environments, young people are consistently let down by the people closest to them and the systems supposedly there to support them.

Tama grew up in single-parent family, in a multi-storey, low socio-economic subdivision, referred to locally by rangatahi as 'The Bronx'. He speaks of the impact that John, a Te Ora Hou kaimahi, made on his life. John is a white, middle-class, middle-aged Christian New Zealander working as a senior government official and far removed from the image of a stereotypical youth worker to marginalised indigenous youth. Tama, now married with his own family, remembers how him and his mates would try to get John to buy them takeaways, not realising that their crude efforts were willingly supported by John, who valued the opportunity to take time over fish and chips to listen, connect and build a relationship of trust with the boys.

John, like so many other effective Te Ora Hou kaimahi, was an exception in Tama's life—one of too few positive adult role models who offered hope, consistency and an alternative voice, in a kiwi accent. John challenged Tama and his mates in a non-confrontational way with the teachings of Jesus that are embedded in the DNA of Te Ora Hou club programmes. Tama describes how John would quietly present an alternative perspective; when conflicts occurred, he would get the boys to consider the other person's point of view, the role that each person played, while slowly unpacking the events without getting preachy.

For young people like Tama, Te Ora Hou offered a major point of difference that churches and other youth groups struggle to emulate. It wasn't so much about what took place, but how it took place. In Te Ora Hou, mainly volunteer youth workers attempt to genuinely engage with young people, not just on a weeknight activity programme, but meeting their whānau, participating in the community and getting involved in key areas of their lives. As Sam Chapman, a long time urban community development worker and a friend and mentor of Te Ora Hou, puts it: 'their witness is their withness'.[10] Alternative, peaceful lifestyles and ways of being are modelled in simple, down-to-earth ways. Kaimahi build connections, laying the foundation of trust that provides the opportunity for genuine relationships to develop, and the chance to positively influence rangatahi as they make some important life decisions.

Dealing with rangatahi, however, is not without its moral dilemmas. For example, on one trip by the Christchurch Te Ora Hou crew to Hastings for a sports tour, two of the young people were caught getting stoned. Up until then it had been a fantastic trip for everyone. Prior to the trip the agreement was that anyone breaking the rules by possessing or using drugs or alcohol would be automatically sent home, no questions asked, no exceptions. Great in theory, however, in practice it was not so simple. The logistics of getting two young people back to Christchurch raised all sorts of issues. Who will pay for it? Do they fly (very expensive in the mid-1990s), or drive? Who drives? And what does that mean for the other kaimahi? Better consult with the parents . . . hmmm, and there lies the bastard problem. If you tell one of the boys' dads, he will get angry and without doubt give his son a beating when he gets home. And we know the reason the boy gets stoned is because of the violent relationship with his father. At the heart of this lies the need of a broken, hurt young person.

At the heart of the pursuit for peace is reconciliation. Through journeying with rangatahi over many years, we build relationships of trust and attempt to demonstrate an acceptance of life's messiness as the rangatahi reconcile themselves with their world.

Stone Soup

Stone Soup is a community initiative in a socially and economically struggling neighbourhood in Whanganui, a small city on the West Coast of the North Island. It has brought neighbours together socially every two months for the past six years. The initiative began as a response to a tragic gang-related drive-by shooting, which increased tension and pressures in the community: the incident resulted in residents moving out, removing their children from the local school, and requesting transfers from Housing New Zealand to other parts of the city. Greg and Judy live locally and, as part of Te Ora Hou Whanganui, have worked with young people for 25 years. They got together in 2009 with other local people and Housing New Zealand and decided to do something positive as a neighbourhood. This group came up with the concept of 'Stone Soup', which aimed to strengthen community relationships and support networks in order to help prevent violence.

Stone Soup is based on the old story of a traveller coming to a village, carrying nothing more than an empty pot. Upon his arrival, the villagers are unwilling to share any of their food stores with the hungry visitor. The traveller fills the pot with water, drops a large stone in it, and places it over a fire in the village square. One of the villagers becomes curious and asks what he is doing. The traveller answers that he is making 'stone soup', which tastes wonderful, although it still needs a little bit of garnish to improve the flavour, which he is missing. The villager doesn't mind parting with just a little bit to help them out, so it gets added to the soup. Another villager walks by, inquiring about the pot, and the traveller again mentions his stone soup that hasn't reached its full potential yet. The villager hands him a carrot to help out. More and more villagers walk by, each adding another ingredient. Finally, a delicious and nourishing pot of soup is enjoyed by all. The story has traditionally been told as a lesson in co-operation, especially amid scarcity, and in the Whanganui situation, the principle was applied to encourage ownership of the initiative within the neighbourhood.

Through the bi-monthly gatherings, neighbours are getting to know each other, young people are making positive contributions to their community, and trust is being built between people of different ages and cultural backgrounds. Such positive impacts have had a significant effect on the wider community, with residents reporting greater confidence about their ability to effect positive change. A number of resident-led initiatives have already developed out of Stone Soup, and the number of requests for transfers out of the area has also dropped dramatically. While these outcomes may not be solely due to the Stone Soup gatherings, residents have indicated that the gatherings are part of a broader story of renewal and trust-building in their community.

As residents feel better about the place where they live, organisers have noticed them wanting to take responsibility for the appearance and the safety of public amenities like the local park. Tangible changes in the neighbourhood show that people care about the place, and local people are taking leadership roles within the community and building collaborative relationships amongst themselves. These are factors that lead to lower levels of family violence and abuse, regardless of an area's socio-economic status.[11]

In the early days, graffiti was a topic of community concern. Jay, a local youth worker and key supporter of Stone Soup, met with some young men to hear their thoughts on the topic, and found their passion was for music. He rallied support locally and partnered with the local Māori radio station, Awa FM, to support ten young people to write and record their own music, resulting in the release of a music CD. Some of these artists are now performing locally and throughout the country, and have been featured on national television.

Organisers have witnessed changing attitudes and behaviour amongst residents, citing examples like one interaction in which an elderly Pākehā resident commented to an organiser: 'Isn't it good to see the kids having good honest fun instead of making trouble'; to which the organiser replied, 'Yes, and it's good for them to see you relaxing with them instead of seeing you as a grumpy old man.'

Stone Soup events are run in the local park on a Saturday and are designed to help residents open up, access useful resources, talk about issues as a community, and take ownership of those issues. On average, around 370 people attend the Stone Soup gatherings. A flyer is sent to 550 households, asking locals to supply hāngī (traditional earth oven) ingredients, and this has resulted in many residents, especially young people, being involved in the preparation of the shared meal. Te Ora Hou workers have taken a lead role and do a lot of the organising but do not want Stone Soup to be seen as a Te Ora Hou event:

> We are part of the community, using our time and particular abilities as part of our contribution . . . because this is who we are and where we live.
>
> First time—everyone loved it. Second time—everyone thought it was part of some agency's service delivery and started having expectations of us, but after that everyone started to work out that it was just us doing it together.
>
> We don't think of the people involved as clients, we're not providing a service.
>
> Everyone has something to contribute. At least, part of the answer to community issues exists within the community. Some of it is 'us' being able to identify our issues rather than someone else [telling us what the problems are].

Organisers view Stone Soup as a long-term project of building neighbourhood strength and resilience, not a brief intervention to address a specific issue. While a number of workers from various agencies do participate, they do so on a personal basis and are not usually paid to be there. Initial funding was helpful, but the plan has always been for the residents to contribute everything required to make it happen.

Stone Soup organisers are attempting to allow things to develop organically. They think that trying to follow a particular formula may stifle community initiatives that work best for the local people. Public events have been a great way to promote social cohesion, but there is a need to build on that and allow people the opportunity to share their concerns, ideas and plans. The 'Kōrero Corner' at Stone Soup involves 20–30 people gathering after the meal to kōrero (talk) about questions such as 'What things are happening locally?' and 'Where should we go with them?' These discussions have generated new ideas. For example, some people said, 'Stone Soup is great but we want to do it more often', so the neighbourhood is planning

'Potluck @ the Park' once a month. Another group of whānau started a shared garden to contribute to the Stone Soup hāngī in a practical way, and a craft group has started mid-week gatherings. This group has also shared its knowledge with a local youth group, and plans to visit the neighbourhood after-school programme.

Stone Soup has become a rallying point to extract the good from the community, and it is focused on the strengths of the community, not the problems. Consequently, organisers have consciously kept agencies away so that expectations of service provision are minimised. They have instead encouraged neighbourhood leadership by people with organising and event-management skills, to allow people to work to their strengths—some people are good at being friendly, some are great cooks, gardeners, hunters, administrators, and so on. Everyone has something to offer—that is a core message of Stone Soup.

A neighbourhood event in Whanganui co-hosted by the community and Te Ora Hou Whanganui. Source: Greg Tichbon.

Partnering for Peace in Nepal

Te Ora Hou has a strong focus on local communities, but also has a history of connecting with indigenous communities abroad. The organisation has at times taken its young people to such communities in places like the Philippines, Thailand, Fiji, Hawaii, Australia, North America and Canada as a way to challenge and expose them to other realities. Between 2003 and 2008, Te Ora Hou Aotearoa (TOHA) worked with an indigenous non-government youth organisation called Youth Action Nepal (YOAC) on a number of joint human rights and peacebuilding projects in Nepal. Projects included a series of capacity-building initiatives for YOAC (organisation capability building, communications, training for staff and volunteers, and evaluation of projects), a national series of community leadership and peacebuilding training programmes, and projects with young women from ethnic minorities. This work aligned closely with Mahi Tika, the social justice value of TOHA.

Te Ora Hou Aotearoa raised funds from the New Zealand public and secured funding from the New Zealand Aid Programme (then known as NZAID) to support projects led by YOAC Nepal and their partners in communities across Nepal. By 2007, YOAC was undertaking large training and development projects across Nepal with significant support from European, North American and intergovernmental partner organisations. Private foundations based in Europe, Asia and North America also provided hundreds of thousands of dollars to YOAC, due to the work TOHA and YOAC did between 2003 and 2006 to build a solid foundation for the organisation.

This work occurred during the period of the Nepalese Civil War—an armed conflict between Maoist insurgents and the Government of Nepal (1996–2006). The rebellion was launched by the Communist Party of Nepal (the Maoists) with the main aim of overthrowing the Nepalese monarchy and establishing a 'People's Republic'. In this context, YOAC was credited by the National Endowment for Democracy (USA) with preventing violence in a number of regions around Nepal through the training of young leaders committed to human rights and non-violence. TOHA supported YOAC during its first year, when all it provided was a humble radio show broadcast to villages across the country that encouraged young people not to take up arms for the government or the Maoist insurgents. TOHA provided mentoring and advice for YOAC leaders, a computer and digital camera, and a small amount of funds to support basic costs.

Prakash Bhattarai, as one of the founding members and eventual leader of Youth Action Nepal, drove the establishment and development of YOAC. The organisation works with young people and communities on human rights and peace issues, including cultural minority participation, reproductive rights, gender and development education, labour rights, immigration issues, conflict resolution, democracy training, and leadership development amongst young people. Under Prakash's leadership, a team of youth activists and educators worked in both rural and urban communities across Nepal, demonstrating high levels of commitment within national and local contexts of political instability, daily violence and insecurity. YOAC worked through this period to create a national network of young people who trained their peers in human rights and democratic principles, to counter the recruitment of young people into the civil war.

YOAC was recognised during the latter years of the Civil War, by the government and civil society, as one of the most important national youth organisations in Nepal, and it has regularly been engaged by the government and other organisations for input on development, peace and education initiatives. It organised a number of successful national Youth Social Forums that involved thousands of young representatives from communities and organisations across Nepal.

Te Ora Hou and NZAID's seed funding led to impressive impacts in communities across the country, demonstrating how small strategic investments can result in significant returns down the track. YOAC managed the funds carefully and as a result of their effective utilisation the amounts provided to the organisation have had a multiplying effect.

Succession planning for the organisation is an important issue. Prakash led YOAC through the early years and worked hard on plans to raise up another level of young leaders to take his place. The current board and volunteer leaders for various projects and activities continue to share a common vision and purpose for YOAC Nepal; this bodes well for a bright future, as does the ongoing confidence and support of international donors.[12] Prakash has also maintained an active role in supporting YOAC since leaving the leadership role (to complete a Master's in peacebuilding at Notre Dame University, near Chicago, and a PhD on the role of non-state actors in post-conflict contexts at the University of Otago, in New Zealand). Having returned to Nepal, he is now making a name for himself as a political advisor in the difficult post-conflict situation there.

While significant challenges remain for Nepal, which is one of the poorest countries on the planet, it is a safer and better place as a result of civil society organisations like YOAC.[13] Individuals like Prakash are also set to be invaluable assets for their country, not least as they work to progress democratic ideals and practices within the post-conflict, nation-building, political environment. TOHA has contributed to these tasks, too, in its small way, by investing in relationships and sharing its resources. The peacebuilding partnership with YOAC was surprising and remarkable—given the geographical, cultural and political distance between Aotearoa and Nepal—but one that arose naturally out of Te Ora Hou's values and commitments.

Conclusion

The pōwhiri ceremony begins by acknowledging each party's mana and usually ends with an agreement by both parties to work together in peace, often in spite of their differences. This is sealed with the physical closeness of hongi (a pressing of noses), the sharing of one breath, and then a meal together. Within Te Ora Hou, rangatahi are given the opportunity to enter into positive relationships; often they begin with uncertainties and challenges, but when they find acceptance among others, stability and peace can result. Te Ora Hou has also been challenged to respond to the wider community and to make its peace as an independent Māori Christian organisation. Stone Soup was a natural avenue for Te Ora Hou to extend itself into a joint community relationship, to assist the community to build on its strengths. The YOAC of Nepal is a wholly independent body which Te Ora Hou supported to promote peace in another indigenous community. Such ministries are important tests of maturity within Te Ora Hou as it seeks to acknowledge and help meet the needs of others, building peace without having to control the outcomes.

Ā, kia huaina koe, ko te kaiwhakatikatika o ngā taiepa pakaru,
ko te kaiwhakahou o ngā ara hei nohoanga. Ihaia 58:12

May you be called the repairer of the broken walls and the
restorer of streets with dwellings. Isaiah 58:12

9

Icons of Peace

John Chote

In the Suzanne Aubert Chapel within the St Joseph's Church complex in Wellington there is a beautiful Shane Cotton stained-glass window that stretches from floor to ceiling. At the base of this window is an image of an olive tree, an icon of peace, placed in Pōneke (Wellington Harbour).[1] When I talked with Monsignor Gerard Burns, the previous parish priest of St Joseph's, he told me that he sees this olive tree as a symbol of the gospel of peace. The image recalls how the good news of peace has journeyed all the way from the Holy Land to be planted in the suburbs of Wellington.

This chapter examines St Joseph's icons of peace. Over the years, St Joseph's has forged a strong Catholic identity working for peace and challenging injustice, and this is inscribed in the art and architecture of the church. St Joseph's community has also been shaped and formed by the church's sacred materiality, and these reverberations of peace echo throughout the parish community. The centrality of peace is discernible in the lives of many of the key figures who have helped nurture the parish, both historically and today. These too are icons of, and witnesses to, the gospel of peace. This understanding of icons as formative for Christianity identity and worship is indebted to specifically Catholic theology. According to the Church's Catechism,

> the contemplation of sacred icons, united with meditation on the Word of God and the singing of liturgical hymns, enters into the harmony of the signs of celebration so that the mystery celebrated is imprinted in the heart's memory and is then expressed in the new life of the faithful.[2]

The beautiful and the good—whether this is art, Scripture, liturgy or community—can help form in us peaceable habits and inclinations.

Icons, in the traditional sense, are 'windows to heaven', an aid to seeing and knowing the divine.[3] Stylistic iconographic pictures of Christ, Mary and the saints are sacramental tools that illuminate the glory of God. Icons are also 'light coming from heaven'; a channel through which God's grace is made known to the faithful. The stained glass in the Suzanne Aubert Chapel, the Trinity Window, is a perfect example of this double role of icons. During the daytime, outside light, coloured by the glass tinting, shines on to the altar in the small chapel, giving it greater prominence and drawing the focus of the congregation to the Mass, the central ritual of the Catholic liturgy celebrating the mystery of God's presence among us. The window design is tapestry-like, in the medieval tradition, documenting a visual story. The various images in the window, which include traditional Catholic and distinctly New Zealand elements, tell different parts of this story. The Sacred Heart of Jesus symbolises His great love for us. The Alpha and Omega point to the eternal nature of God sustaining us. A fantail (pīwakawaka) symbolises the

Detail of the Trinity Window, by Shane Cotton, which illuminates the Suzanne Aubert Chapel at St Joseph's Church. Photograph by Philip Fountain.

Holy Spirit who is the bringer of peace and comfort. Pōneke, the harbour, represents the kingdom of God's peace, believed in and lived out in Wellington. A fleur-de-lis and a taniwha (monster, powerful water creature or spirit) recall the whakapapa, or genealogy, of the people of God at work in New Zealand through the early French Catholic missionaries and the existing strength of Māori spirituality. Finally, the olive tree symbolises the peace of Christ we receive through reconciliation and communion. Combined, the images in the window guide believers to remember the story of God's peace and remind them again of the call upon them to live this peace in New Zealand today.

A Community Focused on Peace and Justice

Cardinal Thomas Williams, in the foreword to *Church in the World*, a collection of official episcopal statements on social issues published in 1997 while he was Archbishop of Wellington, states that 'Working for justice and peace is not a peripheral activity, with the "real" work of the Church carried out elsewhere. Working for justice and peace is an integral part, a constitutive dimension of the work of evangelization.'[4] This document affirms that genuine Christian witness actively engages the world for the cause of peace and justice. Even while praying for peace, the Church must also seek to live it out.

Moyra Pearce, a parishioner at St Joseph's for over four decades, noted that the parish has long adhered to this theology of peace, encouraged through consecutive pastors who have sought to strengthen this ethos in a robust way. In his history of St Joseph's, Jack Duggan describes the Church as composed of 'strong minded people' who are 'not afraid to ask questions.'[5] It is a community that has taken the gospel call to peace seriously, and it has sought to embody this peace in its everyday practices.

Monsignor Gerard Burns was a part of this legacy. Known for his activism, in 2009 he splattered a mixture of his blood and red paint on the Yitzhak Rabin memorial plaque in Wellington as part of a protest against Israel's air and ground offensive then taking place in Gaza.[6] Father Burns argued that denouncing injustice through such symbolic actions was part of his priestly role: 'I might be failing in my duty if I didn't do it.'[7] While some in the Catholic Church opposed his actions, others have commended his passion for justice and peace. Indeed, he was recently appointed by Pope Francis onto the executive board of Caritas Internationalis, the global Catholic agency for justice, peace, and development.

Monsignor Burns told me that caring for peace often causes controversy as it requires a willingness to stand against violence, including the violence of the state, as well as those that support it. He outlined other examples of internationally oriented peace activism pursued from within the parish over the years. In the 1940s Father John Kavanagh was appointed chaplain for hundreds of Polish refugees escaping from war-torn Europe.[8] In the 1970s the parish engaged again in chaplaincy work with refugees, and Father Carde ensured warm pastoral care for the many Vietnamese refugees who made St Joseph's their home. In the 1980s Father Owen Dolan became parish priest. He had strong Latin American connections, including with activist Catholic priests at the forefront of advocating for the poor and oppressed. On one occasion Father Dolan even met clandestinely with the Nicaraguan Foreign Minister from the radical leftist Sandinista Government. Alongside the priests, parishioners have also been active, with a long history of involvement in Caritas Aotearoa New Zealand; the Society of Saint Vincent de Paul; the Wellington Archdiocesan Justice, Peace and Development Commission; and organisations such as Peace Action Wellington. Members of the parish were also active in the anti-Springbok tour protests of the 1980s and opposition to the Iraq War in the 1990s, and were keen participants in inter-faith gatherings and eco-theological discussion groups.

In fact, the embedding of a peace and justice tradition into the DNA of this community can be traced back to 1899, when Suzanne Aubert and her fellow sisters arrived in Wellington and joined St Joseph's.[9] Sister Mary Joseph, or Mother Aubert as she was also known, was the founder of the Congregation of the Daughters of Our Lady of Compassion, the members of which sought to lead lives of faith, hope and charity. The Sisters' social welfare activities are well known.[10] In 1900 Mother Aubert opened the first Home for Incurables for disabled children. In

1901 she opened St Anthony's Soup Kitchen on Buckle Street, where each day up to 90 men, many unemployed and homeless, would come for meals. In 1907 Our Lady's Home of Compassion was opened in Island Bay to care for disadvantaged children and babies. From these beginnings, the work of the Sisters continued to expand, both in size and in its breadth of social concern. The Order has overcome considerable challenges, including those from within the Catholic Church, to continue to carry out its charitable work today.

This rich history of activism and compassion has bequeathed to St Joseph's a remarkable collection of flesh-and-blood icons of peace; people who, through their behaviour, have operated as windows pointing to the grace of God, while also channelling that grace to those around them. Their participation has gifted to this parish a tradition of peace that continues to inform and shape the community that gathers there.

The Building Complex

The present St Joseph's building complex, which replaced the previous building in a major reconstruction project in 2001–04, is very much a product of the reforms of the Second Vatican Council (1962–65). The building is not just a church, it is a parish centre. It is a place where a community gathers. Vatican II encouraged the assimilation of local culture within sacred ritual and religious expression.[11] Local art, language, music and design could now become sanctioned vehicles for communicating the Catholic faith. In keeping with this spirit, St Joseph's integrates local Māori and New Zealand elements within its design.

The vision of Father Michael McCabe, who oversaw the project, was that the building would be simple and modest while leading people on a spiritual journey and expressing something about St Joseph, the church community's patron and the carpenter-father of Jesus. St Joseph is known in Catholic tradition as a man of practicality, simplicity, and love of Mary, such that he willingly endured the scandal of marrying an unmarried, pregnant teenager. He is the patron saint of fathers, workers, travellers and immigrants. A statue of St Joseph is located in the church's peace garden.

The exterior of St Joseph's Church, Wellington, with the National War Memorial Carillon in the background towering over the church's lobby. The main worship space, the semi-circular nave, is at the left; the Suzanne Aubert Chapel, which houses the floor-to-ceiling Trinity Window, is on the right at the rear; the full immersion baptistery lies in the small area covered in fish symbols in front of the chapel on the right; the peace garden is located below at right. Photograph by Simon Devitt.

For a number of years, I have led groups of Year 12 students from Sacred Heart College on a field trip to visit sacred spaces in Wellington. We start at Sacred Heart Basilica and then visit St Mary of the Angels and the Home of Compassion Chapel, before finishing up at St Joseph's. As students walk into Sacred Heart Basilica they often exclaim: 'I'd love to get married here.' They are in awe of the neo-Gothic beauty of St Mary of the Angels. But at St Joseph's it takes them more time to figure out which parts of the church complex bring them the peace and awe inherent in a holy place. After a lecture and tour they have a chance to settle somewhere and reflect. Some choose the social area that has large ground-to-ceiling windows looking over the Basin Reserve. This space was specifically designed to reflect the church's philosophy of being open to the surrounding community, so the windows allow two-way vision. Some choose to mingle somewhere in the lobby, shaped in the form of a Latin cross and accessible from north, south, east, or west—a concept inspired by the Māori phrase 'ngā hau e whā', welcoming visitors from all four winds. Some love the outdoor aspects of the church. Carved into the outside walls are repeated fish symbols, the ichthus, one of the most ancient symbols of Christianity. The peace garden is full of olive trees; along with statues of St Joseph and others, it also contains a simple Stations of the Cross. Others reflect quietly in the intimacy of the Suzanne Aubert Chapel, or are engaged in the semi-circular nave, with its green ambience and communality. The complex was designed to be composed of distinct spaces that could be inhabited very differently, the sum of which was to facilitate the life of the community of faith. The students intuitively feel their way through these spaces as they wander around the building.

The architects at Studio Pacific Architecture loved the clarity of the St Joseph's dream and ingeniously planned the building to have four primary spaces: a full-immersion baptistery, a tall chapel space, a gathering area for community-based functions, and a large nave for Mass and other events. Overlaid into these four functions are two visual elements: the Latin Cross, a universal Christian motif, and the koru, an indigenous and local spiral motif shaped like an unfurling fern frond. The Latin

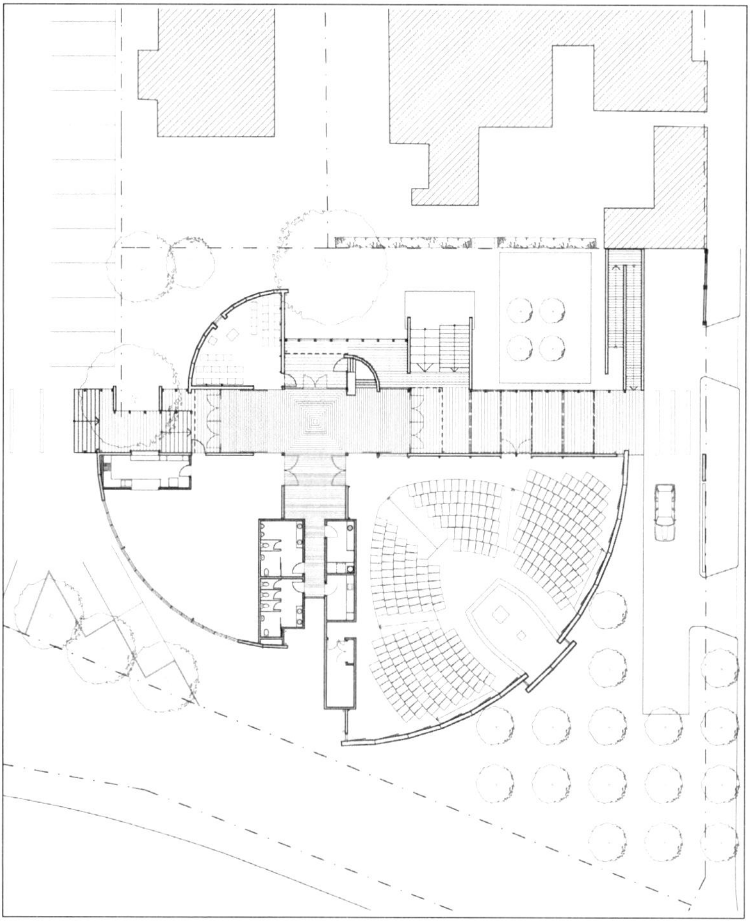

Floor plan of St Joseph's Church. Inspired by the Māori proverb 'ngā hau e whā', four quadrants wrap around the transparent lobby space, creating an overall plan shaped like an abstract koru intertwined with a cross, an image suggestive of new life and spiritual growth. Source: Studio Pacific Architecture.

Cross is the centring floor plan and the koru grows around it, as can be seen clearly in the above floor plan. It begins with a small door into the full immersion baptismal pool, grows into the small chapel, expands firstly into the gathering area and then into the nave, and then finally out into the world. 'In the same way that an unfurling koru shows natural growth, so the transition from baptistery to nave shows spiritual growth—a powerful metaphor for the church's dream.'[12] In this plan, the baptised walk from outside the church into the baptismal waters, where they begin their lives as Christians, and grow or unfurl as they join the church community, then step into the church—literally and sacramentally—and life in Christ. The curved walls of the baptistery, the chapel, the gathering area and the nave are expressions of this koru motif and of this spiritual journey.

Embracing the concept of ngā hau e whā, the invitation of welcome from all directions, St Joseph's envisions itself as a marae, or meeting place, for all people. The church community sees its land as taonga, a precious treasure, and acknowledges its links to the tangata whenua, the people of the land, Te Āti Awa. Te Kāinga, the Māori chaplaincy, advised the parish during the building process and participated in the pōwhiri, the welcome, on the opening day. Moyra Pearce stressed that a part of the peace to which St Joseph's aspires is to be a bicultural community which gives appropriate acknowledgement and respect to the tangata whenua.

The Trinity Window introduced at the start of this chapter speaks to this same desire in its blending of Māori and European motifs. Shane Cotton, the artist who designed the window, has a rich appreciation of heritage and place. Describing his practice Cotton says, 'Biculturalism, how our histories have been interwoven over time, things that have come out of that connection—culture, politics, societal living—have been the driving factors in my work.'[13] Monsignor Burns sees the window as raising important questions that have a gradual influence over time in encouraging this biculturalism: 'I think Shane's question is always going to be relevant: What is growing up here?' In this church, with its Catholic missionary history, there is an affirming connection of spirituality and place, and a rich desire for rangimarie (peace).

The Rite of Peace

While the St Joseph's complex is designed to be used in a variety of different ways, it is also very much intended to be a space of worship. The central ritual in Catholic tradition is the Mass, which at St Joseph's incorporates the use of some te reo Māori. Catholic liturgy has always included a strong emphasis on peace, expressed in a number of ways: in the acknowledgement of the peace that only God can give, as a feature of a right relationship between the believer and God and neighbour, and as a prayer for accomplishing God's ongoing peace-work in the world. Further emphasis was given to this peace dimension when the Rite of the Sign of Peace was reintroduced to the liturgy after Vatican II. Before participating in the Eucharist, the congregation of St Joseph's offer each other a sign of Christ's peace through a handshake or a hug; the peace and unity of His kingdom. In so doing they become, in the theology of the Catholic Church, the body of Christ and also recognise Christ in others.

Recently, there has been high-level discussion in the Church about the appropriate gestures and proper dignity when the faithful share the peace at Mass. The Congregation for Divine Worship and Discipline of the Sacraments sent out a circular letter in 2014 which admonished: 'If the faithful do not understand and do not show, in their ritual gestures, the true significance of the rite of peace, they are weakened in the Christian concept of peace, and their fruitful participation in the Eucharist is negatively affected.' In so doing, the circular drew attention to a theology of practice in which one's actions directly impact one's faith. Further, this statement was placed in the context of a world ravaged by violence and injustice. In response to this, the circular called for a reaffirmation of the centrality of peace in the rituals of the Church: 'That Catholics are today faced with the grave commitment to build a more just and peaceful world, implies a more profound understanding of the Christian meaning of peace and of its expression in liturgical celebration.'[14]

When Mass is celebrated in the large church at St Joseph's, with its semi-circular shape around the ambo, the parishioners can readily feel a part of a community. For Moyra Pearce, who was a member of the committee responsible for designing the new building, 'the shape of the nave brings people together'. This is because it moves beyond a performance-type structure where parishioners sit in rows facing the front. Accordingly, 'gathering around the table of the Eucharist is about relationship and in that sense being at peace with each other enough to be comfortable to do that.' Monsignor Burns agrees, and in his years as parish priest he actively sought to provide 'an inclusive kind of place'. He notes that whether it is through the sacraments or through everyday actions and just actions, peace is achieved through reconciliation, communion and right relationships.

Interior of St Joseph's Church, showing the semi-circular nave surrounding the altar. Photograph by Philip Fountain.

Peacemaking within the Community and Diocese

Within every parish, just as within every community, however, there are times when being at peace with each other is a challenge. While the ideal in a Christian community is that 'we are bound by the love of Christ', this is not an easy thing to maintain in practice. It is when challenges are most difficult and disruptive that real living icons of peace are most desperately needed.

One of the challenges that St Joseph's has faced is a lack of secure status. For over a century, St Joseph's previous buildings were considered 'temporary', and this disrupted the ability of the parish to make long-term plans. Even though St Joseph's now has a permanent complex, there are again questions about its status. These questions arose during the course of a discernment process to decide if and how the four parishes of Wellington South might be combined. This process and the deliberations around the parish's future were often fraught. As Moyra reflected, it is precisely during the times in which tension, anger and grief arise that we must be reminded to again place peace at the centre. 'The process of peace-making is difficult', she says. Monsignor Burns agrees: 'I think it's always a challenge within the community.' In addition to questions about amalgamation, he also points to the challenges involved in welcoming newcomers into the church community. 'The community here has to work at welcoming new groups and working around issues of groups wanting to keep their own identity. There is a challenge on both sides—and it's still being worked on.' In the process of asking questions about what sort of parish they want to be, Burns believes that Suzanne Aubert 'became a very strong unifying force'. She offered to the community a tangible symbol of their history and of the sort of faith they wanted to embody and impart.

Conclusion

The story of St Joseph's over its 130 years of existence has been one of praying for peace and seeking to move toward genuine peace and justice. Archbishop Redwood's sermon, which was delivered in 1899 when he welcomed Suzanne Aubert to Wellington and St Joseph's parish, emphasised the parish as a 'homelike' community with a tight 'family circle'.[15] Through all its struggles and changes, the community has continued to seek to live this vision of peace out. The peace that is sought by St Joseph's is represented in its icons of peace—that is, in its architecture, its art, and the lives of various individuals throughout the community's history—which in turn continue to operate back on the community, inspiring and guiding them into the way of peace. Monsignor Burns suggests that the Trinity Window will have a gradual influence over time, slowly forming its observers, as icons do, raising people's consciousness of what it means to be a witness to the kingdom of God's peace in Wellington. Indeed, the roots of St Joseph's are strong because of its history as a peacemaking community, such that in its journey, growth and struggles, it has flourished like the olive tree.

Te aroha, te whakapono, te rangimarie, tatou tatou e.
Let love, faith and peace be amongst us all.

10

Missionary Peacemaking: New Zealand Activists and the Decolonisation of Southern Africa

Pamela Welch

One striking feature of New Zealand Christianity has been the extent to which it has sent missionaries abroad, though this missionary zeal has been little noticed or understood within New Zealand society at large.[1] Over the period 1890–1930, some 750 Protestant and Anglican Kiwis left for the mission field—60 per cent of them women.[2] By the 1960s, the country was said to be sending out a disproportionately high number of missionaries: in 1973, around 1,500 were serving abroad—1,188 Protestants, 75 Anglicans, and about 200 Catholics.[3] A significant part of the country's Christianity has thus been lived and expressed beyond New Zealand's shores.

Christian missionary activity, while it has assumed a variety of forms and been understood in different ways, has normally been both peaceful in style and transformative in effect—practically as well as spiritually. 'The preaching of peace' between humanity and the divine has characteristically been accompanied by the provision of education and training, better health care and food security. Missionaries have also engaged directly in peacebuilding.

At times, they have found their calling taking a decidedly political form: the pursuit of peace has been inextricably linked with the pursuit of justice and so led to activism, some of it very high-profile. This chapter tells the story of three remarkable Kiwis whose mission work in Africa resulted in such activism. One of them, Garfield Todd, became a figure of international importance in the long drawn-out struggle for racial and political equality in Southern Rhodesia (now Zimbabwe). Two others became engaged in opposition to the apartheid regime in South Africa. Each of these men was linked to and supported by others in their home country. Their stories remind us that New Zealand Christian involvement in peacemaking has sometimes not only cut across deep-seated Kiwi suspicions about religious participation in politics, but also transcended national boundaries.

Garfield Todd and the Struggle for Decolonisation

One of the most notable New Zealand 'political missionaries' of the twentieth century was Garfield Todd—originally from Invercargill—who went to Southern Rhodesia as a Church of Christ missionary in 1934. The posting owed more to his wife's qualifications than his own: the education of the African population was entrusted to government-aided mission institutions and Grace Todd was a teacher.[4] At the remote Dadaya Mission, in Matabeleland, she developed a system of primary education using minimal resources which spread country-wide and was in use until 1980.[5]

Garfield Todd took to Africa the influence of his theological college principal, A. L. Haddon, who taught that life was not to be divided into sacred and secular but seen as a unity: 'Preaching, teaching, governing, farming, building, but in all things serving: this I learned in theory at Glen Leith and practise as best I can in Africa.'[6] Garfield had worked in the family tile-making business. At Dadaya, therefore, while principally engaged in Christian teaching and preaching, he set about transforming the mission, making bricks, building better classrooms and church buildings. He also put to use his basic missionary medical training (and acquired more).

All the while, the Todds built up relationships which differed from those typically found on Rhodesian mission stations, where many missionaries shared the racially exclusive attitudes of their fellow white settlers. The Todds found such attitudes foreign: at home, Todd reflected, with the idealism verging on naïvety that characterised him all his life, 'It was really the other way round—the Maoris [sic] were regarded as rather special people. The colour of their skin was not important'.[7] They nevertheless (as Garfield later admitted) arrived in Africa with a sense of 'superiority', albeit an unconscious one: 'I had no doubts about the role we had come to play. We had come to give: we were the people who knew.'[8]

Conditions in Africa, moreover, were seen as in stark contrast to those of New Zealand, a country 'famous for its enlightened social legislation' which was intended to ensure that '[e]very child is educated, every sick person is ministered to, every old person receives care'.[9] The newcomers found the position of women in traditional African life particularly disturbing. They were:

> poor creatures whose futures were decided by the older people. . . . Here were girls with no rights of their own, promised in marriage to polygamous husbands—promised while possibly small children, taken to live with their husbands at twelve years of age. Here were women, old in appearance while still young in years, bearing children while themselves still immature, walking their way dejectedly through a life of toil which brought them little reward.[10]

From their arrival in Africa, the Todds lived almost entirely among Africans; contact with their 'own kind' was rare. They became increasingly aware of 'a oneness', 'a common humanity' and also witnessed the transforming effect of the gospel upon the lives of African individuals, families and villages. Women 'lift[ed] their heads, finding themselves people with honour and privileges.'[11]

The Todds had also brought with them, in their membership of the Church of Christ, a religious tradition which held to the 'priesthood of all believers' and was 'radically democratic' in origin. They ensured, therefore, that at Dadaya black and white worshipped together—something rare at that time—and the mission was to become unique for the degree to which Africans were trusted colleagues of the missionaries in charge. The Todds lived out theologically based democratic convictions that challenged the racially discriminatory attitudes of Southern Africa.

In 1946, Garfield Todd entered politics and was elected to the Southern Rhodesian Parliament, as member for the local mining district of Shabani. This was not as unlikely an event as might be supposed. Todd had striking looks and an engaging and commanding personality; to the farmers and miners of his constituency, he was considered 'a real enough man' who could 'put a few words together convincingly'.[12] There was also a local tradition of missionary involvement in politics. F. L. Hadfield, the Kiwi missionary who had founded Dadaya, became an MP in the 1920s. Several later federal MPs, elected to represent African interests, were missionaries or ministers of religion.[13] Todd himself entered politics because he had come to believe that the conditions of the African people he served could only be improved by decisions taken at a national level.

In 1953, he achieved high political office. In that year, the three hitherto separate but neighbouring British territories of Southern Rhodesia (Zimbabwe), Northern Rhodesia (Zambia), and Nyasaland (Malawi) were federated. A two-tier system of government was created: a centralised federal government and three territorial governments with limited powers. Todd became Prime Minister of Southern Rhodesia.[14] The politics surrounding the Federation were complicated but progressive circles largely welcomed it and saw it as advancing racial co-operation. The hope was that the Federation would provide a prosperous, enlightened counterbalance to South Africa, its neighbour to the south. In order to entrench white domination, South Africa had in 1948 formally adopted apartheid, a policy of rigid racial segregation and disadvantage to 'Non-Whites' in every aspect of social and political life—housing, business, health, education and even the home. Interracial marriages were banned by law; families as well as communities were torn apart.

Todd was well known for his commitment to reform and during his premiership was able to introduce some legislation which was beneficial to the African population. He was, however, ousted from leadership in 1958. The Federation itself lasted only until 1963. Liberal hopes of a new order in Central Africa were dashed by settler fears of African dominance and African fears of settler dominance. The two northern territories then acquired independence from Britain, while the settler-dominated south (now known simply as Rhodesia), refusing to concede greater political power to Africans, made a unilateral declaration of independence (UDI) on 11 November 1965 and then, for some 14 years, survived threats, international ostracism, economic sanctions and, finally, a bitter guerrilla war.

Many leaders of the African opposition to UDI and in the armed struggle for independence which followed, were friends and associates of Todd: some had been nurtured in the alternative society of Dadaya, his mission station. Many of them were arrested and held in restriction camps. Todd, ever outspoken, became a figure of international interest. He was imprisoned briefly and even held in solitary confinement for a time, as was his daughter, Judith. For over four years he was restricted to his home and forbidden to communicate with the outside world.

Mr R. S. Garfield Todd, Rhodesia, at the Commonwealth Relations Conference, 1959. Source: EP/1959/0139-F, Alexander Turnbull Library.

The Todds were by this point living on a ranch, named after a Southland landmark, the Hokonui Hills. On entering Parliament, Todd, while retaining an overall responsibility for Dadaya, had given up his missionary stipend but as a continued political career was not guaranteed, he had taken an opportunity to buy some 50,000 acres of ranching land. This, when developed, provided an income. Todd also donated some of this land to the Dadaya mission, thereby giving it security of tenure.[15] Now, in the UDI years, he was able from his verandah to count sanctions-busting railway tankers carrying fuel into the country and to report his findings to London. He also gave succour, under cover of darkness, to anti-UDI guerrillas needing food or medicine. Both of these were treasonable offences.

Todd was fortunate in that his international standing and his long support of the African nationalists protected him and his family from any real harm in the war. Most missionaries, caught as they were between two worlds, found their already difficult position exacerbated by the conflict: 30 lost their lives.[16] However, when a plan to assassinate Todd was made by the UDI regime, the (African) men concerned were not able to bring themselves to carry it through.[17]

In 1979, a British governor was once more appointed for Rhodesia and then, following the first election with a universal, non-racial franchise, the territory became independent as Zimbabwe on 18 April 1980. By this time, Todd's achievements were widely recognised. He was awarded a papal medal by Pope Paul VI in 1973. 'Back home' in 1979, he was given an honorary degree by the University of Otago, where he had studied as a young man but never graduated. In 1986, he was knighted by the Queen, at the instigation of the New Zealand Government and with the approval of the Zimbabwean Prime Minister and President-to-be (from 1987), Robert Mugabe, a former teacher at Dadaya and a leader in the liberation war. Mugabe had earlier nominated Todd to the newly created Zimbabwean senate. To black Zimbabweans and to the well-informed elsewhere, these honours were acknowledgements of the part he had played in the struggle for the decolonisation of the country.

Mugabe, however, stripped Todd of his Zimbabwean citizenship shortly before his death in October 2002. Todd had been as unafraid to criticise the new African regime as its settler predecessor: just as he had stood against 'the racism of the past', he stood against 'the terror of the present'.[18] He took an active part, for instance, in uncovering evidence that, soon after independence, a ruthless secret campaign had been waged in Matabeleland to suppress 'dissidents' (in reality, political opponents of the Mugabe government), during which many thousands of people had died.[19] Chris Laidlaw, New Zealand High Commissioner to Zimbabwe (1986–89), described Todd in 2002 as 'the conscience of the country'.[20]

John Osmers and Michael Lapsley: Anti-Apartheid Campaigners

Two other Kiwi ministers of religion—John Osmers, now Assistant Bishop of Lusaka, Zambia, and Michael Lapsley SSM—both Anglicans, have been notable in the struggle for justice and peace in South Africa. They have also provided leadership within New Zealand itself. They travelled (separately) throughout the country, for instance, in 1979 to generate support for the 'Stop All Racist Tours' campaign, which led to the dramatic events of the Springbok tour of 1981 when running battles were fought by supporters and opponents of the tour. By that point, the New Zealand anti-apartheid movement was the largest in the world outside South Africa.[21] In 2010 the former Anglican Archbishop of Cape Town, Desmond Tutu, thanked New Zealanders for their support in the struggle against apartheid, noting that 'psychologically what hit white South Africans was the fact that they were not allowed to play international sport—especially rugby'.[22]

Osmers and Lapsley were feted here in Wellington in 2012, when the centenary of the founding of the African National Congress (ANC), the first political party in South Africa founded by and open to black members, was celebrated and the tour of 1981 was remembered. They were integral to New Zealand's contribution to the fight against racial injustice in Southern Africa.

John Osmers

Osmers was born in 1934, the son of a vicar, in Sydenham, Christchurch. He was also a great nephew of C. F. Andrews,[23] an Anglican missionary priest who spent his life working with Gandhi in South Africa and India and who was instrumental in bringing about the end of the indentured labour system in Fiji.[24]

Osmers' interest in Southern Africa was aroused by the publication in 1956 of Trevor Huddleston's *Naught for your Comfort*, a first-hand account by an Anglican priest working in Johannesburg of the destructive effect the policy of apartheid was having on the lives of black people. After graduating from university, Osmers travelled to England via South Africa. Anglican connections enabled him to meet black South Africans and learn about their experiences of living under apartheid. Alphonse Zulu, a black priest (later also a bishop) alerted him 'to the need for the Church to make a difference for radical change'. This gave Osmers 'the impulse to consider ordination for work in South Africa'.[25]

In England he met Huddleston, who suggested he work in Lesotho, a small independent kingdom in the mountains of Southern Africa. Osmers trained at the theological college run by Huddleston's order, the Community of the Resurrection, in Yorkshire, and by 1965 he was back in Africa, in Lesotho, travelling on horseback around his many scattered congregations and sleeping in African villages rather than the homes of white traders, as did many other expatriate priests.

With help from New Zealand, he became increasingly involved in assisting aspiring African students to obtain access to higher education. After an uprising in Soweto (Johannesburg) in 1976, when hundreds of black youths protesting against the introduction of Afrikaans as a medium of instruction in African schools were gunned down by police, Osmers became concerned with young South Africans who had fled to Lesotho. He—and they—became aligned with the ANC, which had become increasingly militant in its opposition to apartheid (it had been banned, and so prohibited from taking part in any political activity, in 1960). In 1979, Osmers was sent a parcel bomb by the South African security forces and lost a hand in

John Osmers in Dunedin, 1997. Source: *Otago Daily Times*

the explosion. When he toured New Zealand, in that year, he had not long recovered from treatment for his injuries. He cut an imposing figure on the platform or in the pulpit: six feet tall, bearded and 'waving his shorn-off arm as he exposed the brutalities of apartheid'.[26]

The parcel bomb had been sent to Osmers wrapped in a bundle of ANC magazines. This only convinced him of the value of the work he was doing but a year later, having been out of the country on a visit to Europe, he was not allowed back. Lesotho is landlocked and particularly susceptible to pressure from the South African government, which had clearly been applied in this case.[27]

In 1981, Osmers was offered a remote rural post in the church in Botswana. There he remained until 1988, when he had to flee from South African assassins to Zambia, which was already sheltering numerous ANC members and where the movement now had its headquarters. Until this point the ANC had been chiefly associated with the Congress of South African Trade Unions (COSATU) and with another banned organisation, the South African Communist Party, which, unusually among communist parties, was not hostile to religion. As Osmers told me, however, his bombing encouraged other members of the ANC to identify themselves as Christians and so led the ANC leadership 'to see that the Church could be an ally in the freedom struggle'. An open association between movement and Church was instituted with the formation of a 'Church Front' (which later became the 'Interfaith Chaplaincy'). The leader of this ANC Church Front was Thabo Mbeki, subsequently a President of South Africa.

Osmers served as an ANC chaplain until 1990, when the apartheid regime began to disintegrate, the ban on the ANC was lifted and members were free to return home. He remained in Zambia, becoming the first Anglican bishop of Eastern Zambia, 1995–2002. Now, as assistant bishop of Lusaka, he sustains a ministry to refugees, particularly those from Rwanda.

In 2010, Osmers was made a Companion of the New Zealand Order of Merit for service to the Anglican Church and on his 2012 visit he was given the ANC Centennial Award 'to mark an exceptional contribution to the international campaign against apartheid'. In 2016, he was one of three people—along with Kenneth Kaunda, first President of Zambia, and Archbishop Desmond Tutu—to receive the Archbishop of Cape Town's Award for Peace with Justice, in recognition of the part each had played in the ending of apartheid and the ushering in of a new order.

John Osmers pays tribute to the example and friendship throughout of Trevor Huddleston. He was also greatly influenced by the Student Christian Movement, which was in a particularly radical phase when Osmers was a university student.[28] However, when I used the word 'missionary' regarding his work, Osmers demurred. He associates the term with expatriate, externally funded clergy and has himself always worked in Africa at the social and economic level of a local priest. When he was bombed, however, it was a missionary society that flew him to England and paid for his treatment: he is perceived by others as having missionary status.[29]

Michael Lapsley

Father Michael Lapsley, of the Society of the Sacred Mission (SSM),[30] also rejects the designation 'missionary' for himself while being awarded it by others.[31] He was born in Hastings, Hawke's Bay, into a large, working-class Anglican family and left home to join the SSM in Melbourne at the age of 17.[32] In 1973, when he was 24, the Society sent him to Durban in South Africa, where they had a university chaplaincy. He was enrolled as a student as well as becoming a member of the chaplaincy team.

Lapsley had been alerted to the iniquities of apartheid as a child of seven, when the All Blacks had been forbidden to include Māori in a tour of South Africa. 'In our local church there was a petition: No Maoris No Tour.'[33] He was later influenced by the writing of Trevor Huddleston and in Australia became a member of the South Australian 'Committee Against Racism'. Now he was faced for the first time with the grim realities of apartheid. He was, however, through the chaplaincy, able to associate with and minister to students from the various—and separated—racial groups.

Father Michael Lapsley SSM.

Following the 1976 Soweto uprising, Lapsley became increasingly radical and outspoken. In response, the South African authorities revoked his visa and he was given 14 days to leave South Africa, days he spent addressing students at universities throughout the country. He might have returned to the Antipodes but he now considered South Africa his home. A member of his order enabled him to cross the carefully controlled border to Lesotho: he was not to return to South Africa for another 16 years.

Lapsley arrived in Africa a pacifist: by 1977 he was asserting the moral and Christian legitimacy of armed struggle. He became, openly, a member of the ANC, a decision that caused considerable conflict with the Church authorities and members of his order. In December 1982, while he was on leave in New Zealand, South African forces launched a night helicopter raid on ANC houses in Maseru, Lesotho, in which 42 people were killed. Lapsley was believed to have been one intended target of this raid.

Although he returned to Lesotho, his presence there was judged to be dangerous to others as well as to himself and so he was moved to England, where he continued to speak for the ANC—and the South African Communist Party. By 1984, he was back in Southern Africa, but this time in a newly independent Zimbabwe. At university in Harare, he produced a critical study of Anglican attitudes to the struggle for the liberation of the country.[34] He then served, briefly, as rector of a large church, St Michael's, Mbare. He resigned after a disagreement with his bishop and went to work for the development programme of the Lutheran World Federation.[35]

He continued to advocate the liberation of South Africa internationally and so to be at risk. Zimbabwe (like Zambia) had given sanctuary to many South African exiles, and 'bombings, assassinations and unexplained incidents' were frequent. In February 1990, the ANC was recognised as a legitimate political organisation within South Africa and Nelson Mandela, soon to be the country's first black President, was released from a 27-year imprisonment. Members of the security forces opposed to the reform process embarked on a new wave of bloodshed in an attempt to derail it and on 28 April 1990, in Harare, Michael Lapsley opened a parcel bomb. The explosion cost him both his hands and one of his eyes.

Apartheid's demise, however, also saw notably successful attempts to heal and to deal with the legacy of the past. Between 1995 and 1998, a Truth and Reconciliation Commission functioned under the chairmanship of Archbishop Desmond Tutu. In this, victims and perpetrators of racial violence met face-to-face and the proceedings were televised and broadcast. Earlier, in 1993, Michael Lapsley had worked with others to open a Trauma Centre for Victims (later, Survivors) of Violence and Torture. Today he is director of the Institute for Healing of Memories in Cape Town and its work has spread to other countries such as the United States and Rwanda. The Institute is sponsored by the Anglican Church: Lapsley's many battles with church authorities over the years appear to have reached a peaceful resolution.

His own combativeness has been moderated by his ordeal: 'the bombing was like a refining fire that gradually brought me clarity—I would find a way to use my visible brokenness as a tool for healing others'.[36] His contribution to the anti-apartheid struggle has been hailed by Oliver Tambo of the ANC, the novelist Nadine Gordimer, Trevor Huddleston, and President Nelson Mandela himself.[37] Mandela suggested Lapsley's story was a 'compelling metaphor' for South Africa's own story: 'We read about a foreigner who came to our country, and was transformed by what he saw of the injustices of apartheid. He could not remain aloof from the suffering of the people. In order to be true to himself, he had to participate in their struggle for liberation.'[38] The next part of the story, however, with protests against ANC rule in South Africa on the increase and the painful shattering of yet another liberal dream, is difficult to predict.

Conclusion

In this chapter, we have traced the stories of three Kiwis who served as Christian missionaries in Southern Africa during a period of great turmoil. Their views on race, democracy, justice and peace were all shaped by Christian theology and also by their New Zealand upbringing. Their relationships with African friends and colleagues awoke in each of them a desire to tackle the iniquities of racialised politics. They were not always nor necessarily pacifist—for a time Lapsley openly advocated the moral necessity of armed struggle against the oppression of apartheid. Each, however, was deeply influenced by a vision of peace, which led them to challenge state violence directly and condemn racial segregation. Each responded to a call to action and embraced the task of transforming the lives of the politically oppressed. Their work came at considerable personal cost. They were variously vilified, imprisoned and made the targets of attempted assassinations. Todd spent time in solitary confinement and, after many years of working passionately for Zimbabweans, suffered the humiliation of having his citizenship stripped from him. Both Osmers and Lapsley lost hands, and Lapsley an eye, to parcel bombs sent by the security forces of South Africa. Yet a drive to challenge oppression and seek for a better peace endured in them and also in those they encountered. The lives of these transnational sojourners furnish us with remarkable examples of the Christian calling to engage with the sufferings of the world. They still have much to teach us today about the mission of peace.

11

Migrant Peacemakers? African Pentecostals in New Zealand

Dorcas Dennis

With the arrival of African migrants since the early 1990s, New Zealand has witnessed the proliferation of African-led Pentecostal Churches (APC).[1] While APCs are often seen as serving valuable social functions,[2] they are rarely discussed as places of peacemaking. This is, perhaps, unsurprising. Pentecostal rhetoric, with its emphasis on 'spiritual warfare', embraces a confrontational and aggressive language. APC members are also rarely among those that vocally oppose militarism or are at the forefront of peace rallies and protests—despite the early Pentecostal history of profound objection to war.[3]

Nevertheless, there is an evolving concern with peace among APCs, emerging out of migrants' attempts to address their experiences of hostility and tension. The prominent place allotted to peace partly reflects migrants' experiences, since many have faced significant political turmoil in their recent past. It also signals their ambitions for a future of being at peace among themselves and their host community. APCs emphasise hospitality as a vital practice in overcoming tension and hostility—hospitality that fosters relational peacefulness. This chapter, therefore, examines what at first sight may seem to be counterintuitive questions: To what extent, and in what ways, have the APCs sought to be peacemakers in New Zealand? What contributions have the migrant churches made, and what is the character and significance of peace for these churches in New Zealand? In answering these questions the chapter draws upon ethnographic fieldwork at the Christ for Salvation Ministries International (CFSMI) in Wellington.

Sunday Morning at CFSMI

Upon entering the CFSMI at the Maungaraki Community Centre in Lower Hutt, Wellington, on Sunday mornings, as I did on a number of occasions in 2015 and 2016, you are likely to be greeted by a wave of sound. This includes a mixture of clapping, feet stamping and the prayers of worshippers, all of which take place to a backdrop of musicians warming up before the service begins. As you enter the basketball court at the Community Centre, you see worshippers, mostly African migrants, dressed in beautiful and colourful African attire, suits, or jeans. Christ for Salvation Ministries International meets every Sunday morning for two and a half hours. The Church is one of a growing number of APCs in New Zealand.[4]

During one of my visits, kicking off the Sunday service at 10am, Pastor Peace Katumbu, dressed in colourful kaba and slit (African women's attire), invited the congregation to rise to their feet for twenty minutes of intercessory prayer. As is common for most APCs in New Zealand, Pastor Peace and her husband, CFSMI's lead pastor Reverend Willard Katumbu, are migrants themselves, having migrated to New Zealand from Zimbabwe. After this time of prayer, the congregation moved into Bible study, praise and worship, announcements, and finally preaching. In her introduction, Pastor Peace outlined the themes for the prayer time. These included church growth; the prosperity of worshippers; peace in the lives of individuals; unity within families, among Church members, and among the churches in New Zealand; and the peace and security of New Zealand—especially in terms of protection from terrorist and other violent attacks. She also asked the Church to pray for favour, peace and love, and against all discrimination, hostility and prejudice that destabilises the smooth integration of migrants and New Zealanders. For this type of prayer, all the members prayed together at once.

The emphasis on peace and prejudice is not accidental. CFSMI is predominantly composed of African migrants from a range of countries. The worshippers include people from Zimbabwe, Ghana, South Africa, Kenya, Liberia, Nigeria, Malawi, Uganda and Somalia, as well as from Jamaica, the United States, India and Fiji, alongside Māori and Pākehā New Zealanders. African migrants to New Zealand are relative newcomers compared with other migrant groups.[5] A significant wave of African migrants arrived in New Zealand between 1992 and 2001, including about 3,000 refugees and asylum seekers coming mainly from Southern Africa.[6] The emigration of the African migrants into New Zealand largely coincided with significant political and social upheavals in the sending countries, including the Somalian civil war, the Rwandan genocide, armed conflicts in Northern Uganda and the Democratic Republic of Congo, and political repression in Zimbabwe.[7] The migrants' concern for peace arises out of the factors that motivated and conditioned their migrations to New Zealand. Many of these migrants are familiar with profound displacement and situations of hostility, tension and political turmoil.

At the end of the time of intercessory prayer, Pastor Peace, who also works as an air traffic controller, asked the Church to pray for New Zealand. She implored:

> Lift up this land to the Lord. Pray for God's protection and peace of the land. God entreats us to pray for the peace of the city wherein we dwell, for as it prospers, we also prosper. God brought us here not by accident, besides many of us came here as refugees and asylum seekers. Begin to pray. . .

Worshippers started into prayer, some clapping their hands or speaking in unknown tongues, others kneeling or lying on the floor in prayer amidst musicians playing worship songs. In this prayer theme, peace is decidedly spiritual and is given supernaturally. The worshippers believe that they have divine instruction to spiritually activate and promote the peace of the land they live in as migrants. They also believe that their own ability to flourish in New Zealand is intimately connected to the peace of the land.

After about five minutes of prayer, Pastor Peace asked the worshippers to focus their prayers on the churches in New Zealand:

> Many churches here are closing down or decreasing in growth due to internal conflicts due to racial, ethnic, social or age-gap

> tensions. Christians are not at peace with one another. . . . These are attacks of the enemy, and we are not immune to such. Pray and destroy these demonic attacks. . . .

The pastor's prayer guidance explicitly identified internal church conflicts and tensions as having spiritual dimensions; indeed, she describes the causes of conflicts as demonic. Through prayer, these causes can be 'attacked' and 'destroyed'.

Preaching forms the climax of the Church's worship. During his preaching about 'Kingdom Models for Overcomers', Pastor Willard Katumbu encouraged the Church to live with 'Christian Kingdom models'. He explained that these models included being careful about what they heard and talked about, the friends they associated with and the places they went to. Neglect of these models bred conflicts, brawls and hatred within the Church and between ethnic communities. 'We have all come from different backgrounds. . . . However, as a people of God, we are a holy nation of God's Kingdom within the nation of New Zealand, and we have to live the lives that reflect the Kingdom living'. Pastor Willard's sermon sought to cultivate an understanding of the Church as a unified community, undivided by ethnicity or nationality, with social harmony emphasised as a central congregational goal. The pastor added:

> No matter the ethnicity, God entreats us to live in peace with one another. . . . More so, there is the spirit of indecent competition among us just to outdo one another and show off. That spirit of 'I came here first, so I must make it [succeed] before others' destroys the unity and breeds rancour and hatred in our community.

He continued:

> We like priding ourselves with our nationality and ethnicity. . . . We only focus our attention on how to make money, establish careers and professions, and send remittances to build our homelands. We forget that we live here and for us to 'make it', the nation that is hosting us must continue to be safe and peaceful for us to accomplish our desires.

The message was a directive to his congregation to actively contribute to the peace of New Zealand.

Pastors Willard and Peace Katumbu, of the Christ for Salvation Ministries International (CFSMI) in Wellington.

The Significance of Peace in Worship

If we are to understand how migrants cultivate and activate peace, it is important to pay attention to their worship. As the opening ethnographic vignette shows, in CFSMI worship services the language of peace is pervasive, even if the meanings of the term are rarely articulated explicitly. The usage of 'peace' language in their worship and in everyday relationships among church members is a reflection both of migrants' experiences and their ambitions for a future of living in harmony among themselves and the host community. According to Willard, the Church's stance on peace includes but also goes beyond the absence of war, conflicts and tensions, to experience relationships of sustained security, tranquillity, contentment, unity and love with respect to God, nature, self and others.

Crucially, the basis and means for procuring peace are seen as having both physical and spiritual dimensions. Drawing on a Pentecostal theology of human and divine agency, the worship at CFSMI stresses that human efforts are not enough if there is to be a lasting, meaningful peace; to be sustainable, peace must have a supernatural origin. In the same way, supernatural elements have the capacity to destroy peace or prevent its materialisation in the physical world, by manipulating people to engage in activities that disrupt peaceful experiences and relationships. These understandings of peace are played out in the worship of the Church, and in other communal practices aimed at encouraging cordial relationships. In this case, peace is also the preservation of the integrity of communities; it 'means order, harmony, and equilibrium' in that community, as indicated in the opening vignette.[8]

A series of interviews with the pastors of CFSMI helped illuminate their prioritising of peace by weaving together Pentecostal theology and migrants' experiences of hostility, tensions and homemaking. During one such discussion with Willard, I asked him why the Church placed such great emphasis on peace in its worship. He sighed with a sense of heavy burden and explained:

> The nations that most of us fled from were and are still not stable; conflicts here, war there, and crises everywhere. . . . Some of the Church members here were sent from Zimbabwe into exile at the age of eighteen. . . . We cannot continue running and moving, we have to settle some day, and New Zealand has given us that opportunity.

He added that the worshippers must contribute as individuals and as a church to the peace they enjoy, and not just move on to Australia or elsewhere. To him, it was important that his congregation seek the peace of New Zealand as the place they now call home. He emphasised,

> I am not afraid to say that I am not a Zimbabwean or African. . . . I am Kiwi. My children were born here. I live here, and so what concerns New Zealand concerns me too. Some of these members of the Church are married to Kiwis and other migrants, this is their new home.

He concluded by stating that he had received complaints of how some African migrants had married local spouses and, after gaining residency, or sometimes after having started a family, hostility and tensions set in. He had also heard stories about how some members had engaged in fighting, gossip and conflict, both with other members of the Church and, just as importantly, other people in the communities where the migrants lived. For the pastor, behaviour like this destroys the fabric of peaceful relationships. It also creates negative perceptions of migrants as being violent and unable to integrate well into their new society—perceptions that are harmful, and ultimately make life more difficult for all migrants.

Pastor Peace explained her emphasis on peace during the intercessory prayer session by stating that,

> Those who just arrived in the year 2010 upwards, especially the students from Nigeria, Ghana or Liberia, or those who were born here, may not understand. . . . The peace, safety and security of this land mean a lot, especially to those from Zimbabwe, Uganda and Somalia, who experienced the absence of peace in our homelands.

She paused and focused on the Zimbabwean experience:

> At the time [in the 1990s], the only food we knew was sugar and water. Moreover, we will never forget how in 2002 New Zealand relaxed work permit requirements for Zimbabwean nationals who were in the country as at 30 April 2002. . . . Zimbabwe is still the same; it has even become more chaotic and divided today. . . . Our lives here and those who depend on us in the homeland are tied to the peace of New Zealand.

In this case, the significance of the theme of peacemaking during the worship lies in its direct connection to the members' history and livelihood as displaced migrants.

Conflict in the Church and among Migrants

From the opening vignette of the CFSMI worship, it is important to note that the emphasis on peace was also a recognition of existing tensions within the Church, and of conflict faultlines among migrants more generally. These faultlines were based on tribal, racial, ethnic, regional, social and religious boundaries. They were both internal (within the Church community) and external (within migrant communities, other religious groups, and more broadly in New Zealand society).

The CFSMI in Lower Hutt is an extension of the same denomination in Zimbabwe. Pastors Willard and Peace Katumbu told me they started the Church in October 2008, 'with the aim of continuing the work of God to serve the Zimbabwean migrant community in Wellington.' The initial membership was three Zimbabwean families, including Shona, Zezuru and Ndebele ethnic groups. By 2016, Church membership had increased to over 40 people. Because of this growth, and an increasingly diverse congregation, the pastors restructured their practices in 2012 to include other nationalities. Yet, according to the pastors, ethnic chauvinism, inter-ethnic conflicts, interracial violence and xenophobic rhetoric lingered within the Zimbabwean migrant community. Many Zimbabwean members shared with me how a 'Shona-centred' regime led by Robert Mugabe in Zimbabwe had been extended to New Zealand. In this regime, the Shona ethnic group dominated the other groups, creating a sense of Shona ownership, self-absorption and superiority. This situation pitted Shonas against the other ethnicities in the migrant community. Some members wanted the Church to maintain the Shona language and style of worship, as was typical of the denomination in Zimbabwe. Disagreements about this created tension, which resulted in discord and even brawls within the Church between 2010 and 2012.

Church members also experienced some initial hostility from outsiders, partly as African migrants, and at times on account of their Pentecostal practices. Negative stereotypes about African migrant youth involvement in gang violence and crime resulted in a sense of anguish among the broader African migrant community. Some Church members shared that derogatory comments and stereotypes created disconnection and hostility between migrants and members of the host community. Tafa, who plays guitar for the Church, explained that 'Young Africans were described as troublemakers and unable to integrate'. In addition, the Church's African Pentecostal practices were also not readily accepted. According to Clifford, a Kiwi member of the Church, the CFSMI was described as having unconventional Pentecostal practices compared to Pentecostals in New Zealand. Clifford thought that other Pentecostal churches and religious groups in Wellington held a negative perception of the Church and viewed them as 'violent and unruly'. He and his Māori wife (Julie) joined, however, because 'the Church offered something different'. In a separate interview, Julie told me that she had experienced tensions with her own family for her decision to join 'the African Church'. Such perceptions created significant obstacles. Apparently, these experiences also triggered the Church's approach to proactive peacemaking in New Zealand.

CFSMI and Peacemaking

Since 2013, following these experiences of suspicion, conflict and hostility, peacemaking has become central to the Church's worship. The character of the Church's peacemaking must be understood against the background of traditional values. Africans who convert to any form of Christianity neither dispense with their traditional understandings nor embrace their new faith with empty hands. Migrants do not repudiate their traditions; rather, there is an ongoing dialogue between the old and the new.[9] According to Willard, 'it is easier to build on the traditional understandings of peace as the foundation because the migrant members are able to connect to and share in those familiar understandings. Also, members who are natives of New Zealand and elsewhere appreciate our style'.

The pursuit of peace informs and shapes the dynamics, trajectories and strategies of the Church's worship. As a result, the Church seeks to establish dialogue, collaboration and mutual respect between ethnic groups. Members are encouraged to build peace utilising traditional practices of migrants as well as norms that are more common in New Zealand. The Church organises special meetings on peace, tolerance and reconciliation for the different ethnic groups, person-to-person relations, families and other migrant churches. These meetings deploy dialogue and counselling techniques to settle conflicts. Quarrels, disputes, fights and rivalry within the community are taken seriously. Respect for diversity is emphasised, and different cultural practices are encouraged. Shona members seek to maintain respect among themselves and for others by maintaining their traditional greeting style: they clench their hands while clapping and bow before speaking, especially to the older members of the Church. Ghanaians, Māori and other groups also extend their traditional styles of greetings.

There are also weekly reconciliation activities. One of these is the practice of compulsory 'kingdom' hugs, every Sunday. New members get special hugs from all the members, symbolic of an atmosphere of peace and acceptance. This practice has been specifically created to counteract the distancing strategies of some members, who have preferred not to sit next to members from different ethnic groups. Although hugs are common in many Pentecostal churches, which aim to cultivate a sense of 'family', the Church's ethnic diversity and experience of pervasive ethnic conflict forms a crucial and distinctive part of the background for the CFSMI. According to one churchgoer, Machida, the gesture is symbolic of the peace, love and joy that the Church projects. It is part of a deliberate and more general attempt to address hostility by extending hospitality across ethnic divisions.

Weekly 'feast and fellowship of the nations' lunches, after every Sunday service, are another expression of this hospitality. Members contribute towards these lunches, where the sharing of different ethnic and national food forms a symbolic part of the goal of overcoming ethnic tensions and hostility. For the Church, the act indicates a truce: suspension of hostilities, reconciliation and forgiveness. During the 'feast', members lay down the 'weapons of warfare', including grudges, hatred, suspicion and bitterness, and share the meal of other nations, races and ethnicities. Church member Rumi says that this practice establishes peace, which in turn creates a congenial atmosphere where tensions, intolerance and phobias can be given space for resolution.

In parallel with the offering of hospitality to the different ethnic groups, the Church also aims to facilitate the creation of a more unified body of believers. In this respect, the Church has created statements that are emphasised at every meeting. These statements are not all expressed using explicit 'peace' language, yet according to the pastor they are meant to promote peace and unity. One statement is: 'We are a Bible-believing Church with the aim of preaching Christ to everyone, everywhere, and at any time'. The statement directs members towards a singular agenda as migrants, regardless of ethnic, racial or national differences. Through such an agenda, the Church aims to overcome conflicts and promote practices of peace that it wants to share with New Zealand.

In addition, the Church organises joint services with other African migrant churches and an Indian Pentecostal church in Lower Hutt. The aim is to enable them to team up and put their resources together, but also to promote unity, co-operation and peaceful coexistence among the churches. These joint services are marked by collaborative effort, with the migrant churches seeing themselves as sharing the same mission. One example of this was the 2014 and 2015 'Change' conferences, where the CFSMI invited churches in Wellington to their events. The conferences hosted prophets and apostles from the United States (most of whom were African Americans) and from Africa.

Moreover, since 2013 the Church has organised revivals and annual conferences for prophecy, deliverance and healing, in collaboration with other Pentecostal churches in Wellington and Auckland. During these, participants share in the songs, dances and national dress of other worshippers. The 2013 and 2014 conferences, organised by the CFSMI with the Jabula Aotearoa Ministries and Elim Christian Centre from Auckland, included 'Haka Praise' dances. In this context, peacemaking practice includes an attempt to link up the churches in New Zealand, especially by emphasising church unity amid ethnic and cultural diversity. Part of the understanding here is that the Church's vision of proselytising New Zealand necessitates interaction, connection and amity with churches in the host community.

Peacemaking is also grounded in ritual dimensions. According to Pastor Peace, the Church practices social harmony as an element of its mission, but it also ritually invokes peace. She explained that sometimes, when physical efforts have proved futile, spiritual peace is needed. The understanding is that 'humans cannot generate lasting peace. A lasting peace is a gift from God'. So the Church performs rituals to invoke peace. They demonise 'terror activities' shown in the media and 'pray out' conflicts, disputes and hatred in New Zealand. During the 2014 conference with Apostle Yemi Adefarasin from Nigeria, Adefarasin called for individuals to 'stand in' for various racial, national and ethnic groups. He asked the representatives to confess the sins of the groups they represented—sins that included hatred, witchcraft and violence. After the confession, Adefarasin anointed them with olive oil, declared peace, tolerance and acceptance for the groups, and mandated the individuals to be 'watchmen' for the groups they represented.

The ritual aimed to channel the lasting peace of God towards New Zealand, as well as the nations of the individual migrants within the church. Crucially, in this context, peace was presented as necessary for the survival of the church and the migrant community. These Africans come from 'a continent wounded by the "roughness" of ugly struggles in political, social, and religious spheres.'[10] As migrants and refugees, many fled war zones and obtained asylum in New Zealand. No strangers to conflict, their pursuit of peace leads them to seek divine empowerment in order to overcome legacies of hostility and violence in a new land.

Conclusion

This chapter has argued that APCs like the CFSMI provide safe havens for migrants to create new identities and rally social and spiritual resources. More than this, these churches are increasingly understanding their task in terms of contributing to peacemaking in New Zealand. Concern for peace shapes the language and worship of the CFSMI, and the way that it understands its mission; it has also led to ritual innovations. The Church's peacemaking intent is expressed broadly, through a focus on building congenial relationships between migrant members, the migrant community and the churches, and within New Zealand society more generally.

Emphasis on peacemaking within the APCs partly reflects members' experiences of violence, conflict and hostility prior to migration. It is also a response to experiences of conflict within the Church and beyond it in New Zealand. These experiences have bred a desire to witness to peace by bridging social, racial, ethnic and religious divides. Peace is therefore more than the absence of war, but involves cultivation of harmonious relationships—and even engaging in aggressive 'spiritual warfare'. For peace is believed to have both physical and spiritual dimensions. Consequently, rituals of repentance and forgiveness are seen to be as important as reconciliation and dialogue. There is also a pragmatic dimension at play, for the APCs evidently view 'peacemaking' in instrumental terms, as something that can help to change negative perceptions about migrants and smooth their integration into New Zealand society.

Just as the ethnic makeup of New Zealand has changed dramatically in recent years, so too the character of New Zealand Christianity has been increasingly shaped by new patterns of migration. The charismatic forms and distinctive concerns of churches like the APCs may be invisible to many New Zealanders, but they form a growing part of the nation's religious landscape. The CFSMI story demonstrates that desire for 'peace' is a powerful motivating factor for many migrants. It also highlights that ideas about peace are shaped by particular experiences, and may be embraced for various reasons. In considering how Christianity promotes or undermines peace, we need to recognise the significance of ethnic diversity as a source of conflict and tension, and the churches' contributions in this regard. We should also pay attention to what the migrants' churches are doing.

12

Ploughshares at Waihopai

Adi Leason

A Last Supper

It was after 5pm when Manu and I finally arrived in Picton. Sam and Father Peter were waiting for us in a rental car. We joked around about a 'last supper' and I suggested the local Irish pub, which served up a mean cottage pie; eventually we agreed on fish and chips. Nerves were starting to get a little on edge by now. Catching sight of our reflection as we passed a Four Square shop window, even I was starting to feel that we looked a little suspicious.

While we were waiting for our feed, a guy walked up to the counter to order. I noticed that he was dressed tidily, like a detective, and was wearing some kind of earpiece; I pointed it out to the others and we decided to wait across the street. Collecting our order, we wandered down to the waterfront and found a table. Next minute, this same guy strolled past at a safe distance. We all sat there wondering the same thing. Sam turned to Peter and said, 'Shall we tell them now?' He replied, 'You might as well.' 'Tell us what?' I asked. Sam pulled out a small newspaper cutting that he had found in the local community rag. It was a letter to the editor, enquiring about a convoy of large black SUVs with tinted windows spotted driving around the country roads of Renwick. The writer asked for an explanation, as these vehicles looked strangely out of place. We were all silent.

Just then, three Iroquois helicopters came over the hills. They flew directly over us, and then turned west in the direction of the Woodbourne Airforce Base, not far from Waihopai. We again sat in nervous silence. Peter and Sam looked anxious, and Manu had a strange smile on his face. One by one, we started talking;

next we were all talking at once. What does this mean? Where were the helicopters going? Who uses large black SUVs? What about that guy at the takeaways? Were they on to us? Had there been a leak? Had one of us been bugged? Then someone said what we had all been thinking: 'Should we call it off? Cancel, go home, and forget the whole thing? If they are on to us, surely that would be the smart thing to do?' 'Quiet up everyone,' I said. 'I think I've got it.' We huddled a little closer, and I said: 'Either the authorities know. . . or they don't know.' It was meant as a joke, but no one was in the mood for laughing.

It was almost dark. We fed the seagulls the remains of our cold chips and headed back to the rental car, squeezing four big fellas in a Nissan Micra. The conversation turned back to reflection on our story thus far. We were so focused on what was about to happen that we had lost touch with all that had happened to bring us to this carpark in Picton on a late-autumn Tuesday night. We became aware that we had all become very close to one another—emotionally, spiritually, ideologically and, in this small car, even physically.

An Activist Education

In the winter of 1993 I visited the Suzanne Aubert Catholic Worker house in Addington, Christchurch.[1] Trapped in this damp dwelling during the mother of all snow storms, I became acquainted with the veteran Aussie Catholic activist, Ciaron O'Reilly—held up for five days with nothing but our breath and a mountain of donated blankets to keep us warm. So began my Catholic radicalisation.

Ciaron taught me about the Catholic Worker Movement's beginnings: the teaming up of journalist Dorothy Day and itinerant philosopher and day labourer Peter Maurin; the 1 May 1933 launch of the *Catholic Worker* newspaper in New York.[2] The idea of the movement was to promote the biblical promise of justice and mercy. The Catholic Worker Movement was grounded in a firm belief in the God-given dignity of every human person; it emphasised voluntary poverty and the Works of Mercy as a way of life.[3] Dorothy Day spoke of 'sacrifice, worship, a sense of reverence'.

A few days into the blizzard, Father Jim Consedine came around to say Mass. Various homeless men arrived—guests at Joseph Cardijn House, another Catholic Worker home across town. A candle was lit, symbolising the fragile light of Christ in the world. After Mass, Jim continued my education by describing how the Catholic Workers opened their first 'house of hospitality' in Brooklyn, New York, where the homeless, the hungry and the forsaken would always be welcome. Peter Maurin said, 'In the Catholic Worker we must try to have the voluntary poverty of St. Francis, the charity of St. Vincent de Paul, the intellectual approach of St. Dominic, the easy conversations about things that matter of St. Philip Neri, the manual labor of St. Benedict.'[4] Farms and houses of hospitality have since multiplied, as Maurin hoped.

As the cold snap continued, Ciaron added to my elementary understanding of the traditions of the Ploughshares Movement, in which small communities practice direct, non-violent disarmament of one of the many mighty weapons that terrorise our age. Ploughshares communities take their name, and gain permission, from the prophet Isaiah, who spoke of a time when 'They will hammer their swords into ploughshares and their spears into sickles. Nation will not lift sword against nation, no longer will they learn how to make war.'[5] They seek to enact the prophet's vision of a future of peace. Ciaron had only just been released from a year in a United States prison for his role in the 1991 disarmament of a loaded B-52 bomber on the runway at Griffiss Air Force Base, while it was on standby for deployment over Iraq.[6] He spoke about his involvement in the unlawful destruction of government property—property designed for destroying sacred human life—and the profound effect it had on him.

Despite the cold, my heart was strangely warmed by the stories of dozens of Ploughshares actions around the world. Each action had employed similar liturgical elements: community-building and prayer, organisation and research, symbolism and theatrics, disarmament and destruction. Most Ploughshares actions involve an attempt to convert a weapon into a gardening tool. Most also expose the myths of omnipotence and legitimacy surrounding great weapons of warfare. The activists usually stay at the scene of their action, to continue witnessing against the real criminals—the weapon barons, the politicians and military leadership. Ploughshares actions involve a witness for peace in the media, in courtrooms and often ultimately in prison. Most involve crazy acts of courage that risk the activists' own personal safety.

The pathway to each Ploughshares action is unique. For my wife Shelley and I, 9/11 was a major turning point. In 2001, we were living with our three young kids in a slum house in Central Thailand. The Twin Towers had barely hit the ground before the drums of war began beating; the call for payback was instantaneous. As we sat in our house, we pondered the build-up to the imminent aerial bombardment of Kabul.

Contrary to some well-intentioned advice, our family made some banners and travelled down to Bangkok. We set up a picket line in front of the United States embassy, having told the authorities and media of our plan to demonstrate for peace. Eighteen heavily armed US marines blocked off the front gate. The kids had made their own signs saying 'Jesus loves the little children' and 'Who would Jesus bomb?' A blindingly hot and humid Bangkok afternoon was interrupted by torrential monsoon rain. We held our ground as the ink in our signs began to run. Finally, sopping wet and tired, we said our goodbyes to the marines and headed home. The following morning some Thai friends came over with the *Thai Ruth*—a national newspaper with a daily circulation of over one million. On the front page was our small peace demonstration, daring to suggest that 'thou shalt not kill' and 'God is love'.

Making a Decision

Seven years later, in Otaki, 2008, I found myself facing the biggest ethical dilemma of my life. Having just returned from a Catholic Worker hui (gathering) in Jerusalem, up the Whanganui River, my mind was reeling with details of the brutal realities of the US-led invasions of Afghanistan and Iraq. I could not plead ignorance regarding the illegal invasion of Iraq. But what to do now? It wasn't more education that I needed, but avenues for action and engagement.

Then one day it hit me. I was in the garden and an image from the *Dominion Post* returned to my mind—a picture I had seen several years earlier. I had cut it out of the newspaper and literally cried over it. It was a photo, taken in Iraq, of a man holding his beautiful granddaughter in his arms. The child was covered in dirt and blood, with a torn skirt and loose skin. A US cruise missile had destroyed her apartment block, killing most of her family and leaving her legs ripped off at the knees. With her eyes closed, she looked strangely peaceful in her grandfather's arms. What gripped me was the face of the old man. That could be my face; that pain, that despairing, heartbroken cry. 'I can relate to that; I could cry like that if you were my precious child', I thought. 'This cannot happen, this must not happen again, not on my watch. This man is my brother and his dear one is most sacred to me.' Direct action was needed if kids just like mine were to remain safe.

Three of us had remained in regular contact since our Catholic Worker hui: Sam Land, a 24-year-old subsistence farmer from the Hokianga, Peter Murnane, a Dominican priest in his late 60s, and me. We resolved to carry out a Ploughshares action that we hoped would prevent the death of innocent civilians in Iraq. But at what cost? Shelley and I considered the implications. As we talked, we realised a worst-case scenario would mean losing my current teaching job, and even worse my teacher registration. This would leave us hard-pressed to maintain our mortgage payments; we could potentially lose our farm. We also had to consider the possibility of my going to prison. What would that mean to our family, for the kids and for our relationship? How would this affect our relationships with the community? If this worst-case scenario developed, would the benefits of our action be worth it?

Shelley finished making the sourdough for the following morning's bread. We banked up the fire and put down the dampers. Our four littlest ones were all asleep, peacefully in their little, cosy, safe room, all squeezed in together. Shelley and I stood there holding hands, looking at our little darlings. At that moment the cost was counted. The decision was made. We knew what had to be done; it was personal now.

Sam, Peter and I decided that our action would take place at Waihopai, a surveillance facility run by the Government Communications Security Bureau (GCSB). Waihopai was part of the Five Eyes global intelligence network. Information gathered from this communications base was utilised as part of the US-led invasions of Afghanistan and Iraq, and directly implicated New Zealand in those campaigns. If we could shut down Waihopai, even for a day, how many lives could be saved?

Towards the Domes

In the early evening of 29 April 2008, we arrived at the storage yard where Cotton Jenny, our Hiab truck, was parked. The yard manager opened up, we paid our account, and I drove Cotton Jenny out to the others waiting nearby. We drove off in convoy and parked the truck, with its purpose-built crane, at an old quarry for picking up again early the next morning. We then headed back towards Blenheim, where we stayed the night in a motor camp. Peter had already prepaid the cabin as it was unlikely we would be back again anytime soon. We had about four hours to fill, and so we went over our plans. We discussed how Moana Cole had once said to us, 'If you ever get arrested for anything never make a statement at the time. Always wait and speak to your lawyer first, always.' She knew from personal experience that you can't defend charges until you know what they are.[7]

The alarm went at 2am and I awoke suddenly out of a deep and peaceful sleep. It was time. Grabbing our few belongings, we headed out in the rental car back to the quarry and Cotton Jenny. Manu took a few pictures on his phone as we unloaded our gear and repacked. A light drizzle had settled in and the temperature had dropped. A growing anxiety about the weather, and how the truck would fare in the paddock next to the electrified fences, led to a late change in the plan. Sam and Peter went first to check the paddock. Before they drove off, Peter gave me a spare cell phone and said, 'We'll call you when we're sure everything is OK.' After a long wait of almost two hours I was getting worried and so I eventually called Peter to find out what was going on. 'What's happening up there?' I said. 'Where are you?' said Peter. 'I'm still here, at the quarry,' I replied. 'Didn't you get my text? I sent it nearly an hour ago!' said Peter. 'What's a text?' I said. 'I can't explain all that now, just come, just come now.'

The Hino Fuso 840 truck was never designed for fast cornering, and handles more like a tug than a tinnie. Driving through the Renwick night-time countryside in light rain, I was aware of my need to remain calm and drive to the conditions. I was likely to be in enough trouble without getting a ticket on the way to the spy base. Sam and Peter were waiting about one mile from the main road entrance to the base. Manu had driven the rental car to a nearby ridge where he could see the base and the domes; when the dome came down he would launch our web page publicising the action. Peter climbed in the cab with me, while Sam untied the ten-speed bicycle we had brought with us. Before Sam headed off into the dark, we reconfirmed our plans for where to meet up: 'Meet ya there in fifteen minutes, all going well.'

Sam's task was to place a chain and padlock on the entrance to the base. We knew we might be hard pressed for time once we set off the security alarms; delaying the police at the front gate would buy us just a little bit more. Meanwhile, Peter and I drove Cotton Jenny along a dirt road in a vineyard. We had checked this route out before and knew the track led to the base perimeter in the northwest corner. The track was comfortably wide, but was becoming muddy as the rain settled in. We could clearly see the huge illuminated domes away off to the left, both white, each with a small flashing red light on top. My heart raced as we finally approached our destination. It was then that something unexpected happened. As I took a corner on that muddy track I could feel the truck begin to slide; I braked and turned as we skidded, but it was too late. The truck slipped off the track and landed in a ditch, almost tipping over onto its side.

Peter remained calm, almost prayerful, as we climbed out of the cab and assessed the situation. I was somewhat less composed. After some consideration, I moved into problem-solving mode and found various lengths of timber to block under the rear tyres, to try and get some traction. After half an hour of struggling in the mud I was tired, wet and anxious for some success; and there was still no sign of Sam. Then it occurred to me what we had to do: use the crane on the back of the Hiab to pull the truck out of the ditch. However, try as I might, there was no way the truck was going anywhere. (It turns out there are various laws of physics that prevent a crane lifting itself up.) So Peter and I just stood there, staring at the truck, with its crane and all our gear getting wet. Just then Sam showed up, with blood on his head, looking a little dishevelled. 'What happened to you?' I asked. 'What happened to you, don't you mean?' Sam replied. 'I asked you first,' I said. After a while we told Sam our story, and he told his. Sam had hit a fence while riding back over the paddocks after locking up the front gates—the bike got tangled in the wire and he went through the air and landed awkwardly.

Sam checked out the truck. 'Not good,' he said. We walked around and looked at the situation from various angles. 'Not good,' he said again. We stood still for a while by the truck as the drizzle got heavier. 'What now?' I said. Eight months of prayer and planning—all our hard work getting the truck and doing repairs, all our weeks of training and community building—lying there in ruins. We stood for what seemed like ages, looking on at Cotton Jenny in the ditch. Looking back, it was so sad, it was almost funny.

This was decision time: would we, or wouldn't we, carry on? Our hope had been in our plan and in Cotton Jenny; she would get us over that fence and past all those dangers. Now the truck was gone. How much did I really care for people in war zones—for little kids who I would never meet? Was I really prepared to lose everything I cared about for them? Was I now ready to get hurt entering this base for the sake of maybe just one kid? What would Shelley say?

'Well, we either give up and go home, or we carry on and see what happens,' I said as cheerfully as I could. We unloaded the banners, the bolt cutters and our friend Graham's dented trumpet. Peter gathered what he needed for the shrine he was planning to build at the base, and we started walking. We stuck to the track, as planned. After a few minutes the track took a bend and suddenly there in the middle of the roadway was a small encampment. We froze in our tracks, then as quietly as possible sneaked into the rows of grapevines on our left and hoofed it as fast as we could. A dog barked, but not for long. No lights came on. No movement. We were safe. We were all thinking the obvious thought: if we hadn't driven off the road where we had, we would have turned that corner and been right on top of that little campsite. The noise would have woken the vineyard workers and that would have been that. This realisation inspired a growing sense of hope: maybe we were not alone, maybe providence was at work, maybe all those dear ones murdered in war were cheering us on.

After winding our way through the vineyard, we came to the edge of the base—without our truck, but with a growing sense of hope and determination. The floodlit facility created an eerie light as the fog hung over it, with the domes towering over the base. I felt small and helpless against the looming might and authority of this high-tech facility. But sometimes things aren't what they appear. I knew the base was mixed up in some of the most frightening things happening in the world, but perhaps it wasn't as impenetrable as it seemed. We crawled across the paddock toward a small grove of conifers near the perimeter fence. Everything was still and quiet in the base; the only sound was the humming of the great fans that held the domes up with air pressure.

Sam began working on the hurricane netting wrapped around the fenceline. Behind this netting were high-tension parallel 40,000-volt steel wires. They were spaced about a foot apart. Cutting four of these would create enough space for us to wriggle through. I suggested to Sam that we give the bolt cutters to Peter. (If you are ever involved in anything like this yourself in the future, having a Catholic priest along is a great idea.) Peter raised his hand and said a prayer over the electric wires, but without touching them. 'Give me the cutters,' he said. Opening the cutters, Peter raised them near the first wire. He pushed forward and closed the cutters at the same time. Sam and I watched from a little way away. The wire sparked and broke but did not electrocute him. The second wire was cut without any signs. The third wire sparked and twanged when it broke and still Peter was unhurt; and the fourth wire was the same.

Sam crawled in and we quickly passed the gear through to him. Security cameras and motion sensors were easily in view and we expected the alarms to go off at any moment. At the second fence Sam used the bolt cutter to chomp through the vertical steel bars. After this we worked through the third fence—a twelve-foot, steel-bar, razor-wire security fence. It wasn't long until we were through all the defences and standing inside the base compound. I could hardly believe it.

Sam pulled two gardening sickles out of his gear bag and gave one to me. They had been bought from Bunnings on special for ten dollars each. The three of us looked at each other and smiled. I put one hand on the dome and called out over the noise of the fans: 'In the name of Jesus Christ we disarm you!' I stuck the point of the sickle into the dome and a great rush of warm air poured out against my hand. I proceeded to cut a large slice around the bottom of the dome while Sam cut a huge cross into it. I must have cut forty foot around the base of the dome before I realised that it was deflating quite quickly and collapsing in my direction. Luckily Sam had finished his crosses, and he cut a hole for me to squeeze through before I was crushed under the weight of the deflating dome. All this time, Peter had been setting up his shrine on the grass near the dome. This consisted of a simple box covered by a red velvet cloth, upon which a candle struggled to survive in the light drizzle. A cross lay on the altar beside an icon of Archbishop Oscar Romero.[8]

There was the tiniest bit of pre-dawn light appearing over the eastern hills as we knelt together in prayer. We sang, we prayed for the dead, and we cried. After what seemed like ages we saw torch lights coming from around the side of the dome. Two security guards spotted us and then froze. I stood up and called out to them: 'We have come here to pray. Would you like to join us?' They called back 'No'. One of them ran off, I guess to call the police. The woman security guard stayed with her torch shining on us, waiting; after a while it felt a little awkward. Sam handed over the keys to the front gates. 'You might need these to let the police in,' he said. 'Thank you,' she replied. Peter then took the bolt cutters, cut off three small inch-long pieces from one of the cut steel bars, and gave one to each of us; that felt a little weird.

Just before sunrise, we saw the flashing lights of the police coming out from Blenheim, bright against the still black hills of the valley. They were moving at high speed, but without their sirens going as a courtesy to the neighbourhood. We saw them drive straight past the base, missing the front gate; we heard their brakes squeal as they turned around and then drove back up the road. The New Zealand police must surely be the best in the world. Most officers are caring, professional, ordinary Kiwis who work hard, often in difficult or unpleasant situations that not many people would tolerate. Sure, there might be a few bad eggs, but that was not our experience that day. Mike was the arresting sergeant; he and the other officers walked up very calmly and introduced themselves. I'm sure I saw a small smile on Mike's face as he approached—not a smirk, but a real, genuine smile as he took in the whole situation. Cops have seen most things before, but this was probably a little outside of the box. After being told our rights and asked all the usual questions, we were handcuffed and put in the police van, each of us in a separate compartment in the same vehicle. Before we got inside, the last thing we reminded each other was 'no statement until after we speak with a lawyer'.

As we drove back up the spy base driveway I could see the sun on the clouds as the rain lifted. The van slowed at the front gate and I looked out the window to see our friends Justin and Tom with their Bibles in their hands, smiling towards the tinted windows of the van. I waved and shouted hello. They couldn't hear me, but that didn't matter; they knew we were there. That day Justin had a disposable camera in his pocket. At the moment we left, the sun shone through the clouds and the most beautiful rainbow poured out of heaven, filling the sky with wonder and landing on top of the very spy base dome we had just deflated. Justin caught the moment on film and gave me a copy a few weeks later. I still have the photo, and I treasure it to this day.

At the point of leaving the Waihopai base, a rainbow burst through the clouds, landing on top of the deflated dome.

Conclusion

It was years before the court cases were all resolved—which is another story in itself. Many were shocked that a jury of our peers finally found us innocent of any crime. While we were certainly relieved, Peter, Sam and I never presumed this outcome. Our action was undertaken in the full expectation that we would be held accountable. Indeed, this was why we had sat around the Waihopai base waiting to be arrested. Even in a relatively peaceful society like New Zealand, an action that disrupts our commitment as a nation to violence almost invariably carries a cost. The possibility of a prison sentence or a substantial fine was not something we desired, but it was something we were willing to bear if it came to that.

The Catholic Worker Movement emphasises our need to take responsibility for making peace in a violent world. Rather than being overwhelmed by the scale of destruction or the apparently unassailable might of those in power, we should do what we can. This includes all kinds of attempts to disarm, practically and symbolically, our addiction to violence and war. For Catholic Workers, this is not only an individual's task, but rather is something that requires community. Commitments to peace have to be formed and learned in communities of risk-taking and prayer. Through cultivating a way of life which is characterised by radical simplicity, hospitality, inclusion and compassion for those about us, we can learn the art of peace.

13

Restoring Karioi: Ecology, Community and the Practice of Peace

Andrew Shepherd

It's a humid Saturday afternoon in early October and the spring sun radiates on 40 or so people gathered on the edge of the gravel road. They are an eclectic bunch: middle-aged Pākehā sporting paunches and the latest in outdoor rainwear, octogenarians with broad smiles and skinny legs standing alongside fit and lithe adolescents, young enthusiastic women in active wear and muscular Māori men wearing hunting garb and gumboots. Against the background hum of cicadas and bird calls, a hubbub of human conversation and laughter. People mill around enjoying the warmth of the day and each other's company. Eventually instructions are issued and the activity of loading packs begins. Gentle debate and discussion ensues as individuals determine whether they will carry one, two, or three of the ten-kilogram DoC-200 stoat traps. The octogenarian asserts that he is fit enough to carry a trap and take the most difficult route up the mountain . . . others are less sure. With a mixture of diplomacy and humour some suggest another option, which ticks health and safety checklists and still leaves the individual's pride intact. The 36 traps are loaded onto packs and laughter gives way to grunts as the packs are hoisted onto backs. Further instructions are given and after jovial farewells, small groups are led off into the bush by Māori guides to begin their slow ascents.

Hours later the intriguing assemblage reconvenes. A mix of cultures and occupations are represented—Māori, Pākehā, Sri Lankan and African, freshwater scientists and full-time mums, builders and biblical scholars, artists and activists, surfers and students. Together, they offer karakia (prayers) of thanksgiving for safety and for kai (food), and then, over a shared meal, they recount their afternoon adventures: the steepness of the terrain made more treacherous by recent rainfall, the encounters with birds, the awe-inspiring coastal views from higher up the mountain.

The trap deployment is part of the Karioi: Maunga ki te Moana (Mountain to the Sea) project—an ambitious community conservation project that seeks to restore the ecological health and well-being of Mount Karioi, a forested, extinct volcanic cone that sits to the south of Whāingaroa/Raglan Harbour on the west coast of the North Island. The project is led by A Rocha Aotearoa New Zealand, a Christian organisation that works in practical community conservation and environmental education.[1] Originating in 2009 with a small-scale predator-trapping project on ten hectares, nine years later the Karioi project has expanded to the management of 2,500 hectares and is regarded as one of the most significant community biodiversity projects in the Waikato region. Each month 40-plus local volunteers walk forest tracks, traverse ridges and clamber up slopes to clear and rebait 800-plus traps deployed to kill mammalian predators. The understanding that human well-being and flourishing is tied up with the health and well-being of the land and other species is one that is integral to Māori culture and also the Christian tradition. But to appreciate the pursuit of shalom (wholeness/well-being of life in personal, communal and ecological realms) that lies at the heart of the Karioi Project, it is necessary to understand the history of the maunga, the broader ecological history of Aotearoa New Zealand and a little more of the community involved in the practical conservation work.

The Ancient Past: The Sleeping Lady and Seabird Islands

Karioi maunga is a 2.4 million-year-old basaltic and andesitic volcanic cone, the earliest and most westerly of a line of four volcanoes (along with Mounts Pirongia, Kakepuku and Te Kawa) that run inland on a south-east axis. For Tainui hapū (subtribes) of Tainui ki Whāingaroa, Karioi is a tupuna (ancestor).[2] Karewa was married to Karioi but flirted with her younger sister, Pirongia. On discovering this infidelity, Karioi fled to the coast, pursued by Karewa. Reaching the shore, she ignored the conciliatory advances of her wayward husband, forcing him out into the ocean. Te Toto Gorge, on the western coast of Mount Karioi, is the heel mark left from where Karioi 'gave the boot' to Karewa. Today, Karewa (Gannet Island) sits offshore, while Karioi, the wahine moe (sleeping lady), looks out to sea, waiting for him.[3]

Prior to the arrival of *Homo sapiens* in Aotearoa, the far-flung islands of this archipelago in the far south of the Pacific were an avian paradise. Over millennia of biogeographic isolation, Aotearoa, with no land mammals except two species of native bats, evolved into an aviary of weird and wonderful birds.[4] Many of them, without the threat of mammalian predators, chose to live on the ground and eventually lost their ability to fly—kiwi, weka, takahē, kākāpō, and also nine species of moa, among the largest flightless birds ever to exist, which were preyed upon by one of the largest birds of prey ever to exist—the Haast Eagle. And alongside these iconic forest birds, the islands also teemed with pelagic bird life. They must have been quite a sight—and sound. Eighty per cent of New Zealand's landmass was covered in dense forest, and over millions of years more than one billion seabirds returned annually to the forested coastline to breed. They brought with them nutrients from the sea and left behind guano, dead young and eggshells. It is these deposits, along with the leaves and rotting wood from the forest canopy, that created New Zealand's fertile soils. Much of the land where farms, orchards and gardens now prosper was once dense forest honeycombed with seabird burrows.

Two waves of human migration (Polynesians from 1100 to 1300 CE, and then Europeans from the late 1700s), with their accompanying mammals, had a catastrophic impact on the archipelago's unique ecosystems. Unused to mammals, many ground-nesting seabirds, like their better-known forest cousins, were extremely vulnerable to predation. Yet even now, after a thousand years of gradual decline in ecological health, Aotearoa is still a wonder to behold, regarded as the seabird capital of the world.[5] Today, many mainland seabird colonies have been eliminated, and the remnants are threatened by

Mount Karioi as seen from the south—Ocean Beach, Kawhia, June 2016. Photograph by Matt Brandon.

introduced pests—possums, rats, mustelids (stoats, ferrets and weasels), hedgehogs, and domestic cats and dogs. However, on the flanks of Mount Karioi, one species of seabird, oi (the grey-faced petrel), continues to return. Ultimately, it is these seabirds that are critical to the healthy functioning of this coastal forest ecosystem. Accordingly, the monitoring and protection of this oi population has become the centrepiece of the biodiversity restoration work. The project's vision: to restore Karioi to a seabird mountain.

The Recent Past: Conflictual Community

Over the last 30 years Raglan has grown and changed from a quiet fishing village to a significant tourist destination. Surfers from around New Zealand and the world venture to Raglan to catch waves on the famous point breaks. Like other wild west-coast beaches in New Zealand, Raglan also has something of a magnetic attraction for artisans. However, while a sense of connection to place and an affinity to nature is elemental to many recreationalists and artists, until recently a number of barriers prevented the local Raglan community from participating directly in restoring the declining health of Karioi.

On a practical level, access to the mountain is difficult. Karioi encompasses 1,800 hectares of forested land, but the land around the base of the mountain is privately owned (90 per cent farmland and small-block holdings, and the remainder hapū land). There are only three access points to enter into the Crown-owned forested land, which is administered by the Department of Conservation (DoC) as part of Pirongia Forest Park. Karioi's topography further exacerbates the problem of accessibility. Andesitic volcanic rock eroded over two millennia means that the mountain is characterised by steep and dissected slopes. A traverse of the maunga involves a five-hour trek, with chain-ladders in places to assist the descent of near vertical cliffs!

But beyond these physical barriers, the greatest obstacle to overcome was the strained and broken relations that existed within the community. The arrival of Europeans not only brought change to the ecological balance of the islands, but also dramatically altered the ability of Māori to exercise mana whenua (authority over the land). As elsewhere around Aotearoa, over a century and a half, hapū around the Whāingaroa harbour had witnessed the gradual loss of their land through a mixture of Crown confiscation, legislative stealth and questionable land purchases.

In 1855, the tribe of Tainui gifted Karioi to Queen Victoria while retaining a reserve for themselves. Eight years later, under pressure from settlers, the colonial government invaded the Waikato region, seeking both to claim land for new settlers and to break the power of the Kīngitanga (King Movement). They confiscated 150,000 acres of coastal land at Te Akau (north of Whāingaroa harbour). In 1923, hapū gifted over 28 acres of land at Te Kōpua, Whāingaroa—the tūrangawaewae (home, or standing place, where one belongs and has rights of residence through kinship and genealogy) of the people of Tainui hapū—to the local council. In 1941, a further 75 acres of Te Kōpua was taken under the Public Works Act so that the government could build an airstrip for defensive purposes. At the conclusion of the Second World War this land was not returned. For many years, Te Kōpua was then leased out by the Raglan County Council, until in 1969 a lease was given to the Raglan Golf Club to build a nine-hole golf course. In the 1970s the golf club was extended to an eighteen-hole course and thus golfers began traipsing across the ancestral cemeteries of Te Kōpua. At this point, Tuaiwa Hautai Kereopa (Eva Rickard) entered the fray. Her arrest in February 1978 and her ongoing battle with the Crown for the return of Te Kōpua became a significant turning point, not merely for local hapū, but also nationally, in the struggle by Māori for rangatiratanga (self-determination) and for recognition of their ongoing role as kaitiaki (custodians, guardians) of their lands, waterways and resources.[6] Given this history, a particularly uneasy and troubled relationship existed between the local hapū and DoC, the government agency tasked with managing the maunga.

As elsewhere in the forests of Tāne,[7] a century and a half of mammalian predators had a devastating impact on the ecosystems on and around Karioi. Possums, wild goats and pigs have had deleterious impacts on forest health and diversity, and this was compounded on Karioi by the predation of rats and mustelids on forest and sea birds. While hapū were engaged in possum control on 500 hectares of their land, elsewhere on the mountain, predator control mainly consisted of a five-yearly dose of 1080.[8] And the issue of 1080 had itself become a major battleground, with many local community members deeply unhappy about the aerial application of poison. Hunters were annoyed that 1080 impinged on their ability to hunt wild pigs and goats. Local landowners and residents expressed concern at 1080 making its way into waterways.[9] And, for local hapū, the power of authorities such as DoC and local councils to dump toxins from above onto the 'sleeping lady' was an ongoing affront to both her mana and their mana whenua. As Malibu Hamilton, a local Māori environmental activist, states:

> Being tangata whenua (people of the land) we had to take it back, it's not right what they [DoC] were doing, it still isn't. . . . because they somehow got the colonial rule over us and start imposing their Western war onto us, we have to suffer the indignity of it all. . . . but we'll never not protest.

Malibu remembers that community consultation meetings run by DoC prior to 1080 drops in 1994 were 'packed to the rafters . . . the walls of the town hall were bulging.' Community outrage led to the establishment in 1994 of Te Whakaoranga O Karioi—an incorporated society with the stated aim of restoring the health of Karioi.

Initially, however, the incorporated society was essentially a protest mechanism—a vehicle for expressing dissent and disagreement. Throughout the 1990s and into the turn of the century, disgruntlement over management of the mountain simmered away, reaching boiling point each time DoC began a community consultation process over major management plans—usually 1080 drops. Fiona Edwards has been involved in a range of environmental initiatives within the Raglan community, most notably the highly successful and esteemed Whāingaroa Harbour Care. But at that time, she was the local community liaison officer for DoC. She remembers well the rancour of 1080 consultation meetings: 'I was the most hated person living in Raglan. People used to hurl abuse at me across the street.' Indeed, relationships were so antagonistic that when officials from DoC and Waikato Regional Council heard that representatives from Te Whakarongo O Karioi and/or hapū were coming into their offices in Hamilton, some would find reasons to be absent.

The personalities, history and politics of Karioi all made practical community involvement in the ecological restoration of the maunga seem impossible. Those within the community with a passion for ecological restoration turned their attention towards other areas.[10] Over time these other projects grew and became more successful, while Karioi, the sleeping lady, patiently waited.

Christian Faith and Collaborative Conservation

In 2007, Kristel van Houte returned home to Raglan after time overseas working as a marine biologist in American Samoa and at a conservation project in Kenya run by A Rocha Kenya. At the heart of A Rocha is the belief that to follow the person of Jesus Christ is to participate in Christ's action of reconciling all things, of bringing wholeness (in biblical terms, 'shalom') to the nexus of relationships that comprise life on our planet.[11] This belief, that peacemaking involves both human and ecological well-being, expresses itself in collaborative community conservation projects.

Inspired by her time in Kenya, Kristel, with others, helped establish A Rocha Aotearoa New Zealand, and discussions began about potential projects that this fledgling conservation organisation could be involved in. As a university student Kristel had volunteered on a restoration project on another nearby volcanic cone, Kakepuku. One day, driving across the hills that separate the inland city of Hamilton from Raglan, Kristel had an epiphany:

> I came across the rise, and I was like, wow, you know, there's this mountain. . . . It's right by the sea, it was really beautiful, and it was really accessible. . . . I guess that an idea formed in my head. . . . Every volcanic cone around the Waikato has a community project—like Kakepuku, Maungatautari, and Pirongia. And I thought 'oh, and Karioi doesn't'.

Kristel van Houte holding an oi chick at Mount Karioi, 2017. Photograph by Bexie Towle.

Kristel began conversations with Malibu Hamilton and John Lawson from Te Whakarongo O Karioi and other stakeholders within the community about the possibility of a restoration project on the mountain. Kristel recounts:

> Malibu said 'We've just been more reactive rather than proactive. Why don't you, as part of A Rocha, try and do something?' They basically had this big list, a database of people . . . and he said 'Email these people and see who wants to get on board and do something proactive.'

Malibu remembers these early conversations too: 'I got Kristel involved because we were wanting an alternative. We need to take our Tupuna Maunga back off the Crown, off them administering our maunga because they are doing it badly.'

In 2009 Kristel wrote up a small project proposal and met with DoC staff:

> I met with some people at DoC and said 'Look, this is what we want to do . . . how do we go about it?' I think because I was a new face with no history with them, they were more open. In light of the past, I guess any relationship I had with them was positive.

Buoyed by the encouragement and practical support of both Malibu and DoC, Kristel sought to find broader community interest. Initial community meetings to discuss the potential for a community-led restoration project on Karioi did not get off to a great start, however. 'One of our first consultation meetings in town was quite negative,' Kristel recalls:

> There were a few people that turned up that didn't really have much positive stuff to say. In fact the tone was very negative. There was a DoC guy present, which probably created some of the friction. After the meeting the DoC guy said to me, 'Look, just hang in there', and I said 'okay' . . . 'maybe'. . . .

Despite being a marine biologist by training, and feeling out of her depth with regard to terrestrial ecology and the science of predator control, Kristel did have suitable skills for the role. As well as being free of the emotional baggage from previous conflict over 1080, first and foremost, Kristel understood her vocation to be that of a scientist, not a protestor or activist.

Also, working as a scientist for the National Institute of Water and Atmospheric Research (NIWA), Kristel was able to speak in the language of funding, project proposals and data that management agencies such as DoC employed. Malibu says: 'You know that that's another reason that Kristel is so successful with me, she's a marine scientist so she's got academic skills, she's got understanding. And if there is one thing you can actually beat the others with, it's education.'

From its origins, the Karioi project was based around a holistic vision of shalom—not merely one of restoring the ecological health of Karioi, but also of contributing to the health and well-being of the community around it. Central to A Rocha's ethos is the belief that authentic, long-lasting ecological and social transformation requires the involvement of the whole community. While professional conservation scientists have, at times, an important advisory role, ultimately, the pursuit of ecological shalom is best done not by external professionals but by a local community empowered to care for their place in the world. This emphasis on community-led ecological restoration for the benefit of the local community has found expression in four main ways.

First, voluntarism lies at the heart of the Karioi project. Initially all work on the Karioi project was purely voluntary, and then in 2011 funding from A Rocha International enabled Kristel to take on a paid co-ordinator role and to devote time to the development of the project. However, even now—with a project of regional significance involving 2,500-plus hectares, an annual budget of hundreds of thousands of dollars, the co-ordination of large numbers of volunteers, and two successful and oversubscribed environmental education programmes for local children—the project still only employs two full-time-equivalent staff. While wishing for further funding to employ people in critical areas, Malibu says: 'I want volunteers to remain because that's the backbone of people's aroha (love).' For Malibu, 'There is a difference between aroha and giving and being paid to do a position'.

Second, A Rocha's approach on Karioi has emphasised that conservation is an activity that involves the whole whānau (extended family). While the steepness of the terrain makes the task of checking some trap lines an activity for fit adults, from its origins the project has intentionally focused on all-age activities. Advocacy events at Māui dolphin day, rat-trap tunnel-building workshops, and A Rocha hui (gatherings) are all inclusive activities designed to encourage different ages to build relationships and share skills and knowledge with each other.[12]

Third, because the project's vision of restoring a seabird mountain is long-term and will require the energy and commitment of future generations, environmental education is a core component of the project. Local youth participate in a range of environmental programmes that seek to encourage and deepen their relationship with Karioi and its environs—assisting them to grow in their understanding of the interrelationships within ecological contexts and to apply this learning to actions for a more sustainable future.

Fourth, from the beginning, there was the dream that conservation work on Karioi, while being primarily delivered by volunteers, would also lead to local employment opportunities and job creation, especially for hapū. In 2015, as part of a major expansion of the project, members of the local hapū were contracted to cut 30 kilometres of new tracks on Karioi and to assist in the deployment of new predator traps. The event was highly significant for local hapū—giving them the opportunity to actively exercise their mana whenua, not just on hapū-owned land, but over the whole maunga. The qualifications gained and skills learnt by the track-cutters also enable them to tender for further conservation work on Karioi and further afield. In 2017, hapū were contracted again to cut further tracks on Karioi to assist in the hand-laying of poison for predator control.

Speaking of the joy he has regarding the project, Malibu says:

> And so all this about the community, the people in the community have created this wellness, they have created this joy, happiness, and ability to do something. I am proud to go and do something, trip down a bloody track and slip down a bloody rope for Christ's sake and then go and have lunch with somebody. . . . the environment is being nourished, papatūānuku (Mother Earth, the land) is being nourished.

Intergenerational trapping team, Wainui Reserve, Whāingaroa/Raglan, November 2016. Photograph by Andrew Shepherd.

The Future: Conservation—It's All About People!

Despite its successes, the Karioi project always feels fragile. As with all community conservation projects, the search for funding is an ongoing challenge, and volunteers come and go. Undoubtedly, the greatest challenge is the nature of human relationships. One of A Rocha's central values is that of collaboration and partnership. A critical aspect of the success of the project thus far has been the overcoming of divisions and the uniting of diverse and divergent members of a community—surfers, environmental activists, farmers, hapū, local residents, landowners, local businesses, officials from central and local government agencies, Māori, Pākehā—to work towards a common goal.

Kristel acknowledges that the steepest learning curve for her has been around understanding and working with people. Wounds from previous battles have had to be salved, egos massaged, blunt truths delivered and encouragement offered.

Some would typify Kristel as a 'community facilitator', adept at community development and engagement. Yet underlying Kristel's work is a deep Christian faith, and therefore maybe her work can also be understood using biblical imagery. The Apostle Paul urged the early Christians in the city of Corinth to see themselves as 'ambassadors of Christ', engaged in the 'ministry of reconciliation'.[13] The work of Kristel and others can be understood as that of 'ambassadors'—working behind the scenes, building bridges, strengthening relationships, to ensure that a larger strategic aim is met. Such reconciliation work requires the skill of diplomacy—a willingness to listen to others and a desire to be inclusive. Malibu sees this as one of Kristel's strengths: 'Kristel has listened, followed . . . and in her heart she wants to be inclusive. . . . in her heart she knows that tangata whenua and mana whenua in particular, not just Māori, but the ones who have authority, are important.'

Yet collaborating with others requires an acknowledgement of sometimes painful pasts and then the forging of new ways of relating—and this is never an easy task. Kristel acknowledges that over the years there have been more than a few mistakes and misunderstandings, which have led to personal angst, despair and sleepless nights. 'Sometimes,' she says, 'it all seems too hard and I think perhaps I should just give up.' However, beyond these difficulties she also often has glimpses of reconciliation in action, moments which give her great hope:

> It's exciting when we have meetings of the Karioi advisory group and sitting next to each other on my couch are individuals who only a few years ago would have been antagonists deeply suspicious of each other. Now there is a mutual respect developing and they're sitting and strategising together about how to restore the health of Karioi. Likewise, standing on a cliff on a stormy night and experiencing oi returning to the sea-cliffs of Karioi or listening to the increasing bird chorus in the forest makes all the hard work worthwhile.

Undoubtedly the most exciting moment was when Kristel first confirmed that the 2017 breeding season had produced the first successful fledging of oi chicks for many decades. This delightful outcome was celebrated as a major milestone.

But the numbers of oi chicks remain few, and much work is still to be done for this result to be replicated in the years to come. The journey to restore Karioi as a seabird mountain is only just beginning. And the restoration isn't only ecological. As the community have turned their attention to the 'sleeping lady', seeking to restore her mana, so the tupuna Karioi—herself familiar with broken relationships—has begun her work of reconciliation and restoring relationships within the Whāingaroa community.

14

Are Contemporary Christian New Zealanders Committed to Peace?

John H. Shaver, Chris G. Sibley & Joseph A. Bulbulia[1]

If one were to ask members of the general public whether Christians are committed to peace, responses would divide people into two camps. One group would point to the prosocial teachings of Christianity and activism for peace. The other group would point to Christianity's parochial focus, social divisions and ideological uses in war. Which group would be correct? Both. There is more to the story, however. This study examines the influence of Christianity on social attitudes in contemporary New Zealand, especially as they relate to the acceptance of minorities and willingness to participate in war.

Across the world, Christianity has been, and continues to be, influenced by global and local economic, cultural and environmental factors; Christianity is not monolithic.[2] Seemingly contradictory events—from the violence of the Crusades, to the significant positive social change of the American civil rights movement—are part of Christianity's legacy. If one were to attempt to make sense of Christianity's relationship to peace across its incredible historical and geographic expanse, the complexity would be insurmountable.

Christianity is diverse in the social and economic locations of its membership, its institutions and their value commitments. To simplify, we focus on how these differing contexts affect attitudes to peacemaking in New Zealand during the past few years. Fortunately, New Zealand is home to the New Zealand Attitudes and Values Study (NZAVS), a twenty-year longitudinal study that includes several questions relevant to assessing the legacy of Christian peace teachings in New Zealand. In this chapter, we use NZAVS data to address a manageable subset of questions relating to conflict and peace: Do Christian New Zealanders report higher levels of acceptance of immigrants? Are Christians more accepting of Arabs? Are they more accepting of same-sex marriage? Are New Zealand's Christians committed to peace even if a war were to erupt?

Although commitments to peace manifest in many ways, we assume that these questions directly address Christianity's hypothesised peace legacy in New Zealand. If contemporary New Zealand Christians are more accepting of others, then interactions with these groups would be less likely to result in conflict. Attitudes that decrease the likelihood of conflict would provide evidence of a commitment to peace. Likewise, we assume that one of the most significant threats to a person's commitment to peace is when they are faced with the possibility of joining a warring party. Opposition to violence in the face of armed conflict would provide further evidence of a commitment to peace. Thus, while we do not assume that the answers to these questions will provide definite answers to the question of Christianity's influence on peace in contemporary New Zealand, we believe they provide valuable clues.

Are Christians More Accepting of Ethnic and Religious Difference?

In contemporary New Zealand, there are similar numbers of people who claim no religious affiliation (41.9 per cent) as there are Christians (48.9 per cent).[3] New Zealand's social diversity renders it an ideal place to study the relationships between Christianity, peace, and acceptance of difference, because comparisons can be made between people who are demographically and ideologically similar in most respects, but who differ in religious affiliation and levels of religious commitment. The NZAVS data we discuss here were collected in 2014 and include 13,222 participants who were born in New Zealand. Of these, 4,463 identified as Christians, while 8,759 reported no religious affiliation. The NZAVS asks people how warm they feel towards various social groups, including immigrants, on a scale from one to seven, where one indicates the least warmth and seven indicates the most warmth. We measure acceptance by assessing warmth because measures of emotion are strong predictors of social interaction. The study also asks questions about religion, including whether a person affiliates with a religious tradition, and if so, how important religion is to how they see themselves (rated on a scale from one to seven, where one indicates that religion is not important and seven indicates that it is very important). We assume that this measure of religious identification assesses individual differences in the extent to which someone's faith (in this case Christianity) acts as a guiding framework in their life. We can, therefore, address the questions: Are New Zealanders who identify as Christians more accepting of immigrants than those who do not? And are those who identify very strongly as Christian more accepting than those who identify less strongly?

Figure 1 shows the association between strength of identification with Christianity and level of warmth towards

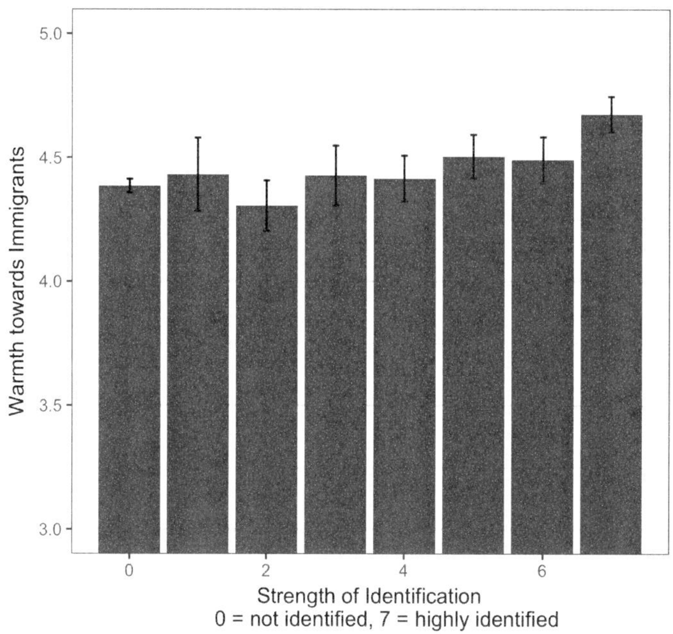

Figure 1. Warmth towards Immigrants by Christian Identification

immigrants. The vertical axis only shows part of the scale (three to five) in order to highlight differences, however the graph shows that New Zealanders are similar in their acceptance of immigrants regardless of the strength of their religious belief. New Zealanders that strongly identify as Christian are slightly more tolerant, but in general there is not much difference between non-Christians and Christian New Zealanders in their reported acceptance of immigrants.[4]

'Immigrants' is a general and somewhat vague category. The NZAVS also tracks warmth towards specific groups of immigrants, and perhaps a difference between Christian and non-Christian New Zealanders will reveal itself when people are asked about their acceptance of a specific group of immigrants. We can ask the question: Are New Zealand Christians more accepting of Arabs, for example? Figure 2 displays the level of warmth towards Arabs among those who report no religious affiliation and those who report varying levels of Christian

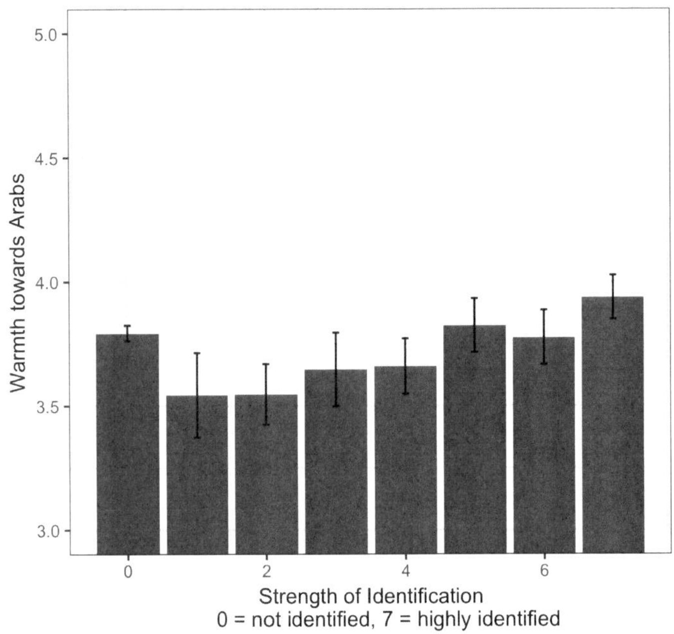

Figure 2. Warmth towards Arabs by Christian Identification

identification. Again, the y-axis is truncated to emphasise differences. Overall, warmth towards Arabs is lower than warmth towards immigrants as a whole, and the data show considerable diversity in acceptance. People who strongly identify with their Christian faith are the most accepting of Arabs. Those who identify with Christianity at low levels, however, are less accepting of Arabs than non-religious New Zealanders. Here we see that attitudes towards a minority group are influenced by the extent to which people identify with Christianity.

We know from other research that there are many drivers of prejudice and that there are many features of a person's life that contribute to acceptance of diversity. For example, men, those who are uneducated, and/or those who are unemployed all tend to exhibit reduced acceptance. When our statistical models adjust for these known drivers of prejudice, we find the same pattern that we report in the previous paragraph: though non-religious people are more tolerant than those who only weakly identify with Christianity, Christian New Zealanders who identify as highly religious report the highest levels of acceptance among the population. This pattern even extends to acceptance of people who follow other religions, including Muslims.[5] That is, highly identified Christian New Zealanders are more accepting of Muslims than those who claim no religious affiliation—though people who are Christian, but only loosely identify with their faith, are the least accepting members of contemporary New Zealand society. It appears, then, that Christianity in New Zealand does lead to increased acceptance of other social groups, but only when it is a highly motivating force in one's life. Importantly, there are few differences in acceptance between Christian denominations; rather, how strongly a person identifies as a Christian predicts larger differences.

Are Christians More Accepting of Personal Freedoms?

The research described above, conducted among a large sample of New Zealanders, reveals that highly religious Christian New Zealanders are more accepting of ethnic and religious diversity. But does this acceptance extend to members of the population who differ in other ways? The NZAVS asks people to indicate their support for the Marriage (Definition of Marriage) Amendment Act of 2013, which allowed same-sex couples to legally marry. Participants were asked to rate their position on the Act, from 'strongly oppose' (one) to 'strongly support' (seven). Attitudes towards the Act are affected by a host of issues; however, responses to this question allow us to address, albeit imperfectly, acceptance of homosexuals. So, are New Zealand Christians more accepting of homosexuals than other New Zealanders?

Figure 3 displays the association between people's position regarding the Act and the strength of their identification with Christianity. Here, religiously unaffiliated participants report much higher levels of acceptance of homosexual unions. Across the entire range of religious identification, Christians are opposed to the Act, with those who identify most strongly with Christianity reporting the lowest levels of acceptance. While highly identified Christians in New Zealand appear more accepting of ethnic and religious diversity, this acceptance does

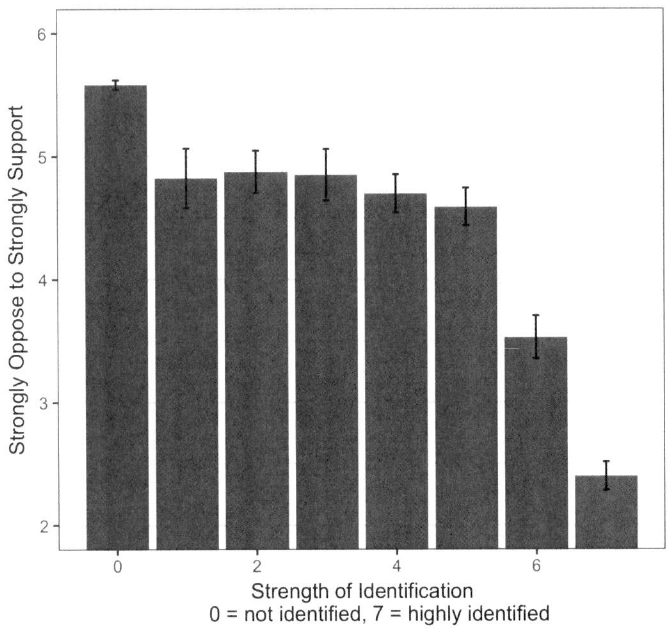

Figure 3. Attitudes towards Same-Sex Marriage by Christian Identification

not seem to be indiscriminate. Unaffiliated New Zealanders are far more accepting of homosexuals than are Christians, and those who highly identify as Christian are the least accepting of legalised homosexual unions. Figure 3 focuses on a larger portion of the scale than Figures 1 and 2 (two to six along the left-hand side of the figure, rather than three to five), because non-Christians and Christians differ more on their stance towards the Act than they do in their attitudes towards ethnic and religious minority groups.

These results challenge simplistic assumptions about Christianity's influence on acceptance in contemporary New Zealand society; rather, the picture drawn by the data is complex. Broadly, this complexity is evident in the two main findings presented above: 1) Although Christian New Zealanders are more accepting of some groups, they are less accepting of others; and 2) there is a wide range of responses to minorities within Christian communities.

Are Contemporary Christian New Zealanders Committed to Peace?

Although the NZAVS does not address commitments to peace specifically, it does ask New Zealanders about their willingness to fight, should circumstances arise. Specifically, we asked participants to respond to the following question, from 'definitely no' (one) to 'definitely yes' (seven): 'Of course, we all hope that there will not be another war, but if it were to come to that, would you be willing to fight for your country?' Figure 4 shows how participants who differ in their religious identification responded to this question. Unaffiliated New Zealanders are significantly less likely to say that they would be willing to go to war than Christian New Zealanders at all levels of religious identification. Moreover, there are no practically important differences in willingness to go to war across levels of Christian identification. We illustrate this finding with a larger portion of the scale (two to six) than in the first two figures (three to five) because non-religious New Zealanders and Christians differ more in their willingness to fight than in their acceptance of diversity.

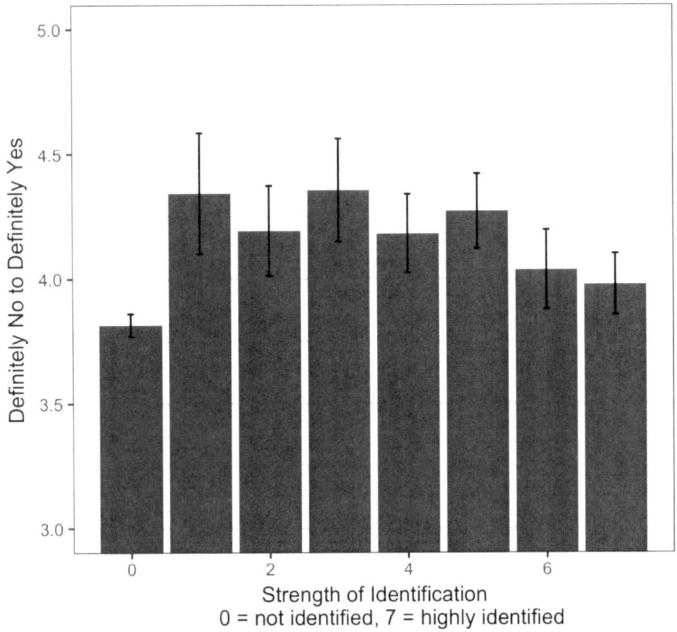

Figure 4. Willingness to Go to War by Christian Identification

Despite a strong historical commitment to peace among some New Zealand Christians, contemporary New Zealand Christians appear to be more willing to go to war than unaffiliated New Zealanders. Interestingly, there are very few differences in attitudes towards war across religious identification, or across Christian denominations. Christian New Zealanders and those New Zealanders who are not religiously affiliated are starkly opposed in their willingness to fight for their country.

Making Sense of the Findings: Christianity and Cross-cultural Variation

We opened by asking questions about whether Christianity is associated with attitudes likely to reduce conflict with other social groups in New Zealand, and whether Christians in contemporary New Zealand would be committed to peace should war break out. We suspected that members of the general population would have strong, albeit largely opposing, responses to the question of whether New Zealand's Christians are committed to peace. The results presented here suggest that both groups would be both partially correct, and slightly wrong. In other words, these data challenge simple assumptions about the effect of Christianity on social attitudes in contemporary New Zealand. In concluding, we place these findings in context in an attempt to make sense of them.

To do so it helps to ask another question: are the greater levels of acceptance of ethnic and religious diversity among Christians found here unique to New Zealand? Or are they similar to those found elsewhere around the world? In the 1950s, when psychologists first started to investigate prejudice—the opposite of acceptance—they found, somewhat surprisingly, that Christians tended to be less accepting of minorities. In fact, in 37 out of 47 studies religious people were observed to be more prejudiced than religiously unaffiliated people, and in only two of these studies did the researchers find that religious people were more accepting of minorities.[6] These findings held regardless of the social group towards whom the prejudice was directed, or how religion was measured: people who reported that they were Christian, or said they believed in God, or indicated that they attended church, were all found to be more prejudiced towards ethnic, religious, sexual and social diversity in all of its forms. These studies, however, were conducted almost exclusively in the United States.

Worldwide acceptance of minority populations differs widely by region. For example, recent research has examined attitudes towards immigrants across historically Christian countries.[7] In countries such as Switzerland, only 3.9 per cent of people report that they would not like to have immigrants as neighbours. Elsewhere, for example in the Czech Republic, this number increases to 29.5 per cent. The other countries of Europe fall somewhere in between these extremes. The effect of religion on tolerance towards immigrants varies dramatically across these countries as well. In some places Christian faith strongly increases tolerance, in others it has little effect, and in some places Christianity appears to increase prejudice.

These cross-cultural findings suggest that the relationship between Christianity and acceptance of diversity is highly culturally variable. While Christian New Zealanders are more accepting of ethnic and religious diversity, they are also less tolerant of same-sex unions. An association between Christianity and an objection to same-sex marriages is not unique to New Zealand, however. Though there are exceptions, the majority of Christians across the world are opposed to homosexual partnerships.[8] So while some aspects of tolerance expressed by Christians in New Zealand are unique, other aspects are not.

New Zealand has enjoyed a relatively peaceful history, one largely free of interreligious conflict. At the national level, principles of freedom, equality and social harmony were codified as early as 1840, in the Treaty of Waitangi. There were some sectarian religious conflicts, particularly between Catholics and Protestants around the period of the First World War, but such conflicts were much less pronounced than in many other areas of the world.[9] Indeed, the other contributions to this volume attest to an enduring Christian peace commitment in New Zealand. Yet, the data reported here clearly show that Christians are more willing to go to war than their non-religious counterparts. In the following, we explain why attitudes towards peace and conflict differ by target group.

Again, we can begin by asking whether or not this finding is unique to New Zealand. Although there tend to be a great deal of individual differences,[10] researchers do consistently find an association between religion and support for the use of violence against out-groups.[11] In this respect, the findings reported here do not appear unique to New Zealand Christianity.

Explaining the Complexity: The Transmission of Religious Cultures

Christianity, of course, did not originate in New Zealand; it was brought to the country by both missionaries and settlers. While New Zealand Christianity shares many things with Christianity elsewhere in the world, it is also unique in many ways, having been subject to local cultural and historical influences. Thus, perhaps we might make sense of our findings by investigating how it is that religions transmit, or change over time: which aspects are most likely to adapt to local factors and which are more likely to be resilient.

All religions bind people together, and the cohesiveness of religious communities is, in part, the result of shared values. People hold different values, to different extents, but those values at the intersection of religion and social conservatism seem to be the most important for binding social groups.[12] Such values include those that encourage loyalty towards group members, a focus on the traditional family, a respect for authority, and purity. Not only do these values function to bond people, they also ensure the transmission of religious cultures: religious cultures transcend generations because they focus on family values, and submission and obedience to authorities. These aspects of religious cultures are relatively inflexible, or else religions would not persist.

The conservative values of European Christianity—such as willingness to fight (i.e., in-group loyalty) and objection to same-sex marriage (i.e., family values)—ensured transmission to future generations. Values that are of lower importance for transmission of religious cultures—such as attitudes towards minority groups—are more likely to shift in response to local cultural and historical factors. The values that underlie acceptance of social diversity are such values. To summarise, we suspect that differences in value conservation and value change, necessary for cultural transmission, are the reason why Christian commitments to peace take the complex form that they do in contemporary New Zealand.

Other NZAVS research provides support for this interpretation. Across New Zealand the proportion of conservative religious people living in an area predicts the portion of unaffiliated people with conservative values.[13] That is, conservative values transmit with such fidelity that even the non-religious neighbours of conservatives come to endorse them. Other values are not as robust and do not spread amongst neighbours. Moreover, people who were low in their religious identification one year reported weaker conservative values the next year, whereas those high in religious identification were more likely to be even more conservative a year later. In other words, high religious identification and conservative values appear linked, and seem to contribute to the remarkable transmission of relatively unchanging conservative religious cultures.[14]

In closing, we would like to emphasise that while conservative values are important for the transmission of religious cultures, this does not mean that they are completely incapable of change. Changes in social attitudes that are motivated by conservative values, however, likely require conscious effort and the acknowledgement that these values are the most difficult to modify. Efforts aimed at increasing Christians' acceptance of homosexual rights would take considerable conscious effort. At the same time, the values underpinning acceptance of ethnic and religious diversity, if our interpretations are correct, are more fragile. Maintaining high levels of acceptance in the future will require further cultivation. The dynamics of cultural transmission of religion help to explain the complex pattern of commitments to peace among contemporary New Zealanders; a more thorough understanding of these dynamics may encourage further progress towards such commitments to peace in the future.

15

Remembering Jesus on Anzac Day: Just War or Just Another War?

Chris Marshall

On Anzac Day 2015, New Zealand observed the centenary of the Gallipoli landings and the disastrous campaign that ensued. There was huge public interest in the commemorations, partly the result of a conscious effort on the part of government over many years, supported by the media, to use Anzac Day as a nation-building exercise. Anzac Day has grown beyond a mere day of remembrance to become a primary focus of our national unity and identity. The ritual observance of Anzac Day, with its mythology of blood sacrifice, heroism and selfless service of country, is the closest thing we have in New Zealand to a civil religion.

The term 'civil religion' refers to the overt use of religious symbols, language, practices and beliefs to sacralise an ethnic or national community by projecting its experiences and values onto the cosmic order, so that society, in effect, venerates an image of itself.[1] While we lack a fully fledged civic cult in New Zealand, the language of 'sacredness' is now regularly attached to Anzac Day in public discourse in a way that never happens anymore for Easter or Christmas, and would be considered inappropriate were it to do so.

Of course, civil religion is a deeply problematic phenomenon, especially for Christians. It was in the name of the civil religion of Rome, with its worship of the emperor, that the early church was persecuted, as the Book of Revelation vividly attests. To say 'Jesus is lord' was, for the first Christians, an act of political dissent from the civil religion of the empire and the violent 'beast' it deified.[2] This alone should give Christians pause in face of the deepening religio-political functions Anzac Day fulfils in our national life.

This is not to say it is inappropriate for nations to recall past military events. One virtue in observing Anzac Day is that it provides us with an opportunity to recall the unbelievable carnage that accompanied the First World War, among others. An attitude of sorrow and repentance, rather than jingoistic pride and manufactured hero making, is surely the appropriate spirit for Anzac commemorations.

Anzac Day can also serve as an occasion for Christians to reflect on fundamental questions about war, violence and discipleship. Should Christians ever go to war? Does the Bible condone or forbid Christian participation in armed conflict? Is it appropriate, even in peacetime, for followers of Jesus to join the military and train for war, to master the skills of violence and the technology of killing in preparation for some future conflict? Should they train as snipers, for example, or as drone operators, whose job it is to assassinate particular individuals? Should they join the Special Forces and serve as the President's personal hit squad, as some Special Ops units in the American military do? Or should they avoid the messier aspects of military violence and support the war machine in other ways?

Historically Christians have disagreed on answers to these questions, and continue to do so. Most would say that, in certain circumstances, it is right and proper for Christians to join the military and fight and kill. Yet at the same time, Christians down through the ages have sensed a deep theological impulse in their faith to engage in the hard work of reconciliation and peacemaking.

This impulse has not typically come from possessing a developed peace theology, which remains very much a minority sport in Christian circles. Very few practicing Christians, and just as few professional theologians, are able to articulate theologically why or how peace is central to the gospel, apart from in some spiritual sense of 'peace with God'.[3] Yet there exists an intuitive *sensus fidelium* that Christianity *is* fundamentally about 'peace on earth and goodwill towards men',[4] that the church ought be on the side of peace not war, that Christians should be known primarily as peacemakers, not as warriors. So where does this instinctive prioritising of peace and non-violence come from?

To suggest there is a normative presumption for peace in the Christian tradition is clearly contestable, since the track record of the institutional church in renouncing militarism and proclaiming peace is far from exemplary. Some would even say that historically Christianity has been one of the world's most violent religions, owing to its entanglement in imperial politics and European colonial conquest, including the colonisation of Aotearoa New Zealand. The extent to which Christianity itself is to blame for the violence conducted under its watch is impossible to say, since the specific role of religious belief in fomenting violence cannot be surgically separated from other contributing factors, as William Cavanaugh's important book *The Myth of Religious Violence* convincingly shows.[5] Nevertheless, it can be said that the official voice of the church has seldom functioned as a major impediment to warfare, and all too often has been commandeered in active support of it.

Yet for all such ambiguity and compromise, there is still, I propose, a pronounced peacemaking predisposition, even a pacifist reflex, located somewhere deep in the bones of the Christian tradition. This pacifist instinct was certainly predominant at the very beginning of the movement in New Testament times, and for several centuries thereafter. Although it was increasingly forced to the margins of the faith following the birth of Christendom in the mid-fourth century, and at times was almost completely submerged from view, it never disappeared entirely. It has resurfaced time and again down through the centuries in radical renewal movements, such as Anabaptism in the sixteenth century and Quakerism in the seventeenth. As the present volume and the recently published *Saints and Stirrers* demonstrate, a pacifist reflex has also repeatedly emerged within Christianity in New Zealand, disrupting and challenging traditions of violence and militarism.[6] Evidently there was something in the originating impulse of the Christian religion that has served to create a deep unease with Christian involvement in fighting and killing, and, at times, to

Crowds gather at the centotaph for the Anzac Day Dawn Service, Auckland War Memorial Museum, 2013. Source: One-Image Photography/Alamy Stock Photo.

nourish a principled commitment to non-violence or pacifism as an inescapable corollary of Christian commitment. There are several varieties of pacifism, but at heart Christian pacifism entails the refusal to participate in war or lethal violence and instead to seek peaceful ways to settle conflicts and overcome evil.

Just War Theory

The former position of deep unease is reflected in the emergence of the so-called Just War Theory. Ever since the time of St Augustine in the fifth century, the official teaching of all major Christian traditions has condoned, even encouraged, participation in war, on the proviso that it falls within the definition of a 'just' war. The just war doctrine is not derived from the Bible and the criteria used for determining it have varied over its lifespan. But essentially the doctrine asserts that war, and Christian involvement in war, is justifiable where two main conditions are met: where there is a *just cause*, that is, where war is required, as a final resort, to put right or prevent some clear wrong; and where *just means* are employed, that is, the violence used is strictly limited and highly targeted (aimed only at enemy combatants) and intended only to prevent them from perpetrating further injustices. These were the considerations appealed to in support of Christians fighting in the First World War, though in many ways it was conceived of as a *holy* war more than a just war, that is, one justified by God's will rather than by utilitarian calculations.[7]

The just war doctrine has several positive features. It may be seen as a praiseworthy effort to restrain violence and limit suffering when conflict is inevitable, and over recent times it has contributed greatly to the development of international laws and conventions seeking to humanise the conduct of war. Though not derived directly from Scripture, its proponents are quick to assert the doctrine's fundamental congruence with biblical and theological principle, and even to depict it as a distinctively *Christian* approach to the problem of war and violence, an impressive application of gospel values to public life.[8] Arguably, this has been the dominant understanding within New Zealand churches; the approach has been implicitly, and sometimes quite explicitly, used in justifying New Zealand's participation in warfare and in legitimating Christian support for Anzac commemorations.

In advancing the just war doctrine, proponents usually feel obliged to repudiate Christian pacifism as being deeply misguided, insisting its simple-minded appeal to the teaching and example of Christ loses touch with reality and slips into a utopian perfectionism that dooms the church to political irrelevance. A case in point is the recent book *In Defence of War* by Nigel Biggar, the Regius Professor of Moral and Pastoral Theology at Oxford University.[9] Alarmed at what he detects as a creeping pacifism in the contemporary church, which he blames on the detrimental influence of theologians like John Howard Yoder, Stanley Hauerwas and Richard Hays, Biggar offers an emphatic restatement of traditional just war thinking—one that manages, incidentally, to defend the slaughter of the Somme and the illegal invasion of Iraq on Christian principle. He also mounts a spirited attack of what he calls the 'virus of wishful thinking' that is Christian pacifism.

Biggar's book has been hailed as 'the most substantial, forceful and provocative Christian defence of the idea of a just war to have appeared in many years', and one that could well become 'the defining Christian text on war and peace for years to come'.[10] But to me the most interesting thing about the book is the reason why Biggar believes a reassertion of just war doctrine is needed at this time, and why he feels compelled to talk down some perceived predilection for pacifism in the contemporary church and warn of 'the evils of peace'.

Could it be that there is something in the DNA of Christianity that irresistibly inclines it towards pacifism, something rooted in the message of the gospel and the work of the Spirit, something that just war theory, for all its philosophical sophistication, will never be able to silence without first silencing the dominant voices of the church's foundational narratives? Could it be that, despite its majority endorsement by all mainstream Christian denominations, just war theory is a deeply flawed tool for Christian moral assessment, one that runs counter to the magnetic pull of the tradition? There are several reasons to challenge the adequacy of just war thinking for shaping Christian thinking on war and peace.

The Nature of Violence

The first challenge to just war thinking relates to the inherent nature of violence. Just war theorists typically dismiss pacifism as idealistic or utopian, but just war theorists are arguably more idealistic and naïve. Just war theory rests on the assumption that, once unleashed, military violence can be controlled by rational rules and agreed-upon limits so that it conforms to the dictates of justice and decency. But organised violence is not like that. It is not some lifeless tool that is taken up and employed instrumentally for higher ends, then put down again without consequence. It is a demonic contagion that always runs amok and overpowers those who seek to control it. Think, for example, of the madness afflicting the architects, Allied and Ottoman, of the brutal campaign at Gallipoli, which, in less than a year of fighting, resulted in almost 400,000 casualties (deaths and injuries).[11] 'Put your sword back into its place,' Jesus told Peter, 'for all who take the sword will perish by the sword.'[12] The lifeless instrument comes to life and has the final word by slaying the slayer.

Nor does just war's endorsement of deadly force as an allegedly last resort exist in a hypothetical vacuum. It demands the existence of material means to carry it out. It requires the establishing, equipping, training and social valuing of military forces. This in turn encourages, and sometimes morphs into, a larger militarisation of social life, a militarism in which collective consciousness is pervaded by military imagery, language, values, myths, forms of entertainment and huge monetary investment, birthing the kind of idolatry against which the biblical prophets railed.[13] It is precisely this danger that should stir alarm over current forms of Anzac Day commemoration.

The just war proposition that political and military leaders will first sit down and objectively evaluate the morality of their cause, and the ethical limits on the means to be used to achieve it, before launching into combat is also, to my mind, unbelievably naïve and utterly devoid of empirical support. Political and military decision-making is not like that. It is never that disinterested, especially in face of perceived threats or opportunities for aggrandisement. Every war that has ever been fought, including the Allied invasion of Gallipoli in 1915, Hitler's conquest of Czechoslovakia in 1938, and George W. Bush's illegal invasion of Iraq in 2003, has been deemed 'just' by its nationalistic architects and court prophets.

The Eschatological Basis of Christian Existence

A second problem with just war doctrine for Christians is that it fails to reckon with the uniquely eschatological basis of Christian existence and moral reasoning—that is, the belief that God's future order has already broken into present history through the coming of Christ, albeit in a partial way, and this changes everything. It therefore fails to view the world through distinctively Christian eyes.[14] How we 'see' the world—that is, how we understand or interpret what is going on around us all the time—is the starting point of ethics. The principal ethical question is not, 'What should we do in this circumstance?' but, 'What do we believe is real? What is the world *really* like?'

Just war proponents typically commend their position as a form of 'realism'. Pacifism, they say, is a wonderful sentiment, a truly noble aspiration, but it is unrealistic to think it can work in the real world. President Obama made this point in the speech he delivered on receiving the Nobel Peace Prize in December 2009. Acutely aware of the disparity between himself, as Commander-in-Chief of the world's greatest ever military power, locked in two major wars, and the example of non-violent peacemaking set by Mahatma Gandhi and Martin Luther King, Obama offered a strident defence of the just war doctrine as a necessary instrument for promoting peace in a violent world. He said:

> I know there is nothing weak, nothing passive, nothing naïve, in the creed and lives of Gandhi and King. But as a head of state sworn to protect and defend my nation, I cannot be guided by their examples alone. I face the world as it is, and cannot stand idle in the face of threats to the American people. For make no mistake: evil

> does exist in the world. A non-violent movement could not have halted Hitler's armies. Negotiations cannot convince al Qaeda's leaders to lay down their arms. To say that force is sometimes necessary is not a call to cynicism—it is a recognition of history, the imperfections of man, and the limits of reason.[15]

For Obama, to 'face the world as it is', with all its existing evils, requires the use of military violence. The alternative is to 'stand idle in the face of threats to the American people', for non-violence can never stop the Hitlers and other perpetrators of mass evil. Perhaps he is right. Many would concur with him on the limitations of non-violence, though to equate non-violence with 'standing idly by and doing nothing to oppose evil' is a travesty of what Gandhi and King truly represented.

But the point to note is that Obama, like all just warriors, counters the normativity of Christian non-violence by appealing to what could be called the 'myth of realism'—the insistence that violence is the only *realistic* option for controlling evil. Such a belief is a myth in both senses of the word. It is a myth because it assumes a larger, and essentially pagan, narrative about the meaning and direction of cosmic history; and it is a myth because its undergirding story, from the perspective of Christian confession, is fundamentally false.[16]

The Christian gospel offers a radically different narrative about reality. While it includes a moral and spiritual code, the gospel must never be reduced to abstract ethical or doctrinal principles. It is, more basically, the explosive claim that with the coming of Christ a whole new world has come into being. It is the good news that the future transfiguration of reality, long dreamed of by biblical prophets and poets, a transfiguration in which the lion will lie down with the lamb and swords will be beaten into ploughshares and spears into pruning hooks, has already begun.[17] It has begun with the bodily resurrection of Jesus from a violent death, an event that marks the definitive defeat of sin's violent tyranny over the world as we know it and the dawning of a new creation.[18]

This, in turn, means that the 'world as we know it' is not the way the world *really* is. Something has shifted in the structures of reality. A dramatic change has occurred. What

Dominic Crossan calls 'God's Great Clean Up Operation' has commenced.[19] This change may be visible at present only to the eyes of faith, but it is still, for believers, objectively real, and one day will fill the earth, as the waters cover the sea.

Christian pacifism, then, is rooted in hearing God's call to participate in a new world that God is building. Awareness of this call comes primarily from attending to the story of Jesus in the Gospels, in the company of the church, and from telling and retelling that story until Christians not only believe it, but actually begin to inhabit it and enact it. Christian non-violence is sustainable only to the extent that it is grounded on the story of Jesus Christ, as the singular paradigm and power of Christian peacemaking.

The Measure of Jesus

This leads to a third criticism of Christian just war theory: it is impossible to square with the teaching and example of Jesus, as recorded in the New Testament, and it is this that constitutes a fatal blow to the theory.

One of the most striking features of New Testament moral teaching is its emphasis on the imitation of Christ as the heart of Christian living and the touchstone of Christian truth. Christ is presented not as one heroic example among many, but as the normative role model for his followers to aspire to because he, in turn, is the perfect human embodiment of the perfections of God. To follow Jesus, for the New Testament writers, is to imitate God.[20]

In this respect, it is hugely significant that Jesus is invariably portrayed as one who utterly rejected the sword and who loved his enemies even to the point of self-sacrifice on their behalf. And it is this dimension of the divine activity in Christ, the dimension of merciful, non-violent peacebuilding, that believers are expressly and repeatedly bidden to emulate. They are to be merciful, for God desires mercy, not sacrifice.[21] They are to make peace, for God is a peacemaker.[22] They are to serve others, 'for the Son of Man came not to be served but to serve, and give his life a ransom for many'.[23] They are to love their enemies and pray for their persecutors, for their Father in heaven 'is kind to the ungrateful and the wicked' and 'makes his sun to rise on the evil and the good and sends his rain on the righteous and on the unrighteous'.[24] They are to forgive, as their heavenly Father has forgiven them,[25] to be forbearing, kind and tender-hearted to one another, as God in Christ has been towards them.[26] They are to endure hostility without retaliation,[27] to live as those who are 'always being given up to death for Jesus' sake'.[28] They are 'to live in love, as Christ loved us and gave himself up for us'.[29]

That is why the New Testament never portrays Christians as being involved in any kind of military action, hostile plotting or violent intimidation. Nowhere do believers carry or wield swords; the one episode where it happens it is severely denounced by Jesus.[30] It also explains why peace language permeates the New Testament.[31] The word 'peace' in its various forms occurs 100 times in the New Testament, and in every book except 1 John. It features in all four Gospels, most notably in Luke, where it occurs 14 times. Indeed Luke sums up the entire ministry of Jesus as 'preaching the gospel of peace'.[32]

The 'peace' spoken of is freighted with the full breadth of meaning of the Hebrew term *shalom,* which occurs between 200 and 350 times in the Old Testament (depending on whether verbal forms and cognates are included). The Hebrew concept of peace is comprehensive in scope, embracing environmental harmony, material prosperity, social justice, physical health, moral integrity and relational well-being. If the ancient Greek notion of peace focused on the interlude between military campaigns, and the Roman concept of peace implied the forced pacification of enemies through military dominance (the *Pax Romana*), the biblical concept of *shalom* denotes the existence of right relationships in all the departments of life.[33]

Biblical peace, then, is more than the absence of armed conflict and bigger than a commitment to physical non-violence. But the messianic reign of peace proclaimed by Jesus and his followers unquestionably entailed the renunciation of lethal violence.

> You have heard that it was said, 'An eye for an eye and a tooth for a tooth.' But I say to you, Do not resist an evildoer. But if anyone

> strikes you on the right cheek, turn the other also. . . . You have heard that it was said, 'You shall love your neighbour and hate your enemy.' But I say to you, Love your enemies and pray for those who persecute you, so that you may be children of your Father in heaven.[34]

As Jesus told Pilate, 'My kingdom is not from this world. . . . If it were . . . my followers would be fighting.'[35]

This pacifist outworking of messianic peace endured well into the post-apostolic period as well. Indeed as far as we can tell, the pre-Constantinian church, which stood closest in time to the ministry and memory of Jesus, was predominantly, if not exclusively, pacifist. There are no records of a known Christian soldier in the Roman army until at least 170 CE. After that there is evidence of Christians in the army, although several Church Fathers, such as Tertullian, opposed the practice and others insisted that Christian soldiers should never shed blood in course of their duties.[36] It was only after the conversion of Emperor Constantine in the early fourth century that Christian soldiers became commonplace; in fact under the reign of Theodosius II (408–50), only baptised Christians could serve as soldiers, a remarkable reversal of requirements.

Thus, as the church's political fortunes waxed, so its vocational distinctiveness, rooted in the way of Christ, waned. Christian theology developed a marked reluctance to take Jesus' function as normative role model seriously, questioning both its ethical feasibility (since, unlike Christ, humans are not divine) and fearing the theological consequences of reducing Christ to a mere moral example (Christ's principal role is as eternal saviour rather than the fountainhead of moral values and praxis). Tellingly, the church's historic creeds are all but silent on ethics in general and the radical demands of Jesus in particular.

This has encouraged what Lee Griffith calls the 'great amnesia' about the normativity of Jesus' human life for the community that bears his name. It is an amnesia that has allowed the church to be seduced by power and wealth and status, and to relegate Christ's call for non-violent peacemaking to the margins of its consciousness. As simple as it may sound, it is the memory of Jesus and continual reference to his example and teaching, not the philosophical principles of just war theory, that is the single most important determinant of Christian moral responsibility in face of violence and injustice. As Griffith urges:

> We must remember Jesus. Wherever and whenever Jesus is not remembered, those who claim the name of Christian have shown a special proclivity to give allegiance to race or ethnicity, wealth or weaponry, empire or liberation army, or any of the other numerous powers laying claim to lordship. When there is failure to remember the one who died on the cross, crucifixion follows. When there is a failure to remember the one who rose from the grave, the graves are filled . . . To remember Jesus, bread is broken, cup is shared, community is formed. *All* violence is an attack upon community. *All* violence by Christians is also an attack upon the memory of Jesus.[37]

Martin Niemöller, the great German Lutheran pastor during the Nazi period, attributed his opposition to the Third Reich to his simple daily motto, 'What would Jesus say about this?' Niemöller survived six years in a concentration camp, and towards the end of his long life as a peace activist and converted Christian pacifist, declared that the only question that really mattered to him was, 'What would Jesus do?'[38]

This is also the question Christians should ask themselves on Anzac Day. The day is often described as a sacred day of remembrance, a time to recall the sacrifices made on distant battlefields on behalf of the freedom and peace we now enjoy. There is nothing wrong with this desire to remember the war dead; one might even consider it a moral duty never to forget the victims of violence, and Anzac Day is an opportunity to do so. But for Christians, it is not the memory of fallen soldiers or the causes for which they fought that is most essential for evaluating Christian involvement in warfare; it is the memory of Jesus.

Christian peacemaking starts and finishes with remembering the story of Jesus, the one who, in St Paul's words, 'came and proclaimed peace to you who were far off and peace to those who were near'.[39] As long as the Christian church attends carefully to this story, and as long as it takes seriously the injunction to 'follow me' which features at the outset of all four Gospel narratives,[40] attempts to justify Christian involvement in killing and conflict by appealing to just war principles, national solidarity and so-called political realism will never be finally persuasive.

16

Afterword: Christianity and the Peace Tradition in New Zealand

Geoffrey Troughton & Philip Fountain

The preceding accounts of Kiwis pursuing peace are held together by one central idea: put simply, we claim that these diverse stories point toward the existence of a significant, sustained and influential New Zealand Christian peace tradition. In this final chapter we turn to this question of a peaceable tradition. We do not seek to present peace as the imagined 'essence' of Christianity, or claim this peace tradition as the necessary historical unfolding of some predetermined centre of the faith. Nevertheless, we argue that the contours of a Christian peace tradition can be fruitfully traced, and that our understanding of New Zealand Christianity, and of New Zealand's history more generally, are enriched by making these connections visible.

A Christian Peace Tradition?

An initial challenge to our claim for the existence of a Christian peace tradition in New Zealand comes from within this volume itself. In their contribution, John Shaver, Chris Sibley and Joseph Bulbulia draw upon remarkably extensive survey data, collected through the New Zealand Attitudes and Values Study (NZAVS), which they argue shows that among New Zealand Christians 'greater religious identification predicts greater willingness to go to war'. This argument finds narrative support in a number of the other chapters. Ormond Burton and Archie Barrington, in Tom Noakes-Duncan's chapter, were rare and persecuted voices within the context of New Zealand's involvement in the Second World War. In fact, Burton had his ministerial credentials revoked by his own Methodist denomination because he refused to stop proclaiming his pacifist stance. Jamie Allen's chapter describes the recent attempts to disentangle St Mary's Cathedral from a militarist past in which the church was firmly aligned with Pākehā settlers during a violent colonisation. In our introduction we noted that Anzac Day services draw extensively on the patterns and language of Christianity in commemoration of New Zealand's participation in warfare. Other chapters also indicate that Christianity in Godzone has frequently been associated with violence, war and discord. This begs the obvious question: How is it possible to argue for a peace tradition when New Zealand Christians have also been enmeshed in violent logics, practices and imaginations?

This kind of questioning assumes an understanding of tradition in which Christianity is supposed to exhibit only a singular, linear and consistent trajectory. We argue that this apparent challenge can be solved through a better conceptualisation of 'tradition', and by carefully explaining why peace-pursuing Christianity should indeed be regarded as a tradition.

The philosopher Alasdair MacIntyre has defined a tradition as 'an argument extended in time'.[1] This approach helpfully points to the historicity of traditions: a tradition is not simply about sameness, and nor is it ever static and fixed. Traditions evolve over time and are characterised by both diversity and contestation. However, MacIntyre's approach to tradition is inadequate for our purposes insofar as it requires the tracing of an ongoing argument. While we do indeed think that peace is a recurring theme in New Zealand Christianity, and while this theme can be fruitfully examined in a range of sites, a striking feature of this volume is that few of the chapters show extensive institutional, theological or personal interlinking. Only few and fleeting attempts have been made to initiate a nationwide, trans-denominational 'argument' for the pursuit of peace, though, as this book has demonstrated, evidence of the theme of peace can be traced right across the denominational spectrum. What do we make of this history of a recurring-and-yet-disjunctive impetus for peace?

We suggest that tradition is better understood in this case with the metaphor of a fertile landscape. New Zealand

Christianity has provided the conditions in which homegrown and transplanted seeds for peace have taken root, grown and flourished. Even without explicit conversation, these disparate attempts can and should be seen in relationship to each other—as parts of a creative and dynamic tradition for the pursuit of peace, extending across the spectrum of Christianities in New Zealand, the elements of which are apparent not only in the high-profile protests of an activist movement, but also in architecture, liturgy, institutional reform and theology. The task of examining this peace tradition is therefore geological as much as it is genealogical; we must examine the soil.

It is not an understatement to note that significant parts of the Christian tradition, in its broadest and most expansive sense, have been preoccupied with the question of peace. When we look at the 'soil', we find scriptures, commentaries, encyclicals, theological writings, sermons, art and architecture, liturgies, rituals, histories, hymns and prayers that serve as repositories and resources for normative Christian ethics. Within these, the theme of peace is a consistently prominent and haunting theme. Peace has been spoken about in passionate ways by Christian authors throughout the Common Era. Its absence has been mourned, and its attainment—fleeting as this often was—has been celebrated and cherished. This terrain has proven to be rich ground for peaceable imaginations.

But merely pointing to the presence of peaceable resources is insufficient. At stake is the question of how such resources have been deployed: how did flesh-and-blood Christians, and their communities and societies, translate these peaceable repositories into practice? We take it for granted that Christianity has, at best, a thoroughly chequered history regarding the practices of peace and violence. A reiteration here of incidents of 'Christian violence' is unnecessary, as most readers will not find it difficult to recall numerous such occasions, given their frequent representation in pop culture, journalism and scholarly work alike. Nevertheless, recalling that Christianity also has a bloody and conflictual past—and present—is an empirical and ethical imperative.

The Landscape of the Tradition

With this in mind, it must be acknowledged that a 'strong' peace stance has rarely been a central feature of New Zealand Christianity. Yet expressions of outright pacifism, conscientious objection, activist protesting and vocal opposition to warfare have been consistently expressed, as have broader commitments to costly reconciliation. Notwithstanding Chris Marshall's plea in his chapter for the normativity of Christian pacifism, and instances of activist peacemaking narrated in this volume, such positions have typically existed as a 'minority report'. In New Zealand, as elsewhere, Christian leaders have often supported the violent practices of the political status quo, or have themselves seen violence as a viable strategy for accomplishing their desired ends.

To point this out is not to deny the existence of a tradition. Christianity is profoundly fragmented along theological, denominational and political lines. Some Christian groupings have been far more active than others in actively cultivating the habits of peace, in nurturing peaceable imaginations and in legitimating public contestations over state-inflicted violence. Similarly, some Christian communities have created more space for enacting peace as reconciliation, social justice and ecological restoration than have others. The inclination toward peace, we argue, arises out of deliberate and concerted formation of particular habits, dispositions and affects. The fact that a peaceable impulse has emerged so frequently in New Zealand Christianity suggests that such nurturing communities have indeed been active in this country's history. In fact, it could be argued that such communities have functioned from the earliest period, from the outset of Christian mission among Māori in the early nineteenth century.[2]

Despite this long history, the few immediate or overt interconnections between the chapters in this book suggest a fragmented tradition, sustained in particular ways in different contexts, with no obvious institutional 'main trunk line'. Such fragmentation partly reflects the dynamics of earlier denominationalism, and more particularly of sectarianism and the sharp boundaries that operate in such forms of community.

Historically, sectarian Christianity has been a primary nurturing ground for strong peace traditions; and for various reasons the 'historic peace churches'—Mennonites, Church of the Brethren and Quakers—only ever had a limited presence in New Zealand. Another factor in fragmentation relates to the serious undermining of the missionary-Māori stream of New Zealand Christianity.[3] For a time, a Christian peace tradition seemed most thoroughly embedded within nineteenth-century missionary and Māori Christianity. Whilst this persisted in some respects, colonialism and the different priorities of settler Christianity eclipsed what might otherwise have been a more broadly influential and subversive feature of the tradition.

Another notable feature is the frequent influence of international events and precedents. New Zealand's tradition never represented the simple unfolding of an internal national history, hermetically sealed off from wider currents. The Waihopai action, as Adi Leason notes, drew on the American Catholic Worker Movement and the strategies devised by Ploughshares. For George Armstrong, it was American Quakers who provided the model that he sought to implement in the Hauraki Gulf. Peter Matheson points to Scottish and European influences on his peaceable politics. Andrew Shepherd writes about a group that initially began in the United Kingdom and was only recently established in New Zealand. All of this suggests a local peace tradition that was open to and shaped by international influences. Yet transnational links can also be overplayed. Global influences and precedents were often catalysts, acting episodically, and leading to sometimes surprising consequences; however, the crucial fact is that such organisations, ideas, models and relationships found a fertile soil in New Zealand. They were absorbed and reconfigured in ways that can only be called distinctly 'Kiwi'. It is hard to imagine the Waihopai action taking place in the manner it did anywhere else in the world, or the development of an organisation like Te Ora Hou.

While New Zealand's Christian peace tradition has been shaped by global Christianity and other international currents, there have also been distinctively local features. Notably, the place of Māori as tangata whenua (the indigenous people, literally 'people of the land') and the increasingly multicultural shape of contemporary New Zealand society loom large in recent history, and in many of the chapters of this book. These chapters highlight the way that growing awareness of the violence, pain and injustice that came with colonisation has shaped Christian thinking and peacemaking priorities. They also consistently highlight threads connecting the pursuit of peace with practices of justice, reconciliation and relationality.

Indeed, another striking feature in a number of the preceding chapters is the extent to which contemporary Christians have often seemed more comfortable referring to justice, reconciliation and restoration than employing explicit 'peace' language—even in relation to goals and practices that are explicitly understood to concern peacemaking. This may reflect a feeling that peace language has become strongly associated with (if not co-opted by) campaigning pacifist and anti-militarist agendas; or perhaps that peace language seems vague and lacks the precision conveyed by these other terms. It may also speak to the limits of a functional peace theology within the churches. Yet it also highlights something of the relative invisibility of New Zealand's Christian peace tradition—both in relation to opposing war, and in connection with broader projects promoting flourishing, wholeness and well-being.

Finally, it is crucial to remember that the New Zealand peace movement exceeds the frameworks, discourses and strategies proffered by Christianity. The Christian peace tradition in Godzone is not synonymous with the New Zealand peace tradition as such. They are certainly connected, and in some ways the broader national movement was birthed and incubated within particular parts of the Christian churches. But they also frequently ran parallel to each other, and they occasionally collided. Within the broad arc of New Zealand history, it is intriguing that the high point of peace activism in the 1970s and 1980s can also be identified as a crucial moment in the decline of institutional Christianity in New Zealand,[4] although it is unclear whether or not this relationship can be considered causal, and if so in which direction. Nevertheless, this conjuncture points to a series of tensions operating between Christian and secular histories of peace in New Zealand.

A Modest Proposal for Future Research

The insights provided in this book are by no means comprehensive or exhaustive. They are merely the tip of the iceberg. Indeed, a key aim of this volume, together with *Saints and Stirrers*, has been to open up debate about the relationship of peace to Christianity in New Zealand and the nature of the peace tradition. We have sought to complicate simplistic tropes that cast religion as a primary perpetrator of violence and discord, but also to stimulate new and better thinking around these issues. To this end, we conclude by offering a modest proposal for future research. Building upon some of the issues raised above, we suggest that further analysis might be focused fruitfully in four key areas.

The first of these areas concerns discourses. Closer examination of the semantics and uses of peace language would reveal much about the place of peace within New Zealand Christianity. Such research would involve addressing a number of central questions. For example: In what ways and contexts, and with what intended meaning, is peace language employed? What synonyms are used, and what are the boundaries of their related semantic fields? Unpacking these themes would help to expose substantive differences in theology and practice. It might also help to clarify the shape of 'the peace tradition' and its relationship to other expressions of virtue, for example, charity and welfare provision.

A second set of issues relates quite simply to practices. We need to know more about the actual practices of Christian anti-militarism, as well as those practices relating to cultivation of 'positive' peace—including the ritual, theological and communitarian bases to these. Among the most important approaches for examining these practices are historical and ethnographic methodologies. Through their attention to particular activities and events, these approaches facilitate a nuanced, textured and detailed understanding. While such approaches are helpfully supplemented and extended through quantitative methods, the value of 'thick' engagements is irreplaceable. In the case of the New Zealand Christian peace tradition, it is important to analyse not only those instances that capture media attention, but also the everyday, quotidian articulations of peace made in the process of apparently mundane Kiwi lives.

Relatedly, a third focus concerns communities. While wartime objectors and organisations such as the New Zealand Christian Pacifist Society are now reasonably well known, there remains much to explore about peace within a wider range of communities. These include Māori and migrant Christianities, Pentecostal and non-denominational churches, and a variety of other Christian groupings, including radical and independent forms. Very little research has been conducted on these increasingly prominent communities, much less on their ethical formations. Within the larger churches, there is more to know about the shape of the 'minority report'. Among smaller groups, many outstanding questions remain: whatever happened to Pentecostal pacifism in New Zealand, for example; and why did Quakers remain so numerically small, while capturing so much public attention? Recent work by Peter Lineham and Harry Ballis has revealed more about poorly understood sectarian groups in the period up until the Second World War, yet their more contemporary contours remain largely unexplored.[5] Beyond Christianity, peace practices and ideologies within other religious and spiritual communities also await investigation.

Finally, we need to understand more about connections. One of our suggestions above, drawn from the evidence of this volume, is that the New Zealand Christian peace tradition appears fragmented and disjointed. That impression warrants closer evaluation. Is the history of Christian peacemaking in New Zealand a history of disjuncture or of connection? The chapters by Peter Matheson and George Armstrong note moments of widespread interaction and co-operation, but it would require more systematic investigation to determine whether such moments have been characteristic or not. To what extent, and in what forms, have there been historical streams of New Zealand Christian peacemaking? What connections have existed between Christians of different stripes, and between Christians and others; and how have these shaped and sustained a peace tradition? Such exploration might extend to a more comprehensive analysis of global linkages and influences, and the similarities and differences between them and peace traditions in other national contexts.

Paying careful attention to these dimensions—discourses, practices, communities and connections—promises to enrich our understanding of the place of peace in New Zealand Christianity, and of the Christian peace tradition. Addressing such issues also promises to reveal much more about peace traditions more generally. More importantly, we believe that considering the pursuit of peace helps us to identify the resources that people deploy which enable human community to flourish even in the most trying and unpromising of circumstances. If the narratives in this volume are any guide, there are many more remarkable stories yet to be told. We look forward eagerly to their telling.

Notes

1. Pursuing Peace in Godzone—Introduction

1 Nicky Hager and John Stephenson, *Hit and Run: The New Zealand SAS in Afghanistan and the Meaning of Honour* (Nelson: Potton and Burton, 2017).

2 See: http://www.newshub.co.nz/home/new-zealand/2017/04/wellington-anzac-dawn-service-marred-by-protest-dispute.html.

3 Ron Johnston, 'Geopolitical Transition and International Realignment: The Case of New Zealand', *Geopolitics and International Boundaries* 2, no. 3 (1997), 43–69.

4 Kevin Clements, *Back from the Brink: The Creation of a Nuclear-Free New Zealand* (Wellington: Allen and Unwin, 1988); Malcolm Templeton, *Standing Upright Here: New Zealand in the Nuclear Age 1945–1990* (Wellington: Victoria University Press, 2006); Rebecca Priestley, *Mad on Radium: New Zealand in the Atomic Age* (Auckland: Auckland University Press, 2012); and Marie Leadbeater, *Peace, Power & Politics: How New Zealand Became Nuclear Free* (Dunedin: Otago University Press, 2013).

5 Johan Galtung, 'Twenty-Five Years of Peace Research: Ten Challenges and Some Responses', *Journal of Peace Research* 22, no. 2 (1985): 141–58; *Peace by Peaceful Means: Peace and Conflict, Development and Civilisation* (Oslo: PRIO, 1996).

6 The term 'Godzone', as used in this book's title, is a longstanding colloquial rendition of this famous phrase.

7 *Global Peace Index 2017* (Sydney: Institute for Economics and Peace, 2017), http://visionofhumanity.org/; John Helliwell, Richard Layard and Jeffrey Sachs, *World Happiness Report 2017* (New York: Sustainable Development Solutions Network, 2017), http://worldhappiness.report/.

8 Cited in Roberto Rabel, *New Zealand and the Vietnam War: Politics and Diplomacy* (Auckland: Auckland University Press, 2005), 161.

9 See: J. E. Cookson, 'Pacifism and Conscientious Objection in New Zealand', in *Challenge to Mars: Essays on Pacifism from 1914–1945*, eds. Peter Brock and Thomas P. Socknat (Toronto: University of Toronto Press, 1999); David Grant, *Field Punishment No. 1: Archibald Baxter, Mark Briggs and New Zealand's Anti-Militarist*

Tradition (Wellington: Steele Roberts, 2008); Geoffrey Troughton, ed., *Saints and Stirrers: Christianity, Conflict and the Peace Tradition in New Zealand, 1814–1945* (Wellington: Victoria University Press, 2017).

10 Vincent O'Malley, *The Great War for New Zealand: Waikato 1800–2000* (Wellington: Bridget Williams Books, 2016); Danny Keenan, *Wars Without End: The Land Wars in Nineteenth-century New Zealand* (North Shore: Penguin, 2009); James Belich, *The New Zealand Wars and the Victorian Interpretation of Racial Conflict* (Auckland: Penguin, 1986).

11 *Building the Future: Children and the Sustainable Development Goals in Rich Countries* (Florence: UNICEF Office of Research, 2017), https://www.unicef-irc.org/publications/pdf/RC14_eng.pdf.

12 Tom Frame, 'Anzac Day: Controversy and Criticism', in *Anzac Day Then and Now*, ed. Tom Frame (Sydney: University of New South Wales Press, 2017), 1.

13 On discussion of the question of New Zealand's reputed secularity, see: Geoffrey Troughton and Stuart Lange, eds., *Sacred Histories in Secular New Zealand* (Wellington: Victoria University Press, 2016).

14 Troughton, ed., *Saints and Stirrers.*

15 Richard Dawkins, *The God Delusion* (London: Bantam, 2006); Christopher Hitchens, *God is not Great: How religion poisons everything* (Crows Nest: Allen & Unwin, 2008). For brilliant, if very different, rebuttals see: William Cavanaugh, *The Myth of Religious Violence: Secular Ideology and the Roots of Modern Conflict* (Oxford: Oxford University Press, 2009); and Terry Eagleton, *Reason, Faith, and Revolution: Reflections on the God Debate* (New Hampshire: Yale University Press, 2010).

16 Timothy Fitzgerald, *Religion and Politics in International Relations: The Modern Myth* (London and New York: Continuum, 2011), 78–79.

17 Religion is best conceptualised not as a fixed essence, but rather as a 'moving target'. See: R. Michael Feener, Philip Fountain and Robin Bush, 'Outlook: Research on Religion and Development', in *Religion and the Politics of Development*, ed. Philip Fountain, Robin Bush and R. Michael Feener (London and New York: Palgrave Macmillan, 2015), 243.

18 John Howard Yoder, *The Politics of Jesus: Vicit Agnus Noster* (Grand Rapids: Eerdmans, 1972); Stanley Hauerwas, *The Peaceable Kingdom: A Primer in Christian Ethics* (Notre Dame: University of Notre Dame Press, 1983); Robert J. Schreiter, R. Scott Appleby and Gerard F. Powers, eds., *Peacebuilding: Catholic Theology, Ethics, and Praxis* (Maryknoll: Orbis, 2010); David P. Gushee, ed., *Evangelical Peacemakers: Gospel Engagement in a War-Torn World* (Eugene: Cascade, 2013).

19 Nicholas Wolterstorff, *Until Justice and Peace Embrace* (Grand Rapids: Eerdmans, 1983).
20 Isaiah 2:4; Micah 4:3.

2. Barrington, Burton and the Challenge of Christian Pacifism in New Zealand

1 Ormond Burton, *The Master of Men* (Wellington: National Committee of the Young Men's Christian Associations of N.Z., 1921), 19.
2 David Grant, *Out in the Cold: Pacifists and Conscientious Objectors in New Zealand during World War II* (Auckland: Reed Methuen, 1986); Ernest Crane, *I Can Do No Other: A Biography of Ormond Burton* (Auckland: Hodder and Stoughton, 1986); John Pratt, *The Prison Diary of A.C. Barrington: Dissent and Conformity in Wartime New Zealand* (Dunedin: Otago University Press, 2016); David Grant, *A Question of Faith: A History of the New Zealand Christian Pacifist Society* (Wellington: Philip Garside, 2004). Also, David Grant, 'The Reverend Ormond Burton and his Antagonists during the Second World War,' in *Saints and Stirrers: Christianity, Conflict, and Peacemaking in New Zealand, 1814–1945*, ed. Geoffrey Troughton (Wellington: Victoria University Press, 2017), 202–24.
3 L. H. Barber, *The Very Rev. James Gibb: Patriot into Pacifist* (Dunedin: Presbyterian Historical Society of New Zealand, 1973).
4 Ormond Burton, *Shall We Fight?* (Auckland: Clark & Matheson, 1923), 30; cited in Crane, 62.
5 According to Crane, Burton's Christian Socialism was perhaps best expressed in his article 'The Saviour of the World', *Methodist Times*, 31 May 1930, and an unpublished work, 'The Politics of Grace'; Crane, 88.
6 Grant, *A Question of Faith*, 26.
7 Allan K. Davidson and Peter J. Lineham, eds., *Transplanted Christianity: Documents Illustrating Aspects of New Zealand Church History* (2nd ed., Palmerston North: Dunmore Press, 1989), 293.
8 A copy of the pamphlet can be found in Crane, 110–11.
9 Grant, *A Question of Faith*, 20–21.
10 Cited in Crane, 114.
11 Archibald Barrington, *Trials of a Pacifist: Being Two Broadcast Talks Over New Zealand YC Stations* (Christchurch: Christian Pacifist Society, 1970), 10.
12 Barrington, 8.
13 Alun Richards was one of a group of theological students training for Presbyterian ministry who from 1927 to 1930 refused to attend compulsory military drill, which resulted in him losing his civil rights for ten years. See Harry R. Urquhart, *Guilty! Religious Objectors Lose Civil Rights!* (Auckland: Reliance Printery, 1929); also, Allan K.

Davidson, 'Compulsion or Conscience: Alun Richards and Opposition to Compulsory Military Training, 1927–1930,' in Troughton, ed.
14 See records of this conference in Crane, 116, and Grant, *A Question of Faith*, 37–39.
15 Pratt, 13.
16 Barrington, 6.
17 Cited in Crane, 118.
18 Crane, 170–71.
19 Cited in Crane, 125.
20 Cited in Crane, 138.
21 Pratt, ix.
22 Pratt, 153–74.
23 Pratt, i–iii.
24 Barrington, 19.
25 Crane, 181, citing Burton's unpublished autobiography, 'A Rich Old Man', 462–63.
26 Allan Davidson, 'Lest We Forget! Remembering War and Those Who Opposed War', paper presented at the Anglican Pacifist Fellowship Study Day, *Anzac Day: Where to From Here?*, St John's College, Auckland, 10 October 2009.
27 Barrington, 17.
28 Lisa S. Cahill, *Love Your Enemies: Discipleship, Pacifism, and Just War Theory* (Minneapolis, MN: Augsburg Fortress, 1994), 246.
29 Burton elaborated this position in greater detail in his rebuttal of Lloyd Geering's attack on the Christian belief in the resurrection, *To Whom Shall We Go?* (Auckland: Forward Books, 1973).
30 Barrington, 16.

3. A Historic Peace Church in Aotearoa New Zealand: Quakers and their Heritage

1 John 14:27.
2 There are three historic peace churches: Mennonites, Church of the Brethren, and the Quakers. Mennonites and Church of the Brethren trace their origins to the radical wing of the Protestant Reformation in continental Europe, Quakers to that in England. All three churches have consistently held to non-violence or pacifism as central to their understanding and practice of Christianity. Of these three, only the Quakers have established groups in Aotearoa New Zealand.
3 Margaret West and Ruth Fawell, *The Story of New Zealand Quakerism 1842–1972* (Auckland: New Zealand Yearly Meeting, 1973).
4 Cited in Edward Smith, *The Life of William Dewsbury* (London: Darton and Harvey, 1836), 29–30.
5 John L. Nickalls, ed., *Journal of George Fox* (London: Religious Society of Friends, 1975), 65, alluding to James 4:1–2.

6 Nickalls, 399–400.
7 Matthew 22:21; Mark 12:17; Luke 20:25.
8 Kevin Clements, 'What's a Quaker Like You Doing on a Committee Like This?,' *Friends Newsletter* (October 1986).
9 The full text is available at http://quaker.org.nz/ym-peace-statement.
10 Marian Hobbs, *A Peaceful World: How Can We Make It So?*, The Quaker Lecture 2016 (Wellington: Religious Society of Friends in Aotearoa New Zealand, Te Hāhi Tūhauwiri, 2016), 7.
11 The interrelation of peace with other testimonies such as equality and integrity is summarised in *Quaker Handbook: The Handbook of Practice and Procedure of the Religious Society of Friends, Yearly Meeting of Aotearoa New Zealand, Te Hāhi Tūhauwiri* (Christchurch: Yearly Meeting of Aotearoa New Zealand, 2000), section 2.4.
12 MS Minute Book I, Dunedin Monthly Meeting (formerly two-months meeting), 10 August 1919, minute 2, held by Dunedin Quaker Meeting.
13 For example, David Grant, *Field Punishment No. 1: Archibald Baxter, Mark Briggs and New Zealand's Anti-militarist Tradition*, with paintings by Bob Kerr (Wellington: Steele Roberts, 2008).
14 Margaret West, Audrey Brodie and James Brodie, eds, *Remembrance of Friends Past: Testimonies and Memorials to Lives and Works of New Zealand Quakers Who Died from 1843 to 1998* (Wellington: Beechtree Press, 1999), 28.
15 West et al., 35.
16 West et al., 56; *Minutes of Aotearoa New Zealand Yearly Meeting*, 1991, 14.
17 Caitriona Cameron, *Go Anywhere, Do Anything: New Zealanders in the Friends Ambulance Unit in China, 1945–1951* (Wellington: Beechtree Press, 1996).
18 West et al., 104, 109.
19 James Brodie and Audrey Brodie, *Seeking a New Land: Quakers in New Zealand* (Wellington: Beechtree Press, 1993), 163.
20 West et al., 97.
21 West et al., 89.
22 Adam Curle, *True Justice: Quaker Peace Makers and Peace Making* (London: Quaker Home Service, 1981), 101, 54, 100. The title of Curle's book alludes to James 3:18 (New English Bible): 'True justice is the harvest reaped by peacemakers from seeds sown in a spirit of peace.'
23 The Committee reported regularly. A useful interim survey of its work and achievements can be found in *Documents in Advance 2003* (Whanganui: Religious Society of Friends in Aotearoa New Zealand, 2003), 57–61.
24 *Advices and Queries of London Yearly Meeting 1840*, quoted in *Quaker Faith and Practice in Aotearoa New Zealand* (Auckland: The Religious Society of Friends (Quakers), Te Hāhi Tūhauwiri, 2003), 3.

25 *Quaker Handbook*, section 2.4.4.
26 Luke 10:29–37.

4. The Peace Squadron Revisited

1 For an early competent account of the Peace Squadrons, see: Tom Newnham, *Peace Squadron: The Sharp End of Nuclear Protest in New Zealand* (Auckland: Graphic Publications, 1986).
2 Bengt Danielsson and Marie-Thérèse Danielsson, *Moruroa mon Amour: The French Nuclear Tests in the Pacific* (London: Penguin, 1977), 55.
3 There was also an indisputably experimental dimension to the Hiroshima and Nagasaki bombs.
4 Though Montpellier accepted that the New Zealanders were right, he also excused his French countrymen on the grounds that their country had been invaded several times and needed a strong arsenal to scare off nuclear-armed adversaries. See George Andrews' meticulous documentary: *Nuclear Reaction: How New Zealand Became Nuclear Free* (Auckland: George Andrews Productions, 1995).
5 Admittedly with some reluctance on the part of Prime Minister Keith Holyoake. Unlike Australia, New Zealand did not send conscripts to Vietnam.
6 Peter Hayes, Lyuba Zarsky and Walden Bello, *American Lake: Nuclear Peril in the Pacific* (New York: Viking Penguin, 1986).
7 For a firsthand account of these events see: Richard K. Taylor, *Blockade: A Guide to Non-Violent Intervention* (Maryknoll: Orbis, 1977).
8 From the early 1970s St John's and Trinity worked in partnership at the St John's campus in Meadowbank.
9 See: Aroha Harris, *Hīkoi: Forty Years of Māori Protest* (Wellington: Huia, 2004).
10 See the recent controversial and seminal book by Swami Agnivesh, *Applied Spirituality: A Spiritual Vision for the Dialogue of Religions* (Noida, India: Harper Collins, 2015).
11 Though the latter is, at least, not without ambiguity. The Bible ironically contradicts itself by picturing the vulnerable David, made mighty by his victory and by seizure of the stunned Goliath's sword, as himself turning brutal and cutting off Goliath's head (1 Samuel 17).
12 David McTaggart, *Greenpeace III: Journey into the Bomb* (London: Collins, 1978), 29.
13 Edward's approach happily contrasts with the current Anglican Bishop of Wellington, Justin Duckworth, who in 2015, at the very same time in which I presented an earlier version of this paper at the initial conference, was actively protesting a global armaments bazaar being held in Wellington. In full episcopal regalia—together with familiar

matching dreadlocks and bare feet—Justin denounced the brazen trading of apparatus designed to turn human beings into body parts. He also decried the willingness of the nation's capital city to play host to such inhuman trading.

14 See: Maire Leadbeater, *Peace, Power & Politics: How New Zealand Became Nuclear Free* (Dunedin: Otago University Press, 2013); also, Kevin Clements, *Back from the Brink: The Creation of a Nuclear-Free New Zealand* (Wellington: Allen and Unwin, 1988). For an account of these dramatic changes that also examines the history of 'pro-nuclear' sentiment in New Zealand, see: Rebecca Priestley, *Mad on Radium: New Zealand in the Atomic Age* (Auckland: Auckland University Press, 2012).

5. Revolution at the Kitchen Tables: Churches and the 1980s Peace Movement

1 Maire Leadbeater, *Peace Power & Politics: How New Zealand Became Nuclear Free* (Dunedin: Otago University Press, 2013).

2 Kevin Clements, *Back from the Brink: The Creation of a Nuclear-Free New Zealand* (Wellington: Allen & Unwin, 1988), 119.

3 Paul Reeves, 'A Pacific Perspective on Peace in the Nuclear Age', January 1985; SJC010/3.00/8, John Kinder Theological Library, St John's College, Auckland (JKTL). Archival holdings of the JKTL and the Archives Research Centre of the Presbyterian Church of Aoteaoroa New Zealand, Dunedin, have provided the basic documentation for this chapter. See especially the Presbyterian records pertaining to the International Relations Committee; the Council for Mission and Ecumenical Cooperation (COMEC); the Public Questions Committee; and the Churches' Agency on Social Issues (CASI).

4 For a thorough report on the effects of nuclear testing in the Pacific see: Tilman Ruff, 'The Humanitarian Impact and Implications of Nuclear Test Explosions in the Pacific Region', *International Review of the Red Cross* 97, no. 899 (2015): 775–813.

5 Christina Steenkamp, *Violent Societies: Networks of Violence in Civil War and Peace* (Basingstoke: Macmillan, 2014), 121–28.

6 Though see, relating to an earlier period: Matthew O'Meagher, 'The New Zealand Campaign for Nuclear Disarmament: Its Birth and Early Years' (BA Hons dissertation, University of Otago, 1985).

7 On earlier pacifism in New Zealand Christianity, see the chapter by Tom Noakes-Duncan in this volume. Also: Geoffrey Troughton, ed., *Saints and Stirrers: Christianity, Conflict and Peacemaking in New Zealand, 1814–1945* (Wellington: Victoria University Press, 2017); Allan K. Davidson, 'Peace and Pacifism: New Zealand Presbyterians 1901–45', in *Reforming the Reformation: Essays in Honour of Principal Peter Matheson*, ed. Ian Breward (Melbourne: Australian

Scholarly Publishing, 2004), 181–96; Kenneth G. Stead, 'Involvement of Members of the Auckland Diocese of the Anglican Church in the Peace Movement since 1945' (MA thesis, Massey University, 1999).

8 Allan K. Davidson, 'Chaplain to the Nation or Prophet at the Gate?', in *Christianity, Modernity and Culture: New Perspectives on New Zealand History*, ed. John Stenhouse and G. A. Wood (Adelaide: ATF Press, 2005), 311–31.

9 Report of Speakers Sub-Committee, 9 October 1957, Folder 1, Auckland Campaign for Nuclear Disarmament Papers (JKTL).

10 *Nelson Evening Mail*, 29 June 1966.

11 *New Zealand Herald*, 15 November 1982.

12 See: Tom Newnham, *Peace Squadron: The Sharp End of Nuclear Protest in New Zealand* (Auckland: Graphic Publications, 1986).

13 See: Ray Galvin, *A Nuclear-Free New Zealand . . . Now!* (Auckland: Belmont Publishers, 1984); also, *The Peace of Christ in a Nuclear Age* (Auckland: G. W. Moore, Ltd., 1983).

14 Lynne M. Woehrle, Patrick G. Coy and Gregory M. Maney, *Contesting Patriotism: Culture, Power and Strategy in the Peace Movement* (Plymouth: Rowman and Littlefield, 2008), 114, argues from recent US experience that committed churchgoers were twice as likely to be engaged in protests and civil disobedience as others.

15 Stead, 72.

16 The Kairos Theologians, *The Kairos Document: Challenge to the Church: A Theological Comment on the Political Crisis in South Africa* (Braamfontein: Skotaville Publishers, 1986).

17 COMEC, 'Nuclear Weapons and Anzus,' presented to the Presbyterian General Assembly in 1986 and 1987; see PGA, 1985, 1986, 1987.

18 This journey is described by Eljean Brash and Alan Brash in *Crossing the Walls: A Journey for Peace* (Christchurch: National Council of Churches, 1984).

19 Stead, 79; see also the chapter by George Armstrong in this volume.

20 Suliana Siwatibau and David Williams, *A Call to a New Exodus: An Anti-Nuclear Primer for Pacific People* (Suva: Pacific Council of Churches, 1982).

21 Methodist-Presbyterian Workgroup for Peace, *Peacemaking: The Christian Imperative* (Christchurch: Council for Mission and Ecumenical Co-operation, 1986).

22 Larry Ross founded the New Zealand Nuclear-Free Peacemaking Association in 1981, and was an outspoken campaigner. An Australian physician and anti-nuclear advocate, Helen Caldicott's writings include: *Nuclear Madness: What You Can Do!* (Brookline, Mass.: Autumn Press, 1978); *Missile Envy: The Arms Race and Nuclear War* (New York: Morrow, 1984).

23 See the Presbyterian Church paper: 'Christian Perspectives on Disarmament: A Contemporary Comment', in PGA, 1982.

24 The Khandallah minister, the Rev. Rhys Pearson, faced protests when he suggested use of retiring collections for peacemaking purposes. Stead, 88, suggests that only a minority of church members ever had a conscious theological motivation.

6. The Treaty, the Church and the Reconciliation of Christ

1 John Bluck, *Wai Karekare Turbulent Waters: The Anglican Bicultural Journey 1814–2014* (Hong Kong: The Anglican Church in Aotearoa, New Zealand and Polynesia, 2012), 27.
2 Claudia Orange notes that the Treaty became known as Te Kawenata o Waitangi (Covenant of Waitangi), especially among Ngāpuhi Māori. Some government agents also promoted this understanding of the Treaty as a sacred compact. See: Claudia Orange, *The Treaty of Waitangi* (Wellington: Allen and Unwin, 1987), 49, 57, 90–91, 150.
3 Bluck, 57.
4 Bluck, 60–61.
5 The Commission comprised both Māori and Pākehā, and over subsequent iterations also included representatives from the Diocese of Polynesia, in recognition of their longstanding relationship with the Anglican Church in New Zealand. This relationship dates back to 1925, when the Diocese of Polynesia became an Associated Missionary Diocese of the Province of New Zealand.
6 Bishop Jabez Bryce, Archbishop Brian Davis and Bishop Te Whakahuihui Vercoe, 1994, Video recording, John Kinder Library.
7 'The Constitution Amendment Statute 1990.' Paper Presented at the Fiftieth General Synod/Te Hinota Whanui, Hamilton, 1992, S-12(a).
8 Ibid.
9 Archbishop Brian Davis, 'General Synod Address 1992.' Presented at the Fiftieth General Synod/Te Hinota Whanui, Hamilton, 1992.
10 Psalm 85:10–11.
11 Jenny Plane Te Paa, 'Theological Hui Report to the General Synod/Te Hinota Whanui.' Paper Presented at the Fifty-Seventh General Synod/ Te Hinota Whanui, Christchurch, 2006, R-121.
12 The question of commitment to the principles of the Treaty continues to be discussed. In 2016 the Treaty/Tiriti Church and Nation Commission called for a Working Group to consider the Treaty Partnership in 2017 and report to General Synod in 2018.
13 Winston Halapua, 'Report of the Commission on Treaty and Partnership Issues.' Paper Presented at the Fifty-Third General Synod/ Te Hinota Whanui, Auckland, 1998, R-106.
14 See: Jenny Te Paa Daniel, 'A Heartfelt Critique of the Three Tikanga Church', Progressive Christianity Aotearoa, https://progressivechristianityaotearoa.com/2014/03/24/critique-three-tikanga/, 24 March 2014.

15 Halapua, R-106.
16 Christopher Tremewan, 'Re-politicising Race: The Anglican Church in New Zealand', in *Public Policy and Ethnicity: the Politics of Ethnic Boundary Making*, ed. Elizabeth Rata and Roger Openshaw (Basingstoke: Palgrave Macmillan, 2006), 95–112.
17 Wayne Rangi Nicholson, 'Ko Te Mea Nui, Ko Te Aroha: Theological Perspectives on Māori Language and Cultural Regenesis Policy and Practice of the Anglican Church' (PhD thesis, University of Auckland, 2009), 212, 214.
18 Muru Walters, 'The Anglican Church', in *Weeping Waters: The Waitangi Tribunal and Constitutional Change*, ed. Malcolm Mulholland and Veronica Tawhai (Wellington: Huia, 2010), 227.
19 Nicholson, 224.
20 Jenny Plane Te Paa, 'On Being Te Ahorangi: An "Underside" Experience of the Constitution of the Anglican Church in Aotearoa', in *Thinking Outside the Square: Church in Middle Earth*, ed. Ree Bodde and Hugh Kempster (Auckland: St Columba's Press, 2003), 318.
21 David Moxon, 'A Trinitarian Theological Reflection for a Three Tikanga Church: For Kotahitanga.' Paper Presented at the Fifty-Seventh General Synod/Te Hinota Whanui, Christchurch, 2006, A-31.
22 Jim Greenaway and Stephanie McIntyre, *Strangers in the Land: Migration. The Aotearoa New Zealand Story and Biblical Reflections in a Three Tikanga Church* (Wellington: New Zealand Anglican Social Justice Commission, 1996), 5.
23 Philip Culbertson, 'Pastoral Theology and Multiculturalism', *Anglican Theological Review* 79, no. 2 (1997): 165.
24 Jenny Chalmers, 'If There is Neither Jew Nor Greek, Slave Nor Free, Why Do We Have a Three Tikanga Church?' *Wellington Institute of Theology Newsletter* (2015): 6.
25 At the 1992 presentation of the revised Constitution, Archbishop Brian Davis explicitly warned General Synod about the danger that they would be 'so distracted by the demands of ecclesial change, that we will have little energy left to do the essential work of mission'; Davis, 7. This concern has subsequently been reiterated by others.
26 For an account of the Hikoi of Hope see: Mike Mawson, 'Believing in Protest: The Liberal Idea of the Separation of Religion and Politics in Two Recent Religious Protests', *New Zealand Sociology* 21, no. 2 (2006): 196–214.
27 John Paterson, 'Address by the Presiding Bishop/Primate/Te Pīhopa Mātāmua.' Paper Presented at the Fifty-Fourth Ordinary Session of the General Synod/Te Hinota Whanui, Auckland, 2000, ix.
28 Nyasha Jasman Gumbeze, 'A Critical Examination of the Three Tikanga Model of the Anglican Church of Aotearoa New Zealand and Polynesia from a Migrant Perspective: Considering the Pastoral

Implications for "Outsiders"' (MTheol thesis, University of Auckland, 2010), 128.

29 An historic General Conference between Māori and Pākehā in Napier just before General Synod in May 2016 set aside any agenda other than open dialogue/kōrero that acknowledged the effects of the Three Tikanga silos and sought for ways to build genuine relationships. Archbishop Philip Richardson reminded those present that the Gospel, the Treaty and Te Pouhere bind them together in ways that mean they must seek each other's good, while Archbishop Brown Turei challenged delegates to practice God's radical hospitality, or manaakitanga, with one another.

30 Gumbeze, 130.

7. Taranaki, Coventry and the Paths of Peace and Reconciliation

1 To our Creator, glorify his name for all time.

2 Danny Keenan, *Wars Without End: The Land Wars in Nineteenth Century New Zealand* (Auckland: Penguin, 2009); James Belich, *The New Zealand Wars and the Victorian Interpretation of Racial Conflict* (Auckland: Penguin, 1988); Tim Ryan and Bill Parham, *The Colonial New Zealand Wars* (Wellington: Grantham House, 2002); Keith Sinclair, *The Origins of the Maori Wars* (Auckland: Oxford University Press, 1974).

3 Margaret H. Alington, *Goodly Stones and Timbers: A History of St Mary's Church, New Plymouth* (New Plymouth, Saint Mary's Church, 1988), 14.

4 *Taranaki Herald*, 4 November 1901, 2; 28 April 1904, 5.

5 Andrew Moffat, 'Their Lives for the Empire: The Memorial Hatchments at Taranaki Cathedral' (2013). Copies of this unpublished booklet are held at Taranaki Cathedral.

6 Alington, 51, 146.

7 See also Elsdon Best, 'Raumahora and Takarangi: A Legend of the Taranaki Tribes', *Journal of the Polynesian Society* 36, no. 143 (1927): 239–59; Tony Sole, *Ngāti Ruanui: A History* (Wellington: Huia, 2005), 81.

8 The occasion was marked by a service led by the Archbishop of York, John Sentamu, kaumatua the Venerable Tiki Raumati, and Bishop Sir Paul Reeves.

9 John O'Leary, 'A Colonial Curiosity: The Maori Poroaki as Victorian Dramatic Monologue', *Kōtare* 3, no. 2 (2000): 42–45; for a full version of the original text, 42–44.

10 On Parihaka, see: Danny Keenan, *Te Whiti O Rongomai and the Resistance of Parihaka* (Wellington: Huia, 2015); Rachel Buchanan, *The Parihaka Album: Lest We Forget* (Wellington: Huia, 2009); Hazel Riseborough, *Days of Darkness: Taranaki, 1878–1884*, rev.

ed. (Auckland: Penguin, 2002); Te Miringa Hohaia, Gregory O'Brien and Lara Strongman, eds, *Parihaka: The Art of Passive Resistance* (Wellington: Victoria University Press, 2001); Dick Scott, *Ask That Mountain: The Story of Parihaka* (Auckland: Heinemann, 1975).

11 Matthew 5:9.

12 Kawe mate is a mourning ceremony, held at another marae (rather than the home marae) subsequent to the tangihanga and burial. It is generally used as a way to acknowledge the links between two groups of people, while both groups recognise those who have passed on and the relationship between their communities.

8. Maungārongo ki te Whenua: Te Ora Hou Making its Peace

1 Mason Durie, *Ngā Kāhui Pou: Launching Māori Futures* (Wellington: Huia, 2003).

2 Lloyd Martin, *One Faith, Two Peoples: Communicating Across Cultures Within the Church* (Paraparaumu: Salt Co. Publishers, 1990).

3 *Positive Youth Development in Aotearoa: Weaving Connections – Tūhonohono Rangatahi* (Wayne Francis Charitable Trust, Youth Advisory Group, 2011). See http://wfct.org.nz.

4 Claudia Orange, 'The Māori and the Crown', in *The Oxford Illustrated History of New Zealand*, ed. Keith Sinclair (Auckland: Oxford University Press, 1999), 21–48.

5 L. Davis, Te Ora Hou National Board Member, personal communication, May 2015.

6 *Boy*, directed by Taika Waititi (Whenua Films/Unison Films, 2010).

7 'Ow' is a slang term used by people who know each other, in this case meaning 'mate' in a slightly derogatory way.

8 *Drug Use in New Zealand: Key Results of the 2007/08 New Zealand Alcohol and Drug Use Survey* (Wellington: Ministry of Health, 2010).

9 Moana Eruera, '"Hooked up": Te Hononga Whaiāipo: Reducing and Preventing Violence in Taitamariki Māori Intimate Partner Relationships' (PhD thesis, Te Whare Wānanga o Awanuiārangi, 2015).

10 Sam Chapman, Te Ora Hou Staff Training, Whangarei, 2005.

11 Di Grennell and Fiona Cram, 'Evaluation of Amokura: An Indigenous Family Violence Prevention Strategy', *MAI Review* 2, no. 4 (2008): http://www.review.mai.ac.nz/index.php/MR/article/view/157/156.

12 International donors include: the Cooperative for Assistance and Relief Everywhere (CARE); the United Nations Population Fund (UNFPA); the National Endowment for Democracy; International Alert; the United Nations Development Fund for Women (UNIFEM); the United Nations Alliance of Citizens (UNAOC); and the United States Agency for International Development (USAID).

13 Bishnu Upreti, *Armed Conflict and Peace Process in Nepal: The Maoist Insurgency, Past Negotiations, and Opportunities for Conflict Transformation* (New Delhi: Adroit Publishers, 2006).

9. Icons of Peace

1 Pōneke is the transliteration of Port Nicholson, the English name for Te Whanganui-a-Tara, the great harbour of Tara (Wellington Harbour).

2 *Catechism of the Catholic Church*: 1162.

3 For a straightforward introduction to the tradition of icons in Christianity see: Elizabeth Zelensky and Lela Gilbert, *Windows to Heaven: Introducing Icons to Protestants and Catholics* (Grand Rapids: Brazos Press, 2005).

4 Chris Orsman and Peter Zwart (compilers), *Church in the World: Statements on Social Issues, 1979–1997 by New Zealand's Catholic Bishops* (Wellington: Catholic Office of Social Justice, 1997), 7.

5 Jack Duggan, ed., *Saint Joseph's Parish Te Aro and Mount Victoria: A Perspective of our Parish History and Catholic Faith, 1885 to 2007* (Wellington: St Joseph's, 2007), 143. Duggan himself exemplifies this by highlighting some very sharp questions around the role of women, the paternalistic and centralised powers of the Church hierarchy, celibacy, married clergy and key beliefs.

6 Yitzhak Rabin was twice a Prime Minister of Israel and co-winner of the 1994 Nobel Peace Prize for his involvement in facilitating the Oslo Accords between the government of Israel and the Palestine Liberation Organization. He was assassinated by an Israeli extremist in 1995. A plaque was erected near Civic Square in Wellington in 2000 to commemorate Rabin's life.

7 NZPA, 'Priest unrepentant over bloody Gaza protest', *Stuff*, 7 January 2009, http://www.stuff.co.nz/national/786200/Priest-unrepentant-over-bloody-Gaza-protest.

8 Michael O'Meeghan, *Steadfast in Hope: The Story of the Catholic Archdiocese of Wellington, 1850–2000* (Palmerston North: Dunmore Press, 2003), 240.

9 These links are evident on the website of the Catholic Parish of Wellington South, to which St Joseph's belongs. Indeed, this parish name is envisaged as an interim name: it will become The Parish of the Blessed Suzanne Aubert, as soon as Suzanne Aubert's beatification (a key milestone on the path to recognition as a Saint within the Catholic Church) is confirmed. See: http://wellingtonsouthcatholic.org/?page_id=426.

10 See especially: Jessie Munro, *The Story of Suzanne Aubert* (Wellington: Bridget Williams Books, 2009), 23.

11 On the changes of Vatican II see: Norman Tanner, ed., *Vatican II: The Essential Texts* (New York: Image, 2012); John O'Malley, *What*

Happened at Vatican II? (Cambridge: Harvard University Press, 2010); Matthew Lamb and Matthew Levering, eds., *Vatican II: Renewal within Tradition* (Oxford: Oxford University Press, 2008). For accounts of its effects in New Zealand see: Pauline O'Regan, *A Changing Order* (Wellington: Allen and Unwin, 1986); Elizabeth Isichei, 'Australia and New Zealand', in *Modern Catholicism, Vatican II and After*, ed. Adrian Hastings (Oxford: Oxford University Press, 1990), 334–44.

12 See: http://www.studiopacific.co.nz/projects/2002/st-josephs-church/.

13 Kay Blundell, 'Artist 'humbled' to receive award,' *Dominion Post*, 9 June 2012, http://www.stuff.co.nz/dominion-post/news/queens-birthday/7069982/Artist-humbled-to-receive-award.

14 http://www.catholicnewsagency.com/news/vatican-announces-desire-for-more-restrained-sign-of-peace-at-mass-36123/.

15 Munro, 235.

10. Missionary Peacemaking: New Zealand Activists and the Decolonisation of Southern Africa

1 For surveys of New Zealand overseas missionary work, see: Allan K. Davidson, 'The New Zealand Overseas Missionary Contribution', in Allan Davidson and Godfrey Nicholson, eds, *'With All Humility and Gentleness': Essays on Mission in Honour of Francis Foulkes* (Auckland: St John's College, 1991), 41–50; Allan Davidson, 'New Zealand', and John Roxborogh, 'New Zealand Mission Boards and Societies', in A. Scott Moreau, ed., *Evangelical Dictionary of World Missions* (Grand Rapids, Michigan: Baker Books, 2000), 687–88; Hugh Morrison, *Pushing Boundaries: New Zealand Protestants and Overseas Missions 1827–1939* (Dunedin: Otago University Press, 2016).

2 Hugh Morrison, '"It is Our Bounden Duty": Theological Contours of New Zealand's Missionary Movement, 1890–1930', *International Bulletin of Missionary Research* 29, no. 3 (2005): 123.

3 David B. Barrett, ed., *World Christian Encyclopaedia: A Comparative Study of Churches and Religions in the Modern World 1900–2000* (Oxford University Press, 1982), 522.

4 Michael W. Casey, *The Rhetoric of Sir Garfield Todd: Christian Imagination and the Dream of an African Democracy* (Waco, Texas: Baylor University Press, 2007), 31.

5 Ruth Weiss, *Sir Garfield Todd and the Making of Zimbabwe* (London: British Academic Press, 1999), 36; Susan Paul, draft authorised biography of Garfield Todd (2016), 65.

6 Todd, 1962, in Casey, 28–29.

7 Weiss, 18. For Todd on his own political 'guileless-ness' see: Norman Harris, *The Fly Away People* (London: Baynard-Hillier, 1971), 154, 168–9.

8 R.S.G. Todd, 'University of Otago Graduation Speech', 7 December 1979, in Casey, 313.

9 R.S.G. Todd, 'Our Timeless Missionary Mandate', World Convention of Churches of Christ, Toronto, 17 August 1955, in Casey, 163.
10 R.S.G. Todd, 'Conference Sermon', Invercargill [April, 1950], in Casey, 128.
11 Todd, 'Conference Sermon' and 'Our Timeless Missionary Mandate', in Casey, 132–33, 163.
12 Harris, 159.
13 C.M. Brand, 'African Nationalists and Missionaries in Rhodesia', in M.F.C. Bourdillon, ed., *Christianity South of the Zambezi, Volume 2* (Gwelo: Mambo Press, 1977), 73.
14 Robert Blake, *A History of Rhodesia* (London: Eyre Methuen, 1977), 273–306.
15 After independence, he gave 3,000 acres to guerrillas disabled in the war and in the 1990s sold the farm and created a scholarship fund for Zimbabwean students. Casey, 87.
16 David Lamb, *The Africans: Encounters from the Sudan to the Cape*, rev. ed. (London: Methuen, 1985), 142; Norman H. Murdoch, *Christian Warfare in Rhodesia-Zimbabwe: The Salvation Army and African Liberation, 1881–1991* (Eugene, Oregon: Pickwick, 2015), 149–57.
17 Weiss, 198, 200.
18 See Casey, 101.
19 Weiss, 220.
20 Casey, 70.
21 Michael Lapsley to Pamela Welch, personal communication, 20 October 2015.
22 Dawn Tratt, 'Tutu Thanks New Zealand on Eve of Retiring', *Otago Daily Times*, 8 October 2010, 6.
23 Elizabeth Gordon to Pamela Welch, personal communication, 17 November 2015. Elizabeth is John Osmers' sister.
24 C.F. Andrews, *What I Owe to Christ* (London: Hodder and Stoughton, 1932); Benarsidas Chaturvedi and Marjorie Sykes, *Charles Freer Andrews: A Narrative; With a Foreword by M.K. Gandhi* (London: George Allen and Unwin Ltd, 1949).
25 John Osmers, '50 Years' Challenge in Southern and Central Africa', *CR Quarterly* no. 449 (2015): 14–17; also 'Fifty Years' Challenge in Southern and Central Africa: Part Two', *CR Quarterly* no. 550 (2015): 9–11.
26 'Honouring the Prophets: John Osmers—a Voice in Africa', *The Common Good* no. 31 (2004); see http://catholicworker.org.nz/the-common-good/john-osmers/.
27 Michael Lapsley with Stephen Karakashian, *Redeeming the Past: My Journey from Freedom Fighter to Healer* (Maryknoll: Orbis Books, 2012), 7.
28 Elizabeth Gordon to Pamela Welch, personal communication, 17 November 2015.

29 John Osmers to Pamela Welch, personal communication, 30 October 2015.
30 SSM originated in England; work was begun in Australia in 1947. See: Alistair Mason, *History of the Society of the Sacred Mission* (Norwich: The Canterbury Press, 1993), 226.
31 Michael Lapsley to Pamela Welch, personal communication, 17 October 2015; Michael Worsnip, *Michael Lapsley, Priest and Partisan: A South African Journey* (Melbourne: Ocean Press, 1996), 1, 136.
32 Lapsley with Karakashian, 36, 37, 43–44.
33 Lapsley to Welch, personal communication, 17 October 2015.
34 Michael Lapsley, *Neutrality or Co-option? Anglican Church and State from 1964 until the Independence of Zimbabwe*, Mambo Occasional Papers—Missio-Pastoral Series No. 16 (Gweru: Mambo Press, 1986).
35 Lapsley with Karakashian, 91–97.
36 Lapsley with Karakashian, 105.
37 Worsnip, 1, 3–4, 5–6; Lapsley with Karakashian, back cover.
38 Nelson Mandela, 'Foreword', in Lapsley with Karakashian, 3.

11. Migrant Peacemakers? African Pentecostals in New Zealand

1 Carl Walrond, 'Africans – Africans in New Zealand', *Te Ara – The Encyclopedia of New Zealand*, http://www.TeAra.govt.nz/en/africans/page-1.
2 Annalisa Butticci, 'Religion in Motion: A Missionary Narrative of Creativity and Survival from the Pentecostal Nigeria Diaspora in Italy', in *Religion on the Move! New Dynamics of Religious Expansions in a Globalizing World*, ed. Afe Adogame and Shobana Shankar (Boston: Brill, 2013), 203–21; André Corden and Ruth Marshall-Fratani, eds., *Between Babel and Pentecost: Transnational Pentecostalism in Africa and Latin America* (Bloomington: Indiana University Press, 2001); Afe Adogame, *The African Christian Diaspora: New Currents and Emerging Trends in World Christianity* (London: Bloomsbury, 2013).
3 See: Jay Beaman, *Pentecostal Pacifism: The Origin, Development, and Rejection of Pacific Belief among the Pentecostals* (Eugene: Wipf & Stock, 2009). Also, on New Zealand: Peter Lineham, 'Sects and War in New Zealand', in *Saints and Stirrers: Christianity, Conflict, and Peacemaking in New Zealand, 1814–1945*, ed. Geoffrey Troughton (Wellington: Victoria University Press, 2017), 163–82.
4 In 2016 there were three APCs in Wellington, five in Auckland, and two in Christchurch.
5 Cynthia Cannon Poindexter, Mark Henrickson, Christa Fouché, Derek Brown and Kay Scott, '"They Don't Even Greet You": HIV Stigma and Diagnosis Disclosure Experienced by HIV-Positive African Immigrants and Refugees in New Zealand', *Journal of HIV/AIDS & Social Services* 12, no. 1 (2013): 99–120.

6 Ibid., 101. This included migrants entering New Zealand on its Special Zimbabwe Residence Policy and subsequent waiver in 2006 that allowed HIV-positive Zimbabweans to apply for residency. See: 'New Zealand Introduces Visas for Zimbabweans', *Africa News Service*, 21 February 2003.
7 Martine Udahemuka and Regina Pernice, 'Does Motivation to Migrate Matter? Voluntary and Forced African Migrants and Their Acculturation Preferences in New Zealand', *Journal of Pacific Rim Psychology* 4, no. 1 (2010): 44–52.
8 David Cortright, *Peace: A History of Movements and Ideas* (Cambridge: Cambridge University Press, 2008), 13, citing Godfrey Igwebuike Onah.
9 John S. Mbiti, '"Never Break the Pot That Keeps You Together": Peace and Reconciliation in African Religion', *Dialogue & Alliance* 1 (Spring/Summer 2010): 4.
10 Jonathan Crush and Daniel S. Tevera, eds., *Zimbabwe's Exodus: Crisis, Migration, Survival* (Cape Town: International Development Research Centre, and Ebrary, Inc., 2010), 1–3.

12. Ploughshares at Waihopai

1 On the New Zealand Catholic Worker Movement see: http://catholicworker.org.nz/.
2 For more about Dorothy Day, Peter Maurin and the Catholic Worker Movement, see: Dorothy Day, *The Long Loneliness: The Autobiography of Dorothy Day* (New York: HarperOne, 2009); Jim Forest, *All is Grace: A Biography of Dorothy Day* (MaryKnoll: Orbis, 2011); Peter Maurin, *Easy Essays* (Chicago: Franciscan Herald Press, 1984); Mark Ellis, *Peter Maurin: Prophet in the Twentieth Century* (New York: Paulist Press, 1981); Patrick Coy, ed., *A Revolution of the Heart: Essays on the Catholic Worker* (Philadelphia: Temple University Press, 1988); Mark and Louise Zwick, *The Catholic Worker Movement: Intellectual and Spiritual Origins* (New York: Paulist Press, 2005).
3 See: 'The Aims and Means of the Catholic Worker Movement', http://www.catholicworker.org/cw-aims-and-means.html.
4 Cited in Stanley Vishnewski, *Wings of the Dawn* (New York: Catholic Worker, 1984). See: https://cjd.org/2006/10/01/meeting-dorothy-day-and-peter-maurin/.
5 Isaiah 2:4.
6 The story of this action is told in Ciaron O'Reilly, *Bomber Grounded, Runway Closed: Prison Letters and Court Notes of a Gulf War Resister* (Marion: Rose Hill Books, 1994).
7 Cole was a pioneer in the Catholic Worker and Ploughshares movements in New Zealand. Alongside Ciaron O'Reilly, she had been

one of the four activists involved in the Ploughshares action at Griffiss Air Force Base in 1991.

8 Oscar Romero was a priest, and from 1977, Archbishop of San Salvador. An outspoken voice for the poor, he stood courageously against poverty, violence and political corruption; he advocated for justice on many fronts, and supported peaceful solutions to the conflicts and national crises unfolding within El Savador in his time. He was assassinated on 24 March 1980 by his opponents while celebrating the Eucharist in a small hospital chapel.

13. Restoring Karioi: Ecology, Community and the Practice of Peace

1 A Rocha is a Christian conservation organisation that started in the early 1980s in Portugal and now operates in twenty countries. For the history of A Rocha see: Peter Harris, *Under the Bright Wings* (Bellingham: Regent College Publishing, 2000); *Kingfisher's Fire: A Story of Hope for God's Earth* (Oxford: Monarch, 2008). See also: http://www.arocha.org/en/our-history/ and http://www.arocha.org/en/values/; and, on A Rocha Aotearoa New Zealand: http://www.arocha.org.nz/. For the Karioi Project see: https://www.karioimaunga.co.nz/.

2 The tribal groups of Whāingaroa, namely Tainui, Ngāti Hounuku, Ngāti Ikaunahi, Ngāti Kōata, Ngāti Māhanga, Ngāti Hourua, Ngāti Tahinga, Ngāti Tamainupō, Ngāti Kōtara and Ngāti Te Huaki, are the kaitiaki (custodians, guardians) of Whāingaroa—of the harbour, sea and waterways, of the land, and of the foreshore.

3 Hapū to the south of Karioi have a variant on this genealogy. To them, Karioi is the husband who formerly stood inland with his wife Karewa. They gave birth to their children, after which Karioi turned his attention to Pirongia. On her discovery of this adulterous affair Karewa fled westward to the coast and out into the ocean. Karioi followed her, but caught by the final rays of the setting sun, was turned to stone. Karioi remains, sentinel-like on the coast, staring out at his estranged wife, while Pirongia remains inland, isolated, living with the shame of her actions. Karewa—approximately seven kilometres offshore—is of significant conservation value, being a winter haul-out station for New Zealand fur seals (200–600 residents per year), and a breeding colony for Australasian gannets (7,000–10,000 residents per year) and oi (grey-faced petrel).

4 For an introduction to the ecological history of Aotearoa see: Michael King, *The Penguin History of New Zealand* (Auckland: Penguin, 2003), 3–17. On New Zealand's unique flora and fauna see: Gerard Hutching, *The Penguin Natural World of New Zealand: An Illustrated Encyclopedia of our Natural Heritage* (Auckland: Penguin, 2004).

5 Eighty-five species of seabirds breed on New Zealand's mainland and offshore islands (including New Zealand's subantarctic islands, the Chatham Islands, and the Kermadec Islands). While 35 of these species are endemic, staying in New Zealand waters year-round, others migrate and only return to these islands to breed.

6 For a survey of this sad history, see: Ranginui Walker, *Ka Whawhai Tonu Matou: Struggle Without End*, rev. ed. (Auckland: Penguin, 2004).

7 In Māori mythology, Tāne, the son of Ranginui (the sky father) and Papatūānuku (the earth mother), is the deity of forests and of birds.

8 The pesticide 1080 is the sodium form of fluoroacetate, a naturally occurring toxin, and is mixed with cereal pellets to be ingested by pest species. See: http://www.doc.govt.nz/1080; http://www.1080facts.co.nz/.

9 Various scientific reports over the years have shown that the 1080 toxin breaks down quickly in water. Despite these findings, the use of 1080 remains contentious within a number of communities around New Zealand. On the controversy and politics of 1080, see the 2011 and 2013 reports on 1080 undertaken by the Parliamentary Commissioner for the Environment: http://www.pce.parliament.nz/media/1294/evaluating-the-use-of-1080.pdf; http://www.pce.parliament.nz/media/pdfs/use-of-1080-update-2013.pdf; also: W. Green and M. Rohan, 'Opposition to Aerial 1080 Poisoning for Control of Invasive Mammals in New Zealand: Risk Perceptions and Agency Responses', *Journal of the Royal Society of New Zealand* 42, no. 3 (2012): 185–213.

10 For example, since 1996, Whāingaroa Harbour Care has grown and planted 1.2 million native trees along streams and harbour edges within the Whāingaroa catchment to stop sediment runoff from land and improve water quality. Xtreme Waste began in the late 1990s after the local landfill run by the District Council was closed. After securing the contract for dealing with Raglan's household and business waste, it achieved a landfill diversion rate of 73 per cent; it now offers 'zero waste' consultancy advice to other social enterprises and councils around the country.

11 1 Cor 15:35–58; Col 1:15–20; Romans 8:1–17; 2 Cor 5:14–6:2. For an introduction to the ecological dimensions of Christian faith see: Stephen Bouma-Prediger, *For the Beauty of the Earth: A Christian Vision for Creation Care* (Grand Rapids, MI: Baker Academic, 2010); David Bookless, *Planetwise: Dare to Care for God's World* (Nottingham: IVP, 2008).

12 Māui's dolphin (popoto) is the world's rarest subspecies of dolphin. In 2012 the adult population was estimated to be just 55. Whāingaroa Harbour is located within the area where the highest density of Māui's dolphins is found.

13 2 Corinthians 5:14–6:2.

14. Are Contemporary Christian New Zealanders Committed to Peace?

1 This research was supported by a Royal Society of New Zealand Marsden Fund Grant (ID: VUW 1321 to JB) and a Templeton World Charity Foundation Grant (ID: 0077 to JB and CS).

2 John H. Shaver, 'The Behavioral Ecology of Fijian Religion' (PhD thesis, University of Connecticut, 2012).

3 Statistics New Zealand, *2013 Census QuickStats about culture and identity* (Wellington: Statistics New Zealand, 2014), 28–29.

4 In this chapter, each solid bar in each graph represents the mean (average) for eight levels of identification—from zero (people who don't identify as religious at all) to seven (people who highly identify as Christians). The small black vertical lines near the top of each solid bar are called error bars; these indicate levels of certainty, and help us to determine whether apparent differences are statistically significant. When comparing two solid bars, if the error bars do not cross each other on the y-axis (the vertical axis), we can say that the means for those two bars are statistically different. If the error bars do cross, then we cannot say that the two means are different. Whether or not the absolute value of the means is close is not important when interpreting difference, it's the error bars that are important.

5 John H. Shaver, Geoffrey Troughton, Chris G. Sibley and Joseph A. Bulbulia, 'Religion and the Unmaking of Prejudice Toward Muslims: Evidence from a Large National Sample', *PLoS ONE* 11, no.3 (2016): e0150209.

6 Charles Daniel Batson, Patricia Schoenrade and W. Larry Ventis, *Religion and the Individual: A Social-Psychological Perspective* (New York: Oxford University Press, 1993).

7 Stefanie Doebler, 'Relationships Between Religion and Intolerance Towards Muslims and Immigrants in Europe: A Multilevel Analysis', *Review of Religious Research* 56, no. 1 (2014): 61–86.

8 Bruce Hunsberger, Vida Owusu and Robert Duck, 'Religion and Prejudice in Ghana and Canada: Religious Fundamentalism, Right-Wing', *International Journal for the Psychology of Religion* 9, no. 3 (1999): 181–94.

9 James Belich, *Paradise Reforged: A History of the New Zealanders from the 1880s to the Year 2000* (Honolulu: University of Hawaii Press, 2001).

10 Daphna Canetti, Stevan E. Hobfoll, Ami Pedahzur and Eran Zaidise, 'Much Ado About Religion: Religiosity, Resource Loss, and Support for Political Violence', *Journal of Peace Research* 47, no. 5 (2010): 575–87.

11 Moira Shaw, Stephanie A. Quezada and Michael A. Zárate, 'Violence with a Conscience: Religiosity and Moral Certainty as Predictors of

Support for Violent Warfare', *Psychology of Violence* 1, no. 4 (2011): 275.

12 Joseph Bulbulia, Danny Osborne and Chris G. Sibley, 'Moral Foundations Predict Religious Orientations in New Zealand', *PloS ONE* 8, no. 12 (2013): e80224; Jonathan Haidt, 'Morality', *Perspectives on Psychological Science* 3, no. 1 (2008): 65–72.

13 Chris G. Sibley and Joseph Bulbulia, 'The Proportion of Religious Residents Predicts the Values of Nonreligious Neighbors: Evidence from a National Sample', *Religion, Brain & Behavior* 3, no. 3 (2013): 219–32.

14 Chris G. Sibley and Joseph A Bulbulia, 'How Do Religious Identities and Basic Value Orientations Affect Each Other over Time?', *International Journal for the Psychology of Religion* 24, no. 1 (2014): 64–76.

15. Remembering Jesus on Anzac Day: Just War or Just Another War?

1 Max Stackhouse, 'Civil Religion, Political Theology and Public Theology: What's the Difference?', *Public Theology* 5, no. 3 (2004): 275–93.

2 Revelation 13:1, 5, 11, 14, 17; 14:9, 11; 17:3; 18:2.

3 Romans 5:1.

4 Luke 2:14, cf. 12:51; Matthew 10:34.

5 William T. Cavanaugh, *The Myth of Religious Violence: Secular Ideology and the Roots of Modern Conflict* (Oxford: Oxford University Press, 2009); also my essay, 'Religious Violence, Terrorism and Restorative Justice', in *Handbook on Restorative Justice*, ed. Daniel van Ness and Gerry Johnston (Uffculme Cullompton: Willan Publishers, 2007), 372–94.

6 Geoffrey Troughton, ed., *Saints and Stirrers: Christianity, Conflict, and Peacemaking in New Zealand, 1814–1945* (Wellington: Victoria University Press, 2017).

7 Philip Jenkins, *The Great and Holy War: How World War I Became a Religious Crusade* (New York: HarperOne, 2014).

8 For a different way of understanding the public relevance of Christian faith, see my essay 'Parables as Paradigms for Public Theology', in *The Bible, Justice and Public Theology*, ed. David J. Neville (Sheffield: Sheffield Phoenix Press, 2014), 23–44 (esp. 30–31).

9 Nigel Biggar, *In Defence of War* (Oxford: Oxford University Press, 2013).

10 Philip Powell, 'Nigel Biggar, *In Defence of War* – A Review Essay', *Ethics in Brief* 20, no. 2 (2014):1–8.

11 See Richard Stowers, *Bloody Gallipoli: The New Zealanders' Story* (Auckland: David Bateman Ltd, 2005).

12 Matthew 26:52.
13 Cf. Deuteronomy 20:1–4; Exodus 14:14; Isaiah 30:15; 31:1–3; Psalm 46:1–10; Micah 4:1–3.
14 For this section, see my essay, 'Pacifism: Cultivate God's Peace', in *Forming Christian Habits in Post-Christendom: The Legacy of Alan and Eleanor Kreider*, ed. James Krabill and Stuart Murray Williams (Elkhart: Institute of Mennonite Studies, 2011), 73–84.
15 http://www.nbcnews.com/id/34360743/ns/politics-white_house/t/full-text-obamas-nobel-peace-prize-speech/.
16 On the universal myth of redemptive violence, see Walter Wink, *The Powers That Be: Theology for a New Millennium* (New York: Doubleday, 1998), esp. 44–48.
17 Isaiah 2:4; 11:6–9; Micah 4:3; Zechariah 9:9–10.
18 2 Corinthians 5:17; Galatians 6:15.
19 John Dominic Crossan, *God and Empire: Jesus Against Rome, Then and Now* (San Francisco: HarperCollins, 2007), esp. 77–88, 115–17.
20 Christopher Marshall, *Beyond Retribution: A New Vision for Justice, Crime, and Punishment* (Grand Rapids: Wm B. Eerdmans, 2001), 259–63.
21 Matthew 5:7; 9:13; 12:7; Luke 10:37.
22 Matthew 5:9; Romans 5:8; 16:20; Ephesians 2:14–22.
23 Mark 10:45.
24 Luke 6:35; Matthew 5:45.
25 Matthew 6:14.
26 Ephesians 4:32; Colossians 3:13.
27 1 Peter 2:21; Hebrews 12:3.
28 2 Corinthians 4:10–11; Galatians 6:17.
29 Ephesians 5:2; cf. John 13:34; 1 John 2:7; 3:11.
30 Mark 14:47; Matthew 26:52; Luke 22:49, cf. v.38.
31 The most thorough treatment is Willard M. Swartley, *Covenant of Peace: The Missing Peace in New Testament Theology and Ethics* (Grand Rapids: Wm B. Eerdmans, 2006).
32 Acts 10:38, cf. Isaiah 52:7.
33 Andrea Bartoli, 'Christianity and Peacebuilding', in *Religion and Peacebuilding*, ed. Harold Coward and Gordon S. Smith (Albany: State University of New York, 2004), 154–5; also Klaus Wengst, *Pax Romana and the Peace of Christ* (London: SCM, 1987).
34 Matthew 5:45–48, cf. Romans 12:14–21.
35 John 18:36.
36 See Louis J. Swift, *The Early Fathers on War and Military Service* (Wilmington: Michael Glazier, 1983).
37 Lee Griffith, *The War on Terrorism and the Terror of God* (Grand Rapids: Wm B. Eerdmans, 2002), 48.
38 Cited in Victoria Barnett, 'Beyond Complicity: The Challenges for Christianity', in *Must Christianity Be Violent? Reflections on History,*

Practice, and Theology, ed. Kenneth R. Chase and Alan Jacobs (Grand Rapids: Brazos, 2003), 105. Barnett observes that Christian rescuers of Jews were usually spontaneous and unreflective, with 'a kind of straightforward ethical simplicity' such as characterises Jesus in the Gospel accounts.

39 Ephesians 2:17.

40 Matthew 4:19; Mark 1:17; Luke 5:27; John 1:43.

16. Afterword: Christianity and the Peace Tradition in New Zealand

1 Alasdair MacIntyre, *Whose Justice? Which Rationality?* (Notre Dame: University of Notre Dame Press, 1988), 12.

2 See Geoffrey Troughton, 'Samuel Marsden and the Origins of a New Zealand Christian Peace Tradition', in *Saints and Stirrers: Christianity, Conflict and Peacemaking in New Zealand, 1814–1945*, ed. Geoffrey Troughton (Wellington: Victoria University Press, 2017), 29–46.

3 Allan Davidson, 'The Interaction of Missionary and Colonial Christianity in Nineteenth Century New Zealand', *Studies in World Christianity*, 2, no. 2 (1996): 145–66.

4 For careful studies of the interweaving of secular and sacred histories in New Zealand, see: Geoffrey Troughton and Stuart Lange, eds. *Sacred Histories in Secular New Zealand* (Wellington: Victoria University Press, 2016).

5 See: Peter Lineham, 'Sects and War', and Peter H. Ballis, 'Adventist Conscientious Co-operators and Jehovah's Witness Neutrals in New Zealand during the Second World War', in *Saints and Stirrers*, 163–201.

Index

Page references in **bold** refer to illustrations